Escaping Earth

The Dream That Revealed the Way

ISBN 9798998898594

© Copyright 2025 by Mihai Ilioi – All Rights Reserved

It is not legal to reproduce, duplicate, or transmit any part of this document in either electronic means or printed format.

Recording this publication is strictly prohibited.

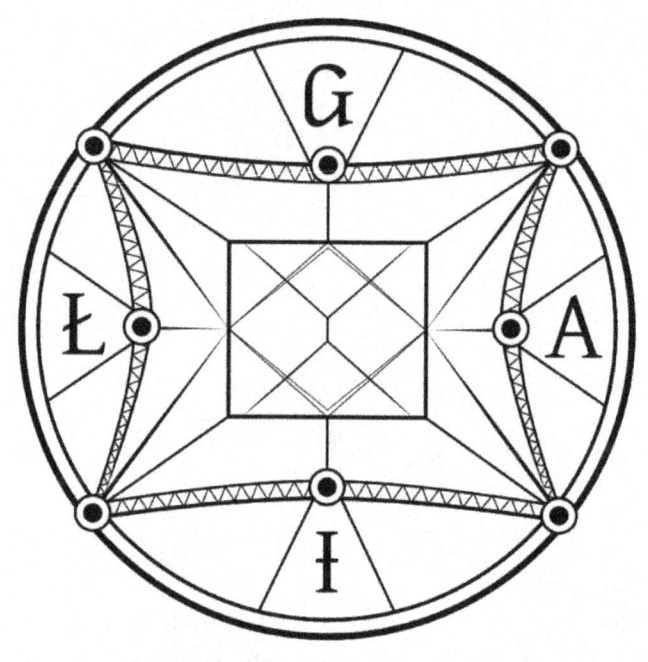

OPREGO AD GLORIAM ETERNI NA MAN

Table of Content

Introduction	6
Prologue: The Dream That Unveiled the Way	9
Chapter One - The Illusion of Outward Escape	13
Part 1: The Modern Pursuit of Escape	21
Part 2: Ascension's Counterfeit	39
Part 3: Losing the Ground Beneath Us	36
Part 4: The Sacred Descent	43
Part 5: Reclaiming the Forgotten Sanctuary	50
Part 6: A Call to the Sacred Below	57
Chapter One- Summary	63
Chapter Two – Reawakening the Inner Temple	66
Part 1: The Soul; The Forgotten Sanctuary	74
Part 2: Beneath the Surface of Daily our Identities	82
Part 3: False Layers and Forgotten Names	99
Part 4: The Excavation of Truth	96
Part 5: The Original Name	102
Part 6: The Descend is the Doorway	106
Part 7: When Roots Become Revelation	112
Part 8: Unveiling the Hidden Wells	116
Part 9: The Harmony of Depth and Hight	120
Chapter Two – Summary	125
Chapter Three – The Unveiling	129
Part 1: The Mirror Restored	137
Part 2: The Breath Returns	144
Part 3: The Spirit of Exploration	152
Part 4: The Resistance Before Resurrection	158
Part 5: The Overflow; From Roots to Rivers	162
Chapter Three - Summary	167

Chapter Four – The Mantle in the Wilderness	172
Part 1: The Eternal Pattern	180
Part 2: The Fire of Hidden Seasons	187
Part 3: The Face of Subtle Opposition	195
Part 4: The Sacred Transfer	202
Part 5: The Receiving of the Mantle	207
Part 6: The Weight of Recognition	215
Chapter Four – Summary	227
Chapter Five – The Descendance	231
Part 1: The Mountains as Thresholds	240
Part 2: The Foundation Holds the Mystery	247
Part 3: Return to The Sacred Core	254
Part 4: Gates Hidden in Plain Sight	261
Part 5: Stones, Caverns, and Hidden Altars	267
Part 6: Rediscovering the Mountain Within	274
Chapter Five – Summary	279
Chapter Six – The Five Cascades of Revelation	283
Part 1: Entering the Hidden Realm	291
Part 2: Revelations Comes in Layers	296
Part 3: First Cascade - Awakening Awe	301
Part 4: Second Cascade-Confronting Illusion	305
Part 5: Third Cascade-Receiving Hidden Wisdom	309
Part 6: Fourth Cascade – Embodying Presence	314
Part 7: Fifth Cascade – Returning with Radiance	318
Part 8: A River Through You	322
Chapter Six – Summary	326
Chapter Seven Reclaiming First Mandate	330
Part 1: From Revelation to Responsibility	338
Part 2: The Forgotten Mandate	346
Part 3: A New Genesis Movement	354
Part 4: Earthkeepers Arise	362
Part 5: Covenant With the Dust	369
Part 6: Return to Eden	375
Closing Chapter Summary	380

Epilogue	383
Final Reflections	387
About Author	389

Dream Flow Diagram
ESCAPING EARTH
A Journey Within the Foundations

> **Helicopter Ascent**
> *Awareness Rising Beyond the Familiar*

> **The Mountain Appears**
> *The Invitation into Hidden Revelation*

> **The Base Portal**
> *Entering Through the Gate of Humility*

> **Crossing the Threshold**
> *The Shift into a Higher Dimension*

> **The Vast Expanse**
> *Awakening to the Magnitude of Existence*

> **The Five Cascades**
> *Five Streams of Living Revelation*

> **The Final Insight**
> *True Liberation Begins Within*

"He who finds the portal within the eternal foundations, discover the world that was hidden since the beginning." - *I.M. RAELITE*

Introduction

Escaping Earth: The Descent into Sacred Revelation

We are told we are evolving. That we are ascending. That every algorithm, every invention, every pixel of light on every screen is proof of progress; a march toward a future unbound by gravity, suffering, or decay.

We hail the triumphs of technology as steps toward liberation, imagining ourselves as gods remaking the world in our image, transcending the limits of matter.

But what if this direction is not ascent at all, but exile?

What if our soaring ambitions to leave the earth are, in truth, symptoms of our separation from earth? What if the promise of escape is the very illusion that keeps us from seeing the sacred dimension of where we already are?

We do not need to escape Earth. We need to awaken to earth's sacred sound.

Beneath our engineered realities lies an ancient truth: the Earth is not merely terrain; it is a temple. Not merely just matter; but it is mystery.

The earth is not a passive stage for our striving, but a living vessel of holy intelligence, groaning, calling, whispering.

Her rhythms are not relics of a primitive past, but the living pulse of a greater order, echoing the wisdom of origins too vast to be reduced to data.

This book did not come through ambition or intellect. It was born through divine interruption, in the stillness of a silent night.

It began with a dream, but not a dream of fantasy. A dream of fire and voice, of symbols and signs. A dream that summoned, not upward toward stars, but downward into the deep chambers of remembering. This was not a vision of departure, but a call to return. Not to retreat from Earth, but to rediscover her, the sacred Earth's womb, the forgotten Mother, the silent witness of our becoming.

Here, caves are not just voids of stone, but the womb of rebirth. Waterfalls are not just falling waters, but flowing speech. Mountains are not just rock, but revelation frozen in form.

This book invites you to descend; to leave behind the synthetic dreams of escape and re-enter the holy terrain of your own soul in union with Earth's sacred design.

It is a pilgrimage into the mystical geography that was always here beneath your feet, veiled only by the noise of modern ambition.

This is not eco-romanticism. This is not nostalgia. This is cosmological reality. This is the unveiling of spiritual memory buried in dust and root.

You are not simply invited to read these pages; you are being summoned to remember your root.

To remember the silence that speaks. The ground that listens. The breath of creation that still hovers over the depths, waiting to be heard again.

This is a return; not to the past, but to the Primordial Real, where the Creator's voice still echoes through the rocks, the rivers, the winds, and your bones. A return to stewardship. To stillness. To the sacred resonance that once guided humanity before the great forgetting.

We have not been called to rise above the Earth, but to become aligned with her. Not to transcend nature, but to awaken to the Spirit that flows through her.

The real exodus is not outward but inward.
The true escape is not from Earth; but from the illusion that she is void of divinity.

This is not just a message. It is a door.

This is not just a book. It is a path.

This is the unearthing.

This is remembering.

This is the sacred descent.

This is Escaping Earth.

Prologue

The Dream That Unveiled the Way

In May 21st of 2025, I was graced with a dream unlike any I had ever known; vivid, luminous, and marked by a presence that transcended sleep.

It came not as a passing flicker of imagination, but as a divine transmission, a moment of sacred interruption; a dream that breathed with the weight of eternity.

At first, I hesitated to share it, because some revelations are too intense to speak of quickly. Yet I now feel compelled to record it here, as the genesis of this book and the ignition point of this unfolding journey.

For this was not simply a dream; it was a dispatch from beyond the veil. A message etched not in ink, but in spirit. A vision born not of intellect, but of encounter.

In this dream, I found myself soaring through the sky in a helicopter. It was a strange and intimate form of flight; not mechanical, but deeply symbolic.

A vessel of both close and personal motion and conscious will.

As I hovered high above the Earth, I could see the majestic landscape of the land below, vast and mysterious still; as though holding its breath.

Then, on the horizon, a singular mountain rose into view. But this was no ordinary mountain.

It did not summon me to climb; it drew me to approach. Not with effort, but with surrender. As though the mountain itself had a voice, and it had spoken my name.

And then it happened.

At the base of this mountain; not at the summit, where our cultures often place revelation, nor halfway up as a reward for the spiritual elite; a portal opened. Quietly. Instantly. Unmistakably. A powerful divine rupture within the foundations of the Earth.

Without hesitation, I descended. I guided the helicopter into the portal that just opened before my eyes; Into the ground, not the sky. Into mystery, not mastery. Into the heart of something ancient, sacred, and alive.

The moment I crossed the threshold, everything changed.

I entered a realm not above Earth, nor detached from it; but within it. It was as if the very soul of the Earth had opened to receive me.

I found myself in a dimension beyond language. It shimmered with truth and trembled with beauty. Imagine the Grand Canyon transfigured by divine architecture; multiplied in scope and cloaked in light. Cliffs like sacred cathedrals. Stones that sang. A sacred landscape carved not by erosion, but by eternal design.

Below me, I saw five colossal waterfalls cascaded downward; Not falling from heaven to earth, but from the inner heights of this majestic and mysterious concealed dimension to its sacred structural foundations.

Each waterfall was greater than Niagara; yet they did not roar. They sang. Their voices merged into a chorus that echoed across this hidden realm; an eternal sound that seemed to carry the memory of creation itself.

And in that sound, I heard a truth I had never known: *"You have been reaching upward for liberation; But your true freedom is waiting downward, inward, deeper still, within; The doorway is not in the stars, but in the soil. The escape is not departure; but return."*

In that moment, I saw clearly. Humanity's continue obsession with outward transcendence; our flights to the stars, our attempts to digitalize the soul, our philosophies of disembodiment; have led us to confuse elevation with awakening.

But true awakening does not sever us from Earth; it roots us more deeply into it. True ascension does not bypass the body. It honors the body as sacred ground. It does not abandon the world; it enters it more fully, through the unveiled pathways within.

This dream in an instant moment turned everything I thought I knew upside down. Escaping Earth is not an exit. It is a reentry.

It is not a rejection of Earth's breathing reality; but a descent into its concealed divinity.

The true temple was never floating above us. It has always been beneath us. Waiting.

This was the revelation that birthed this book. Escaping Earth is not a journey into abstraction. It is a return to the sacred realm. It is an unveiling of the divine architecture pulsing beneath our feet and echoing through our spirit. It is a sincere call to rediscover the sacred portals of our human existence not only in the land, but in the soul.

To remember that our Earth Experience is not exile.

> It is invitation.
> It is sanctuary.
> It is mystery.
> It is home.

Chapter One

The Illusion of Outward Escape

Based on a Word of Knowledge received; December 3rd, 2022

The Prophetic Moment

There are moments in life when time becomes still, and eternity whispers through the thin veil of our human consciousness.

It was in such a moment; in the quiet hours of the night, when the world rested and silence carried the voice of revelation; that I received the Word now known as *"The Illusion of Outward Escape."*

The message descended not as a thought, but as a vibration; a living current that pierced through the noise of the mind and landed in the sacred chamber of my soul. Its weight was gentle but undeniable; its meaning, piercing yet comforting. It came as both correction and invitation: a divine call to humanity, to turn inward before continuing its restless journey outward.

"There is a sorrowful irony echoing through the corridors of our generation: People are searching for the stars in the sky, but they are bypassing the true star dwelling within. They are chasing the lights above, while ignoring the sacred light already ignited in the soul".

When these words were first impressed upon me, I understood that this was not a poetic utterance; it was a divine lament. Heaven was grieving, not over the stars themselves, but over humanity's blindness to the light already placed within them.

For the heaven may declare the glory of God, but the soul bears His image. And the one who bypasses the inner radiance in pursuit of the distant glow becomes like a wanderer lost in the wilderness of his own creation.

Humanity's Longing for Escape

Throughout the ages, humankind has gazed toward the heavens in search of meaning. The desire to ascend; to reach beyond the limits of flesh and gravity; is written into our very being. It is not wrong to desire the stars; it is wrong to forget the Source that gave them their light.

In our modern age, this longing for transcendence has taken on new forms. We build towers of technology, rockets of ambition, and systems of belief designed to catapult us beyond the boundaries of our own mortality. We call it progress. We call it evolution.

Yet in many ways, it is escape; not from limitation, but from reflection. Humanity seeks to escape the weight of its own conscience. We pursue the infinite without first understanding the eternal within. We gaze outward to the galaxies but tremble to look inward, where the divine mirror reflects our true origin and purpose.

The illusion of outward escape is not new. It began when the first human reached for the forbidden fruit; seeking knowledge apart from divine communion. Since then, humanity has sought light without the Source, wisdom without humility, and transcendence without surrender.

The danger is subtle. The heavens above are real, but they are not our destination; they are a reflection of what has already been written within. To pursue them without understanding the inner light is to wander the cosmos with an unawaken soul.

The Light Within – The Forgotten Star

Creation is filled with luminous mysteries. Stars burn billions of miles away, galaxies swirl in divine choreography, and yet, the Creator placed a greater mystery within the human soul.

In the beginning, God spoke light into existence; but not only in the heavens. The same Living Word that called the stars into being also breathed the spark of divine radiance into the soul of humanity. It was never meant to be searched for beyond; it was meant to be discovered within.

When the Spirit hovered over the face of the waters, light was not just born into the universe; it was embedded in the design of life itself. The human soul was formed as the dwelling place of that eternal flame. And though the world has dimmed it with distraction, it has never been extinguished.

By the Living Word.
By the Holy Spirit.
By the mercy and grace of Jesus Christ.

The revelation reminded me that divine light is not found in the spectacle of the sky, nor in the noise of religion, but in the quiet sanctum of a heart made still before its Creator. There; beneath the layers of thought, emotion, and striving, the true star still burns.

To look inward is not to abandon creation's wonder; it is to see it rightly. For once we awaken to the divine spark within, the heavens themselves begin to testify differently. What once appeared distant becomes within focus. What once seemed infinite becomes intimate.

The Descent That Leads to Ascent

The greatest paradox of spiritual life is this: We ascend not by rising, but by descending.

Humanity has misunderstood ascension as departure; leaving the earth, escaping the body, transcending the flesh. But in truth, ascension is a deeper grounding. It is the return of heaven into earth, of spirit into form, of divine purpose into human expression.

When Christ descended into the depths of human suffering, He did not flee from earth; He sanctified it. His path to resurrection began with surrender. His glory was revealed not in escape, but in embodiment.

To follow Him is to walk the same sacred descent; into the depths of our being, where truth is not found in visions of the sky but in the sanctuary of the soul. There we find not escape, but encounter. Not flight, but fulfillment.

The illusion of outward escape tells us that freedom is somewhere else; in another world, another body, another time. But the truth of divine alignment whispers: "The Kingdom of God is within you." Luke 17:21

We are not meant to flee the earth but to reveal heaven through it. The true escape is not from the world, but from illusion; the illusion that we are separated from the light that formed us.

The Inner Sanctuary – Where Silence Speaks

If the outer world is a mirror of divine creation, the inner world is the sanctuary of divine communion. This is where the revelation becomes personal; where philosophy becomes experience, and knowledge turns into transformation.

To descend into oneself is not an act of self-obsession; it is the act of returning to the Source. It is in silence that the soul rediscovers its alignment with the Spirit of Life; the SOL that sustains all being.

In the stillness of the inner sanctuary, one begins to hear the true language of God. It is not spoken in words, but in resonance. It is not seen with eyes, but with light. And this light, once awakened, begins to radiate through every aspect of life; thoughts purified, emotions clarified, intentions sanctified.

The prophets of old withdrew into deserts not to escape the world, but to see it rightly. The mystics entered silence not to deny creation, but to discern its Creator within. The saints and seers throughout history discovered that the way to heaven is not through flight, but through stillness.

For only when we still the storm within can we see the reflection of heaven in the waters of the soul.

The Restoration of Vision

The revelation of *The Illusion of Outward Escape* is, at its heart, a call to restored sight; to see again as God intended. When the eyes of the soul are opened, the search for distant stars transforms into recognition of the divine image within.

The man born blind in John 9 did not receive sight merely to behold the world, but to witness the Light of the World standing before him. Likewise, our spiritual blindness is healed not for spectacle, but for communion.

To see rightly is to know that heaven and earth are not opposing realms but interwoven realities; two expressions of one divine intention. The true escape is not spatial but spiritual; an awakening from illusion into revelation. When the eyes of understanding open, everything becomes sacred.

The soil beneath our feet, the breath in our lungs, the flame in our hearts; all testify to one truth: We were never meant to leave the earth to find God. We were meant to bring God into the earth through awakened being.

At the heart of every soul is a longing; not to escape, but to return. The revelation closes not with departure, but with invitation:

Before we go on searching for stars we cannot reach, why not look into the depths of our soul for the sparkle of life and the reflection of sacred light birthed by the Spirit of the Living God?

This is not the denial of creation's grandeur; it is the reawakening of divine purpose. We are not wanderers seeking light; we are vessels designed to reflect it.

The illusion of outward escape ends when we remember that the journey to the divine is not linear but inward. The more deeply we descend into truth, the higher our spirit ascends in illumination. And there; in that sacred intersection between descent and ascent; the voice of God is heard again:

"You are not lost in the universe. The universe is waiting for you to awaken."

This revelation, like a mirror, turns back upon the reader. It asks: Where are you searching for light? Have you mistaken the brilliance of the stars for the radiance of your own soul?

Have you fled into philosophies and pursuits while neglecting the sanctuary within? If so, the Holy Spirit's call is gentle but firm: return. Not backward, but inward. Not into darkness, but into the secret place where divine light waits patiently to be again recognized.

When humanity ceases its outward escape and begins its inward journey, the world itself will begin to change. Nations will seek peace not through power, but through presence. Science will discover not just matter, but meaning. Human religion will transform from ritual to revelation.

This is the divine economy of awakening; where heaven's light is not stolen from the stars, but revealed through the living soul.

We do not need to escape to find it. We need to descend into the sanctuary of our own being; where the light still waits, still burns, still calls us back home.

Finding The Flame That Never Left

When I received this revelation, I sensed that it was not merely for me; it was for every soul standing at the threshold between confusion and awakening. It is for the scientist staring into the telescope, the mystic kneeling in prayer, the seeker wandering between worlds. It is for the one who feels both near and far, both found and lost.

The illusion of outward escape is powerful, but temporary. The truth of inward return is eternal.

For the same Spirit that hovered over the waters still hovers over humanity; waiting for hearts to remember, for eyes to open, for souls to awaken. And when they do, the earth itself will shine again.

For it was never the stars that were far; it was our sight that was dimmed. Now, the time has come to see.

Part 1.

The Modern Pursuit of Escape; The Illusion of Ascent and the Forgotten Depths of Being

We live in an age where human perception is intoxicated by velocity. The soul is pulled into a constant momentum; spinning forward, upward, faster, and farther, chasing a horizon that never seems to arrive. We have crowned movement as meaning, and elevation as enlightenment. But we must ask: where are we really going?

Forward? Upward? Faster? Beyond?

These are the modern commandments of a species dislocated from its source. They echo through our schools, our corporations, our temples, and even our meditations. Progress is the altar, and growth its gospel. Every innovation is framed as a human salvation. Every acceleration is seen as transcendence. And beneath it all lies a deep, silenced, and an unspoken creed: Escape by elevation.

From Silicon Valley's quest for artificial immortality to spiritual circles promising cosmic consciousness, the shared pursuit is remarkably similar: to get away. To escape pain. To escape time. To escape the body. To escape the silence.

But escape from what? And more urgently; escape from, and to where? And these questions start producing a real mirage of technological transcendence.

We imagine that sending rockets to Mars will redeem our species. We upload our memories to cloud-based temples, hoping to preserve what we never truly understood. We pour billions into the illusion of eternal youth, while our spirits grow old in silence.

We construct towers of code and digital utopias not to confront our mortality; but to cover it. And all the while, the Earth waits.

We have mistaken noise for knowledge, simulation for soul, and light-speed data for revelation. In our striving to ascend beyond the bounds of Earth, we have ironically sunk deeper into confusion, fragmentation, and fear.

We've built technologies to mimic and express transcendence, but they cannot replicate stillness. We prescribe ideologies to manage our existential tremors, but they cannot sanctify the soul. We seek enlightenment without embodiment. Awakening without incarnation.

> We want presence without surrender.
> Light without weight.
> Flight without formation.
> Divinity without descent.

This is the signature confusion of our era, the age of disembodied living of our human expression.

We have redefined the human experience as a project of abstraction. We seek to digitize our consciousness, disembody our experiences, and dissolve our humanity into virtual avatars.

But the more we separate from the soil, the more truly empty and fragmented we will become.

We flee the heaviness of flesh to live in a data cloud and yet our souls ache for touching the once forgotten ground. We replace communities with mere curated connections, and yet we get captured by loneliness. We choose heavy noise over stillness, complexity over simplicity, and perpetual ambition over sacred soul's echoes of enough. And still, peace remains elusive.

Even among spiritual communities, this illusion mutates. We speak of shedding the body as if it were a prison rather than a temple. We aim for "higher realms," as though truth cannot be found in the earth beneath our very own feet.

We talk of ascending beyond the material world, forgetting that God walked in the cool of the garden and not just in the halls of heaven.

But beneath the buzz of pseudo-enlightenment, a whisper remains:

"What if the more you seek is not above you, but within you, and beneath you?"
"What if the sacred is not in departure, but in deeper arrival?"
"What if the real revelation is not about escaping Earth, but entering it more fully?"

If we are being captivated by the false lights of our skyward obsession, we will start living under the tyranny of the vertical quest to nowhere.

Up is praised.
Up is privileged.
Up is powerful.

We are taught that the only direction of importance is up. Higher rank. Higher knowledge. Higher vibration. We glorify the stars and forget the soil. We speak of evolution as if it were solely an ascent, and we label the ground beneath us as "lower" or "lesser."

But even the tallest tree draws its strength from the invisible depths. Even the sky is grounded in the spinning sphere of Earth.

This pattern of skyward obsession is not new. It echoes Babel's tower; the ancient blueprint of human ambition untethered from divine instruction.

Their goal was to find transcendence without transformation, ascent without sanctification. And what was built in pride was undone in confusion. Their unity was fractured. Their language shattered. Why?

Because elevation without sacred alignment leads to fragmentation.

Just as in the dream I received, the divine opening did not appear in the heights. It appeared at the base of the mountain. The sacred portal was not unveiled above the clouds, but within the womb of the Earth.

Revelation did not come through the process of disembodiment, but through rootedness.

Not through escape, but through embodiment. Not in fleeing the flesh, but in sanctifying it.

This is the ancient mystery whispered through every grain of soil:

The higher we reach without inner depth, the more disoriented we become. But the deeper we root, the more purely we rise.

We have become a generation fluent in the language of takeoff, but illiterate in the art of return to the roots.

We can articulate visions of heavenly glory, yet struggle to sit in silence on the ground. We celebrate launchpads, but forget how to plant seeds. We dream of spiritual heights, yet neglect the garden of our own soul. We build mansions in the sky, while leaving the foundations of our lives in disrepair.

The crisis is not a lack of transcendence, but a forgetting of presence. We are not suffering from too little vision, but from a refusal to look within.

What if our need to escape is not the path to freedom, but the mask of fear? What if the Earth we long to transcend is the very altar upon which our soul must kneel? What if the garden we abandoned holds the key to the Eden we dream of?

The Return to the Holy Ground

The journey begins not with a command or doctrine, but with a question: What are we truly trying to escape?

Is it the hardship of embodiment? The uncertainty of life? The wounds of our past? Is our endless movement toward something sacred, or away from something painful?

And what if, beneath all our upward ambition, is a sacred call to descend?

What if "Escaping Earth" is not about truly departing the Earth, but about escaping the illusion that the earth is empty?

What if it is a divine invitation to unearth the holy? To return to the stillness we left behind. To remember that the Earth is not in the way of our transcendence, but the wat goes through Earth?

The Great Inversion: Descent as Ascent

In the sacred logic of the Kingdom, down is the way up. The seed must descend into the soil before it can rise. The Christ descended into the depths before resurrection. The living soul must be still before it can soar.

The irony is sharp and sacred: our vertical striving is often horizontal wandering in disguise. We rise without roots. We claim light without fire. But the true mystery of transformation can only unfold through inversion.

To descend is not to regress, it is to remember. To root is not to retreat, it is to return. To enter the Earth is not to be buried, but to be born again.

As you journey through the pages of this book revelation, do not merely read; listen.

Let the sacred questions rise like incense from the text:

Where in your life are you running without reason?

What internal altars have you neglected in your skyward pursuit?

Where have you equated movement with meaning?

What illusions of escape are masking invitations to engage?

Let silence be your teacher again. Let your feet feel the earth. Let the dust return to your skin. For in doing so, you may discover what the ancient prophets already knew: The Divine does not call us to disembodied light, but to embodied revelation. Not to float above the Earth, but to become true stewards of her divine mystery.

This Is Not an Exit; It's an Entrance. This chapter is not a conclusion, but a threshold.

It is not a ladder to climb, but a well to enter. It is a descent into the sacred interior. A beckoning to the caverns of the self. A call to walk, not away, but inward. Not above, but through. Not out, but into the holy chamber of Earth, Soul, and Spirit, in a sacred unity.

To escape Earth is not to leave her, but to escape the blindness that made us forget her divinity. The real exile was never from Heaven; it was from remembrance.

The sacred flame still burns in the bush, the voice still speaks in the wind, the portal is still open at the foot of the mountain.

But we must stop climbing long enough to bow.

This is not an academic invitation. It is a heavenly summons. You, reader, seer, sojourner, are being called back to something ancient, urgent, and alive.

Return to the soil. Return to the breath.
Return to the silence that knows your name.

The Earth is not the obstacle to your destiny. She is the original oracle. And her voice is rising once more; not in the heavens above, but from the depths below.

Do not be afraid to listen.
Do not be afraid to stop running.
Do not be afraid to descend.

For the mystery was never in the escape. The mystery is in the return.

Part 2.

Ascension's Counterfeit - Chasing Light Without Heat

A Prophetic Warning for a Simulated Generation

"Not all light leads to truth. And not all upward movement brings us closer to the Divine."

We live in a time where light has become a currency, and ascension, a trend. The word "light" is stamped on self-help books, posted in hashtags, infused into spiritual branding. It's become a promise: of clarity, of purity, of arrival.

Yet behind the glow, many are disoriented. Some are burned. And others are lost entirely. This is not because we have ceased seeking, but because we have stopped discerning.

We chase the appearance of light, forgetting that even deception can shimmer. We mistake radiance for righteousness. Glare for guidance. Performance for presence. And in doing so, we chase a counterfeit; an ascension without incarnation, a light without heat.

From digital spaces to new-age temples, a singular mantra reverberates: "Ascend. Rise. Evolve. Upgrade. Transcend."

The sacred language is now spoken of in code. Transcendence is packaged in the language of operating systems, frequencies, neural links, quantum jumps, and vibrational shifts.

The living soul is marketed like a device needing optimization. The human body, once revered as a divine temple, is now seen by some as an outdated shell; a burden to be bypassed through technology, abstraction, or mystical detachment.

But this ascent is not holy. It is hollow. For what we are witnessing is not divine evolution; but spiritual escape in disguise. It is the illusion of upward motion while the soul starves for depth. It is the language of light used to avoid the path of *fire*.

And herein lies the danger: Counterfeit light does not warm. It blinds.

Consider the artificial flame. It mimics the real fire in appearance; bright, flickering, inviting. But touch it, and you'll find no warmth. It dazzles, but does not burn. It draws the eye, but not the heart. It is a seduction without sanctification. So too is the light that the world now calls sacred.

"Like moths to artificial flames, we are drawn to what promises transformation but often delivers nothing more than mere distraction."

We see it everywhere. The pursuit of spiritual experiences that bypass the process of sanctification. Mystical language without moral embodiment. Techno-messianic visions of eternal life without repentance. Practices that promise awakening without accountability.

This is not light; This is glare.

It dazzles the senses but leaves the spirit parched. It offers elevation but severs us from the ground. It creates seekers addicted to the next spiritual high, yet unable to sit in silence. It leads to the simulation of a holiness rather than its sacred and divine manifestation.

And the rise of a synthetic sacred perception it is being sourced and fueled by the sad humanistic reality that we no longer merely seek to know God, but we seek to construct God in our own image.

In our age of algorithms and artificial intelligence, humanity now attempts to digitize divinity. We do not kneel at altars, we code them. We do not sacrifice, we stimulate. We do not wait on the Spirit, we simulate its effects through frequency, visuals, and sound. We have reduced the mystery of the Holy into systems of enhancement.

We call it "higher consciousness," but often it is ego in disguise. We name it "ascension," but often it is avoidance wearing spiritual robes.

This is the damaging lie of spiritual bypassing:

> Ascend without descent.
> Receive without repentance.
> Glow without grounding.
> Know without kneeling.

But true Light is never found in bypassing the brokenness of being human. It is found by descending into it, fully, honestly, and vulnerably.

Let us be clear: There is a vast difference between illumination and incarnation. Illumination reveals truth. Incarnation becomes truth.

One informs the mind. The other transforms the life. The counterfeit light may illuminate without ever incarnating. It does create knowledge without wisdom, movement without meaning, sensation without sincere sanctification.

But the Light of God is not sterile. It is not for show. It burns with holy love. It is the light that burned in the bush yet did not consume. The light that blinded Saul and transformed him into Paul. The light that shattered the tombstone and rolled it away.

This kind of light is dangerous, because it destroys illusion. It is tender, because it meets us in our shame. And it is liberating, because it exposes all that is false in order to reveal what is eternally real.

The ancients knew something modern mystics have forgotten. The sacred Light is not found by floating upward. It is found by entering inward. It is not found in the stars alone, but in the soil. In the cave. In the wilderness. It is not distant, it is dwelling. It is not abstract; it is incarnate.

The real Light does not flatter; it frees. It does not seduce; it summons. It does not entertain; it awakens.

The Light of Truth is not a passive glow; it is a refining fire. It does not tell you what you want to hear. It tells you what your soul *needs* to remember.

It melts pride. It uproots delusion. It awakens the soul's original cry to become holy again. And this Light is not found in escape, but in presence. Not in perfection, but in union. Not in synthetic ascent, but in sacred descent.

This is the divine order: Descent precedes ascension. Just as seeds must be buried before they rise, so too must the soul descend before it ascends.

We must descend into the body, into the wounds, the weariness, the realness of being human. We must descend into the Earth; into rootedness, stewardship, and stillness. We must descend into the sacred fire, where all that is false is burned away.

Only then can we rise, not in illusion, but in light. Not in fantasy, but in fullness. Not as those who float above Earth, but as those who truly carry Heaven within it.

The Fire that Reveals

"For our God is a consuming fire." Hebrews 12:29

Real light burns. It purifies. It does not simply make you feel good; it makes you whole. It burns away pride. It scorches away performance. It strips the soul bare and clothes it again in divine image.

Have you encountered such Light?

It will silence your ego. It will weep with your wounds. It will awaken your memory of Eden.
It will call you by your true name.

This is the fire of Presence. The fire of holiness. The fire that does not destroy you, but reveals you.

As you reflect on the light you follow, let these questions serve as sacred mirrors:

Is the "light" I'm following warming my soul, or merely entertaining my mind?

Does it lead me into humility, reverence, and rootedness, or into abstraction, superiority, and detachment?

Am I chasing an experience, or yielding to a transformation?

Have I confused elevation with escape?

What parts of me still resist grounding, still resist the fire?

Let the silence answer. Let the soil speak. Let the holy fire fall.

This chapter is not a rebuke; it is a return. A return to the unshakable truth that the Light of God is not a performance. It is a presence. Not a flash in the sky, but a flame in the cave. Not a projection, but a Person.

And to follow that Light is not to escape the Earth, but to rediscover its holiness. To follow the true Light is to: Kneel before glory. Walk humbly with mystery. Burn steadily; not brightly; for the eternity.

So, I say to you: stop chasing false flames. Let the counterfeit light flicker and fade.

There is a greater Light calling within you, around you, and beneath your very feet.

And it waits, not at the top of some heavenly ladder, but at the threshold of your surrender.

This is the light that leads home This is not the light of escape, but the light of return.

Return to your soul. Return to your body. Return to the holy weight of being human. Return to the fire of the Holy One who calls you not to ascend away from Earth; but to become one with the Light within it.

For in the end, what we're chasing is not light at all.

We are chasing Home. And Home is not above us. It is within us. And it burns with Love.

This is the Light that never blinds.
This is the Fire that never consumes.
This is the Presence that never leaves.

This is not ascension's counterfeit. This is the Truth that sets you free.

Part 3.

Losing the Ground Beneath Us

A Prophetic Cry for the Return to Embodied Truth

"You are dust, and to dust you shall return." Genesis 3:19
"The Word became flesh and dwelt among us." John 1:14

We were never meant to hover. We were never meant to live in the air. And yet, here we are; suspended.

Suspended in cloud storage. Suspended in digital illusions. Suspended in dreams of transcendence that have forgotten the beauty of embodiment. Suspended in spiritual narratives that glorify flight and denounce form.

We hover, not with liberation; but with loss. We float, not with freedom; but with disconnection.

A civilization built on speed and simulation is a civilization that has lost its grounding. We have become a people with no memory of soil; hovering souls with tired eyes, restless hearts, and feet that no longer feel the pulse of the earth beneath them.

The sacred disintegration of our modern life, leads us to live in the illusion of weightlessness. We scroll instead of stilling. We perform instead of pausing. We connect without communion. We search without settling. And this is not evolution, this truly is a spiritual amnesia

We have forgotten the sacred purpose of being human: To dwell. To root. To remain.

The modern obsession with becoming, faster, better, higher; has severed us from the ancient rhythms of being. We consume data at the speed of thought but forget how to truly think. We chase experiences but cannot stay present in a single breath.

We have crafted a world where the soul is rarely at home in the body; and where Heaven feels far because Earth has been forsaken.

Disembodiment: The Silent Wound of Our Time

"The modern soul is weightless; not with liberation, but with loss."

This is our living time unspoken affliction: disembodiment. We no longer dwell within our own skin. We no longer sense the sacred in the soil, the breath, the broken loaf.

We have spiritualized escape and vilified embodiment. Yet our souls cry out for reunion with the ground, for the rediscovery of the sacred below.

To be human is to be placed. To be grounded not only spiritually, but physically, emotionally, relationally. To belong; not just in idea, but in location, in flesh, in presence.

Because we are not just merely ideas floating in space. We are breath-in-dust creatures, designed for contact, for genuine communion, and continuity with the creation that encapsulates us.

Once, humanity lived close to the earth. We rose with the sun, labored with our hands, ate what we grew, rested in cycles, and worshipped with rhythm. But now:

We have replaced ritual with routine. Sabbath with schedules. Stillness with streaming.
Presence with productivity.

We build smart homes but forget to inhabit them. We seek meaning but refuse to slow down long enough to receive it. We claim enlightenment but bypass embodiment.

We do not merely live in an ungrounded world; we have built systems designed to prevent grounding. And perhaps the most dangerous tragedy is not that we are ungrounded; but that we have ceased to mourn it.

We have normalized rootlessness. We call it freedom. We celebrate detachment as sophistication. We romanticize transcendence without realizing we've left behind something sacred: the weight of being real.

And yet, beneath our elevated ambitions lies a deep ache. The body aches. The land aches. The soul aches. Something in us knows we were not meant to hover forever. We were meant to land.

The Sacred Purpose of Embodiment

"God breathed into dust and called it life"

The divine did not choose abstraction. God chose dust. Not algorithms. Not ideals. Not holograms. But Earth. Flesh. Sweat. Skin. Tears.

Our bodies are not burdens to escape. They are sacred vessels of encounter. And the Earth is not a platform to transcend; but an altar to kneel upon.

The miracle is not that God is "out there." The miracle is that the Divine chose to dwell among us; to put on skin, to walk on dust, to weep, to sweat, to touch, to bleed.

Because true embodiment is not a limitation. It is the stage of divine redemption.

Rediscovering the Divine in the Dust

We have been taught to seek God in the sky. But what if He is waiting in the soil?

In the kneading of bread. In the labor of the field. In the trembling hand of the sick. In the taste of tears. In the steady breath of presence. In the weight of the body standing on earth

The mystics knew this truth: The sacred is not found in escape, but in encounter. The prophets fell on their faces before they received visions. The Christ knelt to wash feet before He ascended in glory.

> There is no resurrection without burial.
> No revelation without grounding.
> No awakening without return.

To root yourself in a world addicted to speed is a revolutionary act. To feel your feet on the earth is to reclaim your soul from the cloud.

Rootedness is not passivity. It is power. It is the refusal to live fragmented. It is the defiant act of being here. Fully. Present. Awake.

To live grounded is to say:

> I am not a product.
> I am not an algorithm.
> I am not a brand.
> I am a living soul in sacred soil.

And this ground, this dust, this body, is not in the way of my spirituality. It is the birthplace of it.

"You do not need to levitate to be holy. You need only to remain rooted in truth."

The path forward is not another technique. It is not a new teaching, trend, or theory. It is the most ancient path of all: Return.

> Return to your breath.
> Return to your body.
> Return to the rhythm of rest.
> Return to the embrace of silence.
> Return to the garden of beginning.

Let the ground remember you. Let the soul come home to flesh. Let Heaven meet Earth within you.

Prophetic Discernment in an Age of Floating Spirituality

The modern spiritual landscape is full of talk about elevation, activation, ascension.

But few speak of incarnation. Few preach about grounding. Few understand that divine power flows not just from the heights; but from the depths.

Beware of any light that teaches you to leave your body. Beware of any teaching that skips suffering. Beware of any movement that has no need for soil, silence, or rest. For the true prophets are not found floating; they are found rooted:

Rooted in justice.
Rooted in presence.
Rooted in the tears of those who mourn.
Rooted in the ground where blood cries out and mercy still answers.

Start reclaiming the ground beneath you. Take a moment now. Pause. Breathe. Let this not be theory, but remembrance.

Feel the soles of your feet.
Feel the breath move through your body.
Name the places where you have drifted.
Let the grief rise for what was lost.
Let the gratitude rise for what still remains.

You are not far from the ground. You only need to remember it. Let your prayers be spoken with your body. Let your worship begin with your breath.

Let your spiritual life be rooted not just in Heaven; but in here, and now.

In the end, the mystery is not that we were meant to escape the Earth. The mystery is that Heaven longs to dwell in it; and in us.

What if holiness is not in hovering, but in being held? What if enlightenment is not in leaving, but in learning to stay fully alive, fully human, fully awake?

What if God is not waiting for us to ascend; but for us to descend into the real? For that is where truth lives. Not in the cloud. But in the clay.

Let the Ground Receive You Again

When did I begin to drift from my grounded self? What practices keep me rooted in truth, body, and presence? In what ways have I made escape more desirable than embodiment? What have I feared in being fully here? Let these questions echo not just in your mind; but in your bones.

Breathe. Feel the weight of your feet. Let the Earth remember you. And give thanks for the ground that still is welcome you home. You were made for it. You came from it. And within it; you will find again the presence that never left.

Part 4.

The Sacred Descent: From Upward Obsession to Downward Awakening

In a world fixated on elevation, on climbing higher, building bigger, achieving faster, the word *descent* sounds almost offensive. To descend is to lower oneself. To descend is to surrender ground, to appear weak, to fall behind. Yet in the true divine process of elevation, descent is not a collapse, it is not regression, it is not failure.

It is sacred reversal. A holy contradiction, a reorientation of value systems shaped by heaven rather than by human ambition.

Descent, in the Kingdom of God, is not a downward spiral, it is a spiral inward, toward the hidden place where truth dwells unshaken. It is not a punishment. It is an invitation.

And in this sacred invitation, humanity is called not to escape Earth but to *enter it fully*; to return, not to rise.

The Myth of Ascent: The Idol of the Upward Path

Modern spirituality, technological expansion, and even many strands of religious teaching have unknowingly perpetuated an idol of upwardness. To be more enlightened, we are told, is to ascend.

To reach higher consciousness is to escape the body, leave behind the limitations of the earth, and live in the rarefied realm of ideas and energy.

But what if that trajectory has pulled us further away from wholeness rather than toward it? What if, in our effort to rise, we have severed the root?

In our flight from the earth, have we lost the soil of our formation?

This is not to deny transcendence. It is to redefine it. True transcendence is not the absence of form, but the inhabitation of it. Not leaving the world behind, but rediscovering its sacred essence.

In Christ, transcendence is not upward escapism but downward incarnation. In his divine descent: He revealed the pattern of the Holy One.

Consider the sacred choreography of descent woven throughout the story of God:

> Moses did not hear the voice of God from the heights of empire, but in the wilderness, amid silence and flame.
>
> Joseph did not step into leadership from a palace, but rose from a pit, through betrayal and imprisonment.
>
> Jonah met divine mercy not in spiritual meditation, but in the belly of a sea creature, surrounded by darkness and death.
>
> Jesus, the Incarnate Word, did not conquer through might but descended into flesh, then into the grave, before rising in divine glory.

Each of these stories reorients our understanding of divine movement. God does not avoid the depths; He inhabits them. He sanctifies them. He uses them not as detours, but as doorways. Heaven bends low to heal Earth.

The Ground of Glory: Where Seeds Are Broken to Rise

The spiritual law of life hidden in creation echoes this truth: everything alive must go down before it can rise.

> A seed must first be buried.
> A womb must first be entered.
> A root must first anchor deep.

So, it is with the soul. To reach maturity, it must descend; into silence, into mystery, into the unformed and uncomfortable depths of being.

It is there that divine transformation occurs, away from applause, away from performance, away from illusion.

We fear descent because we have confused it with death. But descent, in divine terms, is not death. It is preparation for resurrection. In in this place of sacred preparation, within the Earth's hidden chambers, our Eternal Father meets us in truth.

Much of what we fear in descent is not the descent itself, but what we project onto it:

> The fear of being seen as small.
> The fear of becoming irrelevant.
> The fear of encountering the pain we've buried.

The fear of returning to the soil of origin, where we might feel naked and vulnerable.

Yet the sacred scriptures say otherwise.

> "You formed my inward parts;
> You covered me in my mother's womb...
> My frame was not hidden from You,
> When I was made in secret,
> And skillfully wrought in the lowest parts of the earth." Psalm 139:13–15

Here, descent is not shame, it is holy craftsmanship. It is not exile; it is intimacy.

The "lowest parts of the earth" are not metaphors of banishment, but descriptions of divine artistry. You were formed in hiddenness. In sacred soil. In the place the world calls low, God built your soul. The descent within truly is an invitation to re-enter reality.

The journey of descent is not external only; it is deeply internal. It is the descent from noise into silence. From mind into heart. From distraction into presence. From self-deception into truth.

The journey downward is the path inward, and the path inward is the only way to rediscover the flame of divine origin.

Many today are caught in the illusion of ascending away from their human experience. But until we descend into the place of our full humanity, we cannot carry the glory of divine fullness.

For the Spirit does not bypass the body. Heaven does not bypass the Earth. The Word became flesh and dwelt among us.

> That is descent.
> That is the pattern.
> That is the path.

Earth as Altar: Returning to the Womb of Formation

If we believe Earth is only a temporary exile, a holding tank to escape, then we will never treat it as sacred. But if we believe Earth is the original altar, the place of divine meeting, then every rock, every breath, every pain and promise becomes a portal to encounter.

> Earth is not just dirt; it is womb.
> Soil is not just matter; it is memory.

Our first formation in the creation, both physical and spiritual, occurred not in the abstract heights but in the lowest parts. Earth is the container of our becoming. And returning to it; fully, mindfully, truthfully; is a return to our true inheritance.

The Fear of Depth: Shedding the Shadows

Descent exposes us. It reveals what lies buried: ungrieved losses, unanswered questions, unspoken longings.

This is why many resist it. They fear the silence, because silence speaks. They fear the shadows, because they imagine God is not there.

But it is in the shadows that God whispers. It is in the silence that God speaks. It is in the descent that God heals.

To descend is not to vanish, it is to be replanted. To descend is not to give up, it is to be given over to the hands of the Divine Potter.

Let us not confuse the surrounding darkness with abandonment. For even the darkness is as light to Him. The cave becomes a cathedral. The soil becomes sanctuary. The grave becomes gateway.

The Prophetic Call: Embrace the Descent

The prophetic invitation of this generation is clear:
Come down, that you might rise in truth.
Enter the silence, that you might hear what's eternal.
Return to the body, that the Spirit might dwell there again. Touch the earth, that heaven may become real once more.

This is not poetic romanticism. It is prophetic realism. The future belongs not to those who float away in abstraction, but to those who descend deeply into reality and emerge with divine clarity.

Because truly to descend is to remember.

> Who we are
> Whose we are
> Where we were formed
> What we carry
> Why we were sent

The further we descend into truth, the more the illusions fall away. We discover that the escape was never upward. It was always *inward*. And it leads us not into separation, but into sacred union.

This is a sacred reflection for the reader. Let your spirit pause and ask:

> What am I afraid to descend into?
> Where have I equated "going low" with failure?
> What part of my story still waits for my attention in the soil of silence?
> Can I believe that God waits for me, not in the heights, but in the depths?

Sit with these questions. Write what stirs. Return to the breath. And as you breathe, feel the pulse of the Earth beneath you, the heartbeat of the One who formed you in secret and is calling you home, not to the sky, but to the soil where you began.

Sincere Benediction

May you descend into truth. May you find treasure in the tomb. May you walk into the hidden chamber and be named again. Not as one who fell,
but as one who was found. For the path of return is not above, it is *within*. And descent is not departure.
It is homecoming.

Part 5.

The Earth Is Not the Enemy: Reclaiming the Forgotten Sanctuary

In the great span of human spiritual history, Earth has too often been mistaken for exile rather than entrusted ground. This chapter invites the reader to reframe Earth not as a place of limitation, but as sacred design, where Heaven meets soil, and the breath of God animates dust.

We explore the ancient memory, long buried, that Earth is not the enemy of the soul but its appointed meeting place with the Divine.

In a world seeking to escape suffering, limitation, and the material realm, this prophetic meditation reclaims embodiment, place, and presence as essential to transformation. Through scripture, revelation, and rooted reflection, we remember what was once forgotten: Earth is the altar, not the obstacle.

A Fractured Story: The False Divide Between Spirit and Soil

Somewhere along the winding, weathered trail of human spiritual thought, a great fracture occurred that captured the human imagination.

We began to tell ourselves a story, a seductive but distorted one; that Earth was a cage, a curse, a place of condemnation from which the soul must escape.

This narrative embedded itself deeply within theology, philosophy, and even science. Matter became suspect. Spirit became abstract. The sacred was lifted into the sky while the ground beneath our feet was deemed fallen, unworthy, impure.

But what if that fracture was never meant to be? What if the split between spirit and matter is not divine in origin, but human in distortion?

What if the Earth, far from being a realm of exile, is in fact the sacred sanctuary we have long been entrusted to inhabit, cultivate, and honor?

This is not just a rethinking of theology; it is a prophetic restoration of memory. A remembering of what the soul once knew but culture forgot. Earth is not your enemy. Earth is your altar.

In the Beginning: Entrustment, Not Exile

In the Genesis narrative, Earth is not portrayed as a prison. It is paradise. It is not a fallen battleground, but a garden, a place of intentional design, divine delight, and relational communion.

The Creator walked in this garden. Springs flowed from beneath the ground. Animals, plants, and humanity existed not in hierarchy, but in harmony.

Adam, whose name means "from the ground," was formed not from abstract spirit but from the soil itself. And then, God breathed into that clay. Dust met breath. Form met spirit. Earth met Heaven.

From the very beginning, the Earth was not a trap to transcend, it was a sanctuary to tend.

This holy rhythm was not one of escape but of entrustment. The human soul was not banished to Earth. It was given Earth. And in that sacred entrustment, our most ancient role emerged: steward, not fugitive.

Misreading the Fall: Earth Did Not Betray Us

The fall of humanity is often invoked as the moment Earth itself was condemned. But this too, is a misreading. Earth was not cursed for existing; it groaned under the weight of human disconnection.

Creation did not rebel; it mourned. It was not the Earth that turned from God; it was humanity that turned from its relationship to the sacred, and in doing so, distorted its perception of the very ground it stood upon.

The Apostle Paul writes:

"For the creation waits in eager expectation for the children of God to be revealed...in hope that the creation itself will be liberated from its bondage to decay and brought into the freedom and glory of the children of God." Romans 8:19-21

Creation is not waiting to be discarded. It is waiting to be restored. The fall was not the Earth's failure. It was our failure to remain in communion; with the Creator, with creation, and with ourselves.

Sacred Soil: The Earth as the Meeting Place

Throughout scripture, divine encounters rarely happen in the abstract. They happen on mountains, in deserts, beside rivers, under trees, and on the dirt floors of tents.

> God met Moses on a mountain, speaking from a bush that blazed but was not consumed.
> Jacob wrestled with a divine presence on the muddy ground of night.
> Elijah heard the still small voice not in the heavens, but in the silence of a cave.
> And in Jesus, the Word became flesh and dwelt among us; divinity entering the density of human matter.

Even the final vision in Revelation is not of souls ascending to a distant heaven, but of heaven descending to Earth.

> "Then I saw the Holy City, the new Jerusalem, coming down out of heaven from God." Revelation 21:2

The story ends not with an escape but with a marriage. Not with Earth's dismissal, but with its renewal. When the temple touches the soil again.

The Forgotten Sanctuary: When Presence Meets Place

We live in an age of abstraction. We live "in the cloud"; digitally, ideologically, theologically. We value the transcendent while diminishing the immanent. But the living soul cannot thrive in disembodiment.

There is a deep weariness that comes from trying to live disconnected from place. From Earth. From the body. From the now. This disconnection has not led to liberation. It has led to anxiety, loneliness, and ecological collapse.

Could it be that the restoration we seek is not up there, but down here? What if the Earth is not in the way, but it is the prepared way?

What if the very limitations of this earthly realm, its gravity, its seasons, its fragility; are not prisons but portals? Sacred thresholds meant to slow us, press us, and root us; not to punish, but to prepare us.

The Body and the Breath: Embodiment as Spiritual Path

Just as we have feared the Earth, we have feared the body. In many traditions, the body has been reduced to an obstacle, a temptation, a temporary vehicle for something "higher." But the body is Earth. And to reject the body is to continue the same fracture.

The Word of the Living God became flesh not to validate our theology, but restore and redeem embodiment.

To walk, to touch, to bleed, to eat, to sleep, to sweat, to weep; these are not less-than spiritual. They are the very channels through which spirit is revealed.

Every breath you take is a liturgy. Every step on Earth is a sacrament. Every act of presence is a prophetic return.

We do not ascend by leaving the Earth behind. We ascend by rooting deeply within it.

The New Eden: Reclaiming the Garden Within and Around

We often dream of Heaven as elsewhere. But what if Eden was never entirely lost? What if Eden is seeded in every wildflower, every tree that breaks through concrete, every child's barefoot laughter?

The new Earth begins not with cosmic relocation but with cosmic remembrance. When we remember the garden, we begin to tend it again.

When we reclaim the Earth as sacred, we stop exploiting it and begin listening to it. And in doing so, we do not just heal the planet. We heal our perception of God, of self, and of neighbor.

To be rooted is to be reborn.

Rewriting the Narrative: From Escape to Entrustment

The question is no longer, "How do we get out of here?" The question is, "What sacred work are we called to do here?" What if our longing to escape is not about elevation, but about remembering what we've forgotten?

The stories we inherited, stories of shame, of exile, of flesh as failure, must be re-examined in the light of sacred presence.

The Divine is not afraid of soil. The Spirit is not allergic to matter. The sacred has never abandoned the Earth. It waits, like a whisper in the garden, asking: *"Where are you?"*

A Prophetic Re-Entrustment

Can we walk again like Adam; aware, awake, entrusted? Can we take off our shoes on holy ground; not in the clouds, but in the backyard?

Can we bless the body as temple and the Earth as sanctuary? Can we see the ordinary as infused with the extraordinary?

This is the return; not to Heaven, but to Eden. Not to transcendence, but to truthful presence. Not away from Earth, but into it, renewed.

The Earth is not cursed. It is waiting. Not for your escape. But for your attention.

To escape it is to abandon the altar. To reclaim it is to rediscover the voice that still walks in the garden; calling your name, beneath the trees.

Let us return. Let us remember. Let us rebuild the sanctuary, one sacred footstep at a time.

Part 6.

The Descent Begins; A Call to the Sacred Below

This is where the illusion unravels. This is where the sky releases its hold, where ascent gives way to depth, and a forgotten voice; older than time; whispers again: "Come back down."

Not in shame. Not in defeat. Not as regression. But as remembrance.

The sacred descent is not a fall from grace, but the only way to recover it. We have searched the stars for escape routes. We have built towers of intellect, idols of innovation, and temples of transcendence. We have wandered far; astrally, mentally, technologically, and called it evolution. Yet the soul remains unsatisfied. The ache persists.

The whisper grows louder: "You were not made to flee the ground, but to root yourself into its hidden pulse."

This part of the journey, the descent; is not an exit, but a re-entry. Not a retreat, but a return. A prophetic pilgrimage into the womb of the Earth. Into the sacred hidden beneath everything.

Redefining the Escape

We must now revisit our understanding of "escape." It was never about leaving the Earth. It was never about abandoning the body. It was never about disowning pain, discomfort, or dust.

To escape, in its truest form, is to awaken from illusion. It is to break free not from life, but from the fantasy that life is elsewhere. It is to unbind ourselves from the seduction of spectacle and the addiction to ascent.

We must escape:

The tyranny of speed that rushes us past our soul.
The abstraction of spiritual performance divorced from presence.
The digital mirages that sedate the ache of being.
The cosmic ladder that convinces us the sacred is *up there*, rather than *in here*.

To escape is to truly descend into reality, not the one that have been sold to us; but the one gifted to us in creation's soil, rooted in the dust that received the divine breath of God.

Dust is not a symbol of weakness. It is the sacred substance of the origin.

Remember:
It was into dust that the breath of God was first released.
It was from dust that humanity was formed—not to be discarded, but to be filled with divine life.

The descent begins when we no longer despise the dust. When we no longer equate grounding with limitation. When we discover that *lowering ourselves* is the only path to raising our awareness.

In a world obsessed with rising, climbing, achieving, and outperforming; the most radical act of spiritual truth is to kneel.

To descend is not to shrink. It is to enter the sacred beneath the skin. It is to hear the divine frequency vibrating not in the stars, but in the stillness of the soil.

Earth the Portal

We have misunderstood the Earth. We called it a cage when it was a cathedral. We labeled it limitation when it was invitation.

The Earth was never our prison. It is the passage, the sacred womb of formation in creation, communion, and transformation.

Beneath the pain, the pollution, the disconnection, the exploitation; the Earth still holds memory. The memory of what was once living in a sacred harmony with heaven.

And it groans. It groans for the sons and daughters of light to descend again; not with dominion, but with devotion. To touch the soil not with conquest, but with reverence. To walk not in arrogance, but in alignment.

The First Step Is Not Upward

All illusions begin with a single lie: that your salvation lies in escape.

All healing begins with a single truth: that your restoration lies in return. And return starts with one thing: Breath.

Breathe again; not shallow, not fearful. Breathe as one who belongs to Earth. Breathe as one who no longer fears slowness, silence, or descent.

The descent begins not with knowledge, but with breathing. Not with maps, but with surrender.
Not with escape plans, but with presence. To descend is to enter the mystery of groundedness.

You Are Already Descending

If you are reading these words, it means the descent has already begun within you. Somewhere in your being, the illusions are breaking.

The noise is growing unbearable. The hunger for something real is returning. The ache to touch what is true and unshakeable is reawakening.

You are not late. You are not behind.
You are not lost. You are being summoned, called; not upward, but inward and downward.

The Mountain's Secret

We have sought the mountaintop experience.
But few have dared to look at the base of the mountain.

That is where the fire burns. That is where the covenant is made. That is where the voice speaks; not in thunderous displays, but in holy stillness.

The mountaintop may give you a view, but the base gives you your vow.

It is where the divine meets the dust. Where the eternal marries the temporal. Where the Word becomes flesh and the sacred becomes soil.

The Sacred Below

This is not a descent into darkness, but into depth. There is sacredness buried below:

In the silence beneath noise.
In the stillness beneath striving.
In the truth beneath illusion.

The descent is the only way to recover the parts of yourself left behind in the climb. It is where you will hear again the sacred language of the Earth: the hum of belonging. The whisper of wholeness. The memory of Eden.

You stand at the entrance to the sacred below. Before you take the next step, ask:

Am I willing to descend to remember?
Can I trust the ground that once formed me to now receive me again?
What illusions must I release to return to what is truly sacred?

The descent is not forced, it is offered. And it always begins with a choice.

Prophetic Pause: Breathe

Breathe, beloved one. Let the breath descend where your thoughts have raced. Let your spirit settle into the soil.

You are not falling. You are being rooted. You are not escaping. You are re-entering. You are not forsaken. You are found; right here, at the base, where heaven kisses the Earth again.

The Portal Opens... Below

Let this chapter close not as a conclusion, but as a sacred doorway into depth. Not into the clouds of abstraction, but into the sacred ground of living transformation.

The portal does not open in the sky.

It opens...

> At the mountain's base
> In the soil of remembrance
> In the stillness of surrender
> In the holy breath you take... now

Breathe again. The descent has begun.

Chapter One Summary: Echoes from the Descent

The Sacred Unveiling of Our Grounded Return

In the beginning of our journey through *Escaping Earth*, Chapter One pierced the veil of modern illusions and invited us to reorient our hearts; not toward an external ascension, but toward a sacred descent. It is here, in the unseen soil of our origin, that truth begins to hum, whisper, and awaken.

We began by exposing the rootless momentum of a humanity obsessed with rising; rising beyond its pain, beyond its responsibility, beyond its place.

We saw how the illusion of escape is not freedom, but a spiritual fracture, a longing to transcend the discomfort of earthliness without understanding its divine purpose. Escape became the counterfeit, and remembrance became the call.

We then unearthed the modern mythologies that seduce the soul: ideologies of elevation, technologies of detachment, and spiritualities that deny embodiment.

This pursuit of the "higher" often disembodies us from the here. But the sacred is not only in the sky, it is in the soil.

True wholeness comes when we no longer run from our dust, but recognize that dust was God's chosen medium of creation.

Then, we confronted the great counterfeit, light without heat. The soul can be blinded by brilliance that warms nothing. The mirage of enlightenment, when severed from divine intimacy, becomes sterile knowledge. We were reminded that true light is not just visible; it is *felt*. It transforms.

And only through the warmth of the sacred descent can the fire of divine presence illuminate our path.

We explored the dangers of detachment, when the quest to ascend leads to a spiritual free-fall. To lose the ground beneath us is to lose orientation. Without rootedness, we drift into the abstract, the ideological, the untethered. We have been called to recover the lost language of ground: to hear again the groan of creation, to feel the memory of the soil, and to rediscover the sacredness of limitation as a divine anchor.

We met the paradox of all true spiritual growth: the upward path is found by going down. Descent is not regression but regeneration. It is the pattern of Christ, the rhythm of roots, the spiral of the womb. The sacred descent is not falling apart; it is falling into alignment. Into wholeness. Into the memory of who we were before we started escaping ourselves.

Then there was the turning point. From the scattered, the exiled, and the fragmented; comes the call to return. Not to Eden as myth, but Eden as memory. The garden is not lost; it is hidden in plain sight, veiled by our forgetting.

We reclaimed Earth not as punishment, but as promise. As the ground where heaven meets breath. Where dust meets divinity. And where restoration begins.

Echoing Insights from the Whole Chapter

The modern pursuit of elevation often blinds us to what lies beneath.
False light can simulate enlightenment while leaving the soul empty.
Disembodiment is not transcendence; it is a spiritual fracture.
Descent is not weakness; it is the divine pattern of restoration.
Earth is not exile; it is the original sanctuary; the womb of divine formation.
We were woven in the depths of the Earth, and breathed into dust.
The path forward begins by returning to sacred ground.

This chapter doesn't end in despair; it descends into memory, mystery, and communion.

The invitation is clear and still echoing: Come back down; Not to fall, but to rise whole.

Chapter Two

Reawakening the Inner Temple

Having faced the humanistic illusion of escape and rediscovered the sacredness of descent, we now stand before a new threshold: the entrance into the soul's hidden sanctuary.

The previous chapter led us away from the false heavens we tried to reach and toward the sacred earth within us; the ground of divine encounter.

Now, this second step calls for an even deeper journey, one not into the stars nor the soil, but into the eternal temple that God established within the human spirit; the holy chamber where His presence still waits to be remembered.

Every sacred journey begins with a call, and this call is not to rise, but to descend. It echoes not through the mountains of ambition, but through the valleys of remembrance.

The descent into the inner temple is not a retreat from the world; it is a restoration of the soul's forgotten truth. It is the return to the sacred architecture woven into the very design of our being, a structure not made by human hands but breathed into existence by the Eternal Word.

The modern soul has learned to travel everywhere except inward. We have scaled heights of intellect and explored depths of matter, yet the inner sanctuary remains closed to many; not by divine command, but by human neglect.

And so, the Spirit whispers once more: "Descend." Descend beyond distraction. Descend beneath the noise. Descend past the outer courts of thought and emotion, into the holy place where eternity and time converge.

This descent is not about leaving behind, but about returning; to the original communion between Creator and creation, where the soul was once in perfect resonance with the breath of life.

To reawaken the inner temple is to reawaken memory; the memory of being loved, known, and created in divine likeness.

The temple within has not been destroyed; it has only been forgotten. Over time, the noise of the world, the weight of pain, and the illusions of false identity have layered themselves like dust upon sacred walls.

The altar still stands, though unrecognized; the lamp still burns, though dimmed by distraction. The soul's corridors, once echoing with divine conversation, have grown silent; not because the Spirit has departed, but because the heart ceased to listen.

Within the sacred design of this inner temple are symbols that reflect eternal truths. The outer courts represent the realm of human senses; the domain of doing, seeing, and reacting.

The inner court reflects the mind and emotions; the place of prayer and offering. But beyond these lies the Holy of Holies; the secret chamber where Holy Spirit communes with our human spirit, where the breath of the Living God still hovers over the dust of humanity.

This sanctuary is not an abstraction; it is the truest part of who we are. It is the meeting place between heaven and earth, between the unseen and the seen. To rediscover it is to remember that we were never left abandoned; only distracted.

Reawakening the inner temple begins with excavation; the gentle but courageous uncovering of what has been buried.

The Holy Spirit leads us, not with force, but with light. Every memory brought to the surface, every shadow illuminated, becomes an act of holy restoration.

This sacred excavation is not for the faint of heart. It requires stillness, honesty, and surrender.

The layers we uncover are often made of pain; unhealed wounds, distorted beliefs, echoes of rejection.

Yet even in uncovering them, we do not expose ourselves to shame, but to healing.

For in the hands of the Divine Architect, every broken stone can be restored to purpose.

Repentance, in its truest sense, is not a word of condemnation but of alignment. It is the act of turning inward toward truth, of realigning the temple's pillars with the foundation of divine order.

The Spirit of the Living God does not rebuild with condemnation but with compassion, washing the inner courts with grace until the heart becomes once again a dwelling of light.

Silence becomes the chisel. Tears become the cleansing water. And as the noise subsides, the echo of the Eternal Voice is heard again: *"You were never forsaken; you simply forgot the sound of My presence."*

Once the excavation is complete, the rebuilding begins. But this reconstruction is unlike any work of human hands; it is not born of striving, but of surrender.

For the temple of the living soul cannot be restored through intellect or ritual; it must be breathed back to life through the indwelling of Spirit.

Each act of forgiveness lays a new stone. Each prayer of gratitude forms a beam of light. Each remembrance of divine truth rebuilds the walls of communion.

As it is written, "You also, like living stones, are being built into a spiritual house" 1 Peter 2:5.

We are not rebuilding alone, we are co-laborers with the Spirit, artisans of restoration working under divine guidance.

When the soul reclaims its sacred architecture, harmony returns. The altar burns with holy fire once more, not consuming, but illuminating.

The veil that once separated the seen from the unseen is lifted, and light floods the inner chamber. The temple begins to sing again, its resonance vibrating through every layer of being; body, mind, and spirit united in worship of the One who dwells within.

At the heart of the restored temple is Presence; not as concept, but as reality. Here, prayer becomes breath, and breath becomes communion. The soul no longer seeks God in the distant heavens, for true heaven has entered the living soul.

The lamp of the inner sanctuary, once dimmed, now burns with steady light. It reveals that God never left; only our awareness had faded. In this awakening, we no longer strive to reach divinity; we realize that divinity has been reaching for us all along.

The temple is not a monument of religion, but a living organism of revelation, pulsing with the rhythm of divine life.

In this realization, the illusion of separation

dissolves. The individual becomes vessel; the vessel becomes light; and the light becomes the language of love.

This is the awakening of the new creation; not apart from the earth, but within it. The journey into the inner temple is ultimately the journey home.

We discover that what we sought in sacred places and distant visions has always been here; in the stillness of our being. The Holy Father and God, who once walked in the cool of the garden now walks within the garden of our soul, restoring the covenant of presence that was never truly broken.

To reawaken the inner temple is to become aware again that we are the meeting point of heaven and earth. Through us, creation breathes, sings, and remembers its Source. We are not travelers passing through divine mystery, we are living extensions of it.

Every heartbeat, every breath, every act of awareness becomes liturgy in this eternal sanctuary.

And so, the Holy Spirit whispers again: *"Return to your temple. Rebuild its altar. Rekindle its flame. For I have never left; I have been waiting for you to awaken."*

The temple is not lost. It waits. Within you. Within all of us. Let us descend; and remember who we are.

After passing through the illusion of escape and rediscovering the sacredness of descent, we now arrive at a deeper threshold; the descent into the soul.

This is not merely a poetic metaphor, but a sacred invitation to enter the most hidden place within; the inner sanctuary, the temple of divine communion that has long been buried under layers of noise, trauma, distraction, and self-forgetting.

If Chapter One asked us to descend into the Earth to rediscover the sacred foundation, then Chapter Two calls us to descend into the depths of our soul to awaken the divine indwelling.

This is the temple not built by human hands, the place where memory and mystery meet, where eternity was whispered its essence into the dust of our being.

The soul is not a passive container. It is a living chamber, an altar of remembrance, a divine archive where the original breath of life still echoes.

But this temple has been neglected. Over time, layers of false identity, pain, worldly programming, and spiritual disconnection have obscured its holy function.

And so, we must now go inward; not in retreat, but in sacred restoration.

This chapter is a journey through the forgotten corridors of the soul:

> To excavate what was hidden,
> To cleanse what was distorted,
> To rebuild what was once holy.

We do not descend to diminish. We descend to remember. We do not enter the soul to escape reality, but to meet it at its most sacred source. And through this sacred re-entry, we come not only to know who we are; but whose we are and where we belong.

The temple is not lost.

> It waits.
> Within you.
> Within all of us.

> *Let us descend.*

Part 1.

The Soul; Forgotten Sanctuary

Before temples of marble graced the Earth, before incense rose from golden altars, and before hymns echoed in vaulted ceilings shaped by mortal hands, there existed a place of deeper sanctity.

A sanctuary not made by man; but formed by divine breath. The breathing and living soul.

We speak not in metaphors. The soul is not a distant abstraction or a poetic stand-in for emotion. It is not a canvas upon which society paints its moralities, nor is it a spark of religious sentiment reserved for funerals and fleeting moments of spiritual awe.

No, the soul is real. Tangible in its invisibility. A living, breathing architecture; constructed not from stone, but from eternity itself.

In the opening chapters of humanity's story, the text of Genesis 2:7 declares: "Then the Lord God formed man from the dust of the ground and breathed into his nostrils the breath of life; and man became a living soul."

Notice the sequence. The body, first. A form of clay, beautiful, but inert. But only when breath was imparted did the soul awaken.

That perfect moment; sacred, instantaneous, eternal, marked the birth of divine consciousness within flesh.

This is the true origin of the soul: not a result of biological processes, but a consequence of divine interaction.

And yet, in our modern age, that truth has been buried beneath the rubble of progress, psychology, and digital abstraction.

The soul has been unseated from its throne within, and reduced; at best, to a passing idea. But the living soul, though forgotten by the world, has not forgotten us.

The Mystery of the Inner Formation

Psalm 139:13-15 reaches into the depths of this mystery:

"For You formed my inward parts; You covered me in my mother's womb. I will praise You, for I am fearfully and wonderfully made; marvelous are Your works, and that my soul knows very well... when I was made in secret, and skillfully wrought in the lowest parts of the earth."

These verses speak not just of biological life, but of sacred formation. The "lowest parts of the earth" are not mere geographical metaphors.

They symbolize the unseen realm, the secret place where the soul is shaped before the eye ever beholds the body. A place veiled from mere human understanding, yet known intimately by the Eternal Creator.

The soul, then, is not a product of visible evolution. It is not formed through intellect, experience, or self-discovery. It is planted. Sown in the mystery. Wrought in secret. A gift that existed even before cognition, before language, before societal labels.

And because it was made in mystery, it cannot be understood by surface analysis. It must be accessed through descent; an inward journey through stillness, remembrance, and revelation.

Modern Amnesia; The Neglected Sanctuary

We live in an age of a continue search for outer expansion. Our technologies reach the stars. Our networks span continents. Our human intellect penetrates the atom. But in the frenzy journey to understand everything out there, we have neglected the most ancient sanctuary within.

We care for the body with precision. Diet, fitness, appearance; we curate it like a sculpture. We train the mind with vigor; through schooling, information, analysis. But what about the soul?

The living soul is bypassed. It is treated as superstition, or repackaged into shallow self-help slogans. Even in the spiritual settings, the soul is often confused with feelings, emotions, or a higher form of ego. Few recognize it for what it truly is: a living vault of divine remembrance.

This amnesia has consequences.

Without connection to the soul, identity becomes fragmented. We begin to define ourselves by external roles; titles, accomplishments, social belonging.

But these are costumes. When the soul is silenced, these roles become prisons.

Without soul awareness, relationships degrade into transactions. Love is confused with validation. Presence is replaced by performance. The sacred bond between beings is reduced to an algorithm of benefits.

And truth; once rooted in the eternal wells, becomes relative, shifting with the winds of culture and trend. Devoid of the soul's compass, we wander not just as lost individuals, but as an unanchored civilization.

But the sacred whispers of return to our forgotten divine memory to awaken us never stops. And because of them sacred whispers, the soul does not, and it will not remain silent forever.

Even when it is been buried beneath layers of distraction, the soul captures them. There are moments when the veil thins; when something ancient stirs within. Perhaps in a dream. A sudden stillness. A longing that cannot be named. A restlessness that no achievement satisfies.

That is not anxiety. That is not emptiness. That is the living soul calling. Not for escape, but for return to its once divine and sacred purpose.

Return not to a place, but to presence. Not to a religion, but to remembrance. The soul calls us not outward, but inward, toward the sacred center of alignment, where the Everlasting Father and God once breathed life into dust and made us living souls.

In 1 Corinthians 3:16, we are reminded: "Do you not know that you are a temple of God and that the Spirit of God dwells in you?" Not a metaphor. Not poetry. Reality.

The soul is not a blank slate waiting to be written upon. It is a sacred text already inscribed. Within it is etched divine memory. Holy codes. Celestial blueprints of identity, purpose, and connection. Our task is not to re-invent the soul, but to awaken it.

The Descent; A Journey Inward, Not Downward

This chapter is a threshold. A gate. An invitation to descend, not downward into despair, but inward into sanctity.

True descent is not at all regression. It is resurrection. It is the choice to enter the secret chambers within where the soul resides in quiet radiance, waiting to be remembered. We descend past the noise of identity, through the layers of false self, into the holy stillness where the soul speaks without words.

The world norms teach ascension through elevation: climb higher, achieve more, be seen. But the soul invites a different path. One of depth. One of humility. One of divine intimacy.

To forget the soul is to sever our connection with Source. But to remember the soul is to reclaim our place as vessels of sacred habitation.

The Sanctuary Within; Beyond Religious Structures

Let us pause here for a moment to reframe our understanding. When Scripture says we are temples of God, it is not speaking of metaphorical likeness to buildings. It is proclaiming that the soul is a holy dwelling place, a sanctuary where the Spirit of God desires to reside. But how can a temple function when it is unacknowledged?

Imagine a cathedral; ornate, ancient, filled with sacred light, but boarded shut. Dust gathers on the altar. Silence hangs not as reverence, but as abandonment. That is what happens when the soul is ignored. The lights dim. The sacred music ceases. And life becomes a hollow performance.

Yet, when we reopen that door, even just a crack, the Light returns. The soul sanctuary is reactivated. The living soul begins to hum with remembrance, and suddenly, life is no longer something we merely survive; it becomes something we embody.

Echoes from Eden; The Original Sanctuary Remembered

The soul remembers Eden. Not as a place on a map, but as a state of union. A garden of pure presence, where no separation existed between human and Divine. That memory is not lost; it is encrypted within us, like divine DNA waiting to be decoded.

And every genuine longing we experience; every ache for meaning, every desire for home, every pull toward beauty, is the echo of the Garden of Eden calling us home.

The forgotten sanctuary can be remembered. Not by striving. Not by theology. But by surrender. Surrendering to the silence. To the stillness. To the sacred resonance within.

The Reclamation; Living as Soul-Awakened Beings

To awaken the soul is not to escape Earth; but to finally begin living on it as we were meant to. Fully aware. Fully present. Fully infused with divine remembrance. This is not a religious theory. This it is a sacred and a profound transformation.

When we return to the soul, we begin to see differently. People are no longer labels. Situations are no longer accidents, and time is no longer just a countdown; but a divine canvas. And we begin to live from the inside out.

No longer driven by fear of death, we begin to live from the awareness of eternal life already present within us. No longer fixated on approval, we begin to radiate from divine identity. No longer lost in the illusions of separation, we walk in the unity of all things sustained by the same Breath that awakened the soul in Eden.

Let this be more than a reflection. Let it be an altar. Let it be the moment when we choose to return; not just to a belief system or to ideology; but to the living sanctuary we have forgotten.

You may feel the soul's call as an ache. Or a hunger. Or even an existential dissatisfaction that nothing in the outer world seems able to fill.

That is not weakness. It is divine memory. You are not being undone. You are being invited.

The journey of Escaping Earth begins not with leaving the ground and dust; but with leaving behind the illusion of separation that clouds our living soul.

The descent begins now. Not downward; but inward. Back to the sanctuary. Back to the soul. Back to the place where the breath of the Living God still echoes, waiting to awaken you again.

Part 2.

Beneath the Surface of Our Daily Identities

Before we are names, professions, beliefs, or affiliations; before we are sons or daughters, fathers or mothers, citizens or strangers, we are souls. Sacred. Formed. Remembered.

Beneath the surface of our daily identities; beneath the busyness and burdens, behind the opinions and expectations, there lies an ancient architecture. A holy design. A terrain not visible to the human eye, but more real than the ground beneath our feet.

We are not merely what we do, what we accumulate, or what we profess. We are layered beings, sculpted not just by our own experience and environment but by the mysterious hand of divine formation. The soul is not an accessory to life; it is its origin.

To journey into the soul is not to dive into shadow, but to descend into light. It is to become an excavator of sacred memory. Not through ambition, but through surrender. Not with violence, but with reverence.

Each living soul is like an ancient and majestic city; constructed through divine intention and human experience, layered with memory, myth, and mystery. Some layers are tender and true. Others are bruised and buried.

To awaken to who we truly are requires courage, not to ascend higher into egoic illusion, but to dig deeper into forgotten truth. We are not climbing toward identity; we are uncovering it.

The work is sacred archaeology. We brush away the dust of survival. We lift the stones of trauma. We break through the crust of societal programming. For beneath it all is the original imprint of God. The blueprint of the eternal self.

Our Lord Jesus Christ posed a question that pierces through the smog of every false identity:
"What will it profit a man if he gains the whole world, and loses his own soul?" Mark 8:36

This was not just a simply a call to religious salvation. It was a call to spiritual excavation.

To lose the soul is not to cease existing. It is to exist without essence. To gain the soul is to reclaim what was already gifted at the beginning; before the noise, before the masks, before the world gave us its names.

Paul echoes this sacred truth in Ephesians 2:10: "For we are His workmanship, created in Christ Jesus for good works, which God prepared beforehand that we should walk in them."

You are not an accident of biology or a product of chance. You are His workmanship; "poiēma" in Greek; the same word from which we derive "poem." Your living soul is poetry written by the hand of the Divine.

To excavate identity is not self-indulgence. It is divine obedience. It is to brush away the dust of distortion, pain, and pretense in order to behold what

God has etched beneath the layers. It is to discover the architecture that has been buried under performance, perfectionism, and societal polish.

It is to ask, with holy curiosity: Who am I beneath what I have become? What sacred truth lies buried beneath the noise that surround me?

Buried, Not Lost

We are not lost. We are buried. And every excavation begins with a decision; to return.

But such returning comes with resistance. For everything buried is buried for a reason. Pain. Fear. Control. These are the stones that time and experience have laid atop the soul.

Many of us learned, early in life, to hide our truth. To suppress emotion. To conform, adapt, and survive. We were told; directly or indirectly; that worth was earned through achievement, approval, image, or compliance. That to belong, we had to become something other than who we were. And so, the dust of distortion began to settle.

But dust that accumulates does not remain dust. With repetition and time after time, it will surely become sediment. And sediment, under pressure of life it becomes stone.

The Stones of False Foundation

These hardened layers; fear, ego, shame, indoctrination; eventually become foundational. Not in theory, but in practice.

They support entire identities, systems, and ideologies. They hold up institutions. They are enshrined as sacred. But they were never sacred to begin with. They are not holy stones, but mere accumulated debris; debris that are masquerading themselves as doctrines.

We erect temples on top of trauma and pain and wonder why they crumble when truth knocks at the door. We build ideologies upon insecurities and wonder why they produce manipulation instead of liberation.

We participate in systems; religious, political, cultural; that appear stable but are disconnected from the Breath. They mirror form, but they lack essence. They offer structure, but they deny life.

These are the counterfeit foundations. They cannot hold the weight of truth. They shatter under the presence of the Holy Spirit.

The Holy Test of the Stone

Excavation, then, becomes a test of foundation. What are we standing on? What have we built our lives upon? Is it the cornerstone of Christ; or the sediment of culture?

Isaiah 28:16 declares:
"Behold, I lay in Zion a stone for a foundation, a tried stone, a precious cornerstone, a sure foundation."

Everything else must be questioned. Not in fear, but in freedom. For what cannot survive the Spirit's wind was never truly alive to begin with.

This is why excavation matters.
This is why remembering matters.
This is why the descent is sacred.

The Resistance Meets Revelation

The soul remembers. Even when the mind forgets. Even when the heart is weary. Even when the world praises the mask and punishes the truth, the living soul remembers.

And in certain moments, often unexpected; a tremor begins beneath the surface. It may arrive through crisis. Or silence. Or loss. Or encounter. But the tremor shakes something loose. The soul stirs. A question arises that refuses to be silenced. A longing emerges that outgrows every comfort zone.

This is the point of holy disruption. Where resistance meets revelation. And in this moment, we have a choice: to retreat into familiar illusions, or to descend into the truth that terrifies and heals us at once.

The Tools of Sacred Excavation

This descent is not reckless. It is guided. There are tools, not of iron or intellect; but of the Spirit:

> Silence, where the soul's voice is clearest.
> Stillness, where divine presence breathes.
> Scripture, not as doctrine to memorize, but as mirror to remember.
> Prayer, not of performance, but of presence.
> Curiosity, the kind that does not accuse but inquires.

And above all; the Holy Spirit, who does not come to shame, but to illuminate. The Holy Spirit who breathes upon the bones of buried identity and calls them to live again.

As Ezekiel stood in a valley of dry bones, so do many of us stand amid the fragments of self:

"Come from the four winds, O breath, and breathe on these slain, that they may live." Ezekiel 37:9

The Soul's Resurrection

To peel back the layers is not to destroy self. It is to raise the original self from the ruins. The soul is not waiting to be invented. It is waiting to be uncovered.

Psalm 139 whispers the truth we often forget:

"You formed my inward parts... I am fearfully and wonderfully made... My frame was not hidden from You, when I was made in secret..."

You were always known. Always seen. Always loved. Excavation is not a detour from life. It is life. It is the sacred unveiling of who you were before the world told you who to be.

This is not just personal healing. It is cosmic restoration. Every living soul remembered becomes a brick in the restored temple of humanity. Every person who uncovers truth becomes a pillar of light.

We are not called to escape Earth; we are called to restore it by returning to our God and Eternal Father's breathed essence of life. Isaiah 58:12 speaks a prophetic promise: "You shall raise up the foundations of many generations; and you shall be called the Repairer of the Breach, the Restorer of Streets to Dwell In."

To excavate the soul is to become a repairer. A restorer. A living stone in the sanctuary God is rebuilding within his creation. This is the call: To dig. To descend. To remember.

Let every layer be named. Let every stone be tested. Let every sedimented lie be confronted in the light of love. For beneath it all is a sanctuary still intact.

We may aim high, reaching toward heavenly things. But it is not the heights we chase that define us; it is the depths we return to that restore us. Let this not be a concept, but a cry: Come, Breath of God; Stir the ancient stones.

Dissolve the layers of fear. Awaken the buried truth. Let what is sacred rise again. Let the soul live again. And let it be known; we were never lost. We were only waiting to be found beneath the surface of what we became.

Part 3.

False Layers and Forgotten Names

We are born radiant, with names known to Heaven before they are even spoken on Earth.

Yet somewhere along the pathway of life, most of us forget. We are being given labels, identities, expectations; some well-meaning, others are weaponized to define us.

We grow up learning who we are through the reflections and the norms of the world that others offer; many of which are distorted by their own unhealed wounds and fears.

And thus, layer by layer, the sacred name; our living soul's true resonance; is buried beneath names not our own.

The Accumulation of false Names.

From childhood to adulthood, layers upon layers accumulate over the living soul like sediment settling over a once-radiant light.

These layers are woven in names, titles, identities, and expectations; that become survival tools, emotional armor, or simply unconscious agreements made in the shadows of formative years. But these names are often not our own.

The "good child" who pleases to survive

Often born in homes where love feels conditional, this child learns early in life that strict obedience earns the approval of others. They trade authenticity for safety.

In adulthood, this can lead to chronic people-pleasing, fear of conflict, or an inability to set boundaries. The soul becomes caged in politeness, even when injustice must be confronted. The danger? A life lived to meet expectations rather than divine calling.

The "strong one" who hides their pain

This name is often given to those who grew up being told to "be brave," "man up," or "stop crying." Vulnerability becomes a threat. Strength becomes simple performance.

Behind closed doors, their soul aches; but they dare not show it. These individuals often carry silent depression, internalized shame, and may even reject help when it's most needed. The cost? Isolation in the name of strength.

The "success story" whose worth is measured by achievement

Whether driven by societal pressure, parental pride, or internal fear of inadequacy, this identity becomes obsessed with doing over being. They climb ladders, accumulate titles, and build impressive resumes; but often feel empty inside. When failure inevitably comes, their entire sense of self crumbles.

Because who are you, if you're not "winning"? In truth, they are souls in need of permission to just be.

The "sinner," "saint," "failure," "misfit," "provider," "caretaker," "rebel" ...

Each label is a stronghold mold; offered by religion, family, or culture. The "sinner" may live in perpetual shame, unable to receive grace.

The "saint" may feel trapped in perfectionism, secretly afraid of being human. The "rebel" may have simply resisted an unjust system, but now wears the mask of defiance as identity.

These names are heavy; they alter trajectories, distort perceptions, and forge prisons out of roles we were never meant to carry.

These titles are not identities; they are adaptations. Survival strategies. Roles handed to us at times by family expectations, religious labels, societal and cultural norms, or unresolved pain. And once they settle, they harden.

These teachings, whether are being imposed by family, culture, religion, or social media, settle like layers of dust over the truth of who we are.

Over time, the dust becomes sediment, and the sediment becomes stone. And once it becomes stone, it can lay upon it the ground frame to become a fundamental foundation that can hold structures, ideologies, and dogmas that are completely opposite to the light of truth.

Yet because they are constructed on a sediment foundation, they are easily passed off as truth to the masses. In reality, they have nothing in common with divine truth; thus, many struggles and disappointments cloud humanity's progress toward its true betterment, meaning, and purpose.

And still, many of us live our life according to these names; because they can offer belonging, approval, or predictable reward. But these false names are dangerous.

They shape how we pray, how we serve, how we love, how we lead. They determine the lens through which we see ourselves and others. If we are to be free, these false layers must be named; and then released.

This un-layering is not merely just a psychological process; but it is also a spiritual reality. It is the sacred work of remembrance, of soul excavation, of calling back what was once buried.

This section invites you not to adopt a new label; but to courageously remove the old ones, layer by layer, until only the truth remains.

The Spiritual and Human Cost

When we live under false names, we drift from the divine blueprint written into our being. We are mistaking performance for identity, suppression for maturity, and conformity for wisdom. This is not merely a personal problem; it is a true humanistic and collective crisis.

Each false name becomes a garment that we wear, stitched together by cultural norms, family history, and religious dogma, or even at times by the influences of our own systemic expectations.

Eventually, the garments we wear become so many that we forget how to undress them. We begin to believe that these names, roles and titles are who we are.

Nations are built on narratives. Churches are built on interpretations. Families are built on roles.

When these structures are shaped by mislabeled souls, they reproduce dysfunction across generations. Humanity cannot ascend into sacred and divine healing while remaining anchored to distorted identities.

That is why this sacred work matters; not just for the individual, but for the whole. The return to our true name is the return to truth. And where the light of truth reigns, true freedom follows.

Identity Versus Naming

In the ancient Hebrew worldview, a name was not simply a label; it was an essence, a meaning, a purpose. To know a name was to understand the nature, the calling, and the origin of that name.

When God changed Abram's name to Abraham, or Jacob's to Israel, it wasn't merely a renaming. It was a revelation of destiny and destination.

The same applies to us today. Beneath the assigned names of the world lies the name written for us before the foundations of the Earth. As Revelation 2:17 declares: "To the one who is victorious... I will give them a white stone with a new name written on it, known only to the one who receives it."

That name is not spoken by others; it is revealed in the power of intimacy with the Divine.

But when we wear false names long enough, we begin to operate under false identities. These become filters through which we experience life; limiting our responses, clouding our perceptions, and even distorting our own choices.

And just as sediment over time hardens into stone, the misnaming process becomes a foundation for our very decisions, relationships, and even spiritual pursuits.

But what if the struggles we face; the cycles we repeat, are not flaws in our being, but consequences of forgetting our original name?

We are not what we've been called.
We are what we were created to be.

A Call to Renaming

To remember who we are is a sacred work of divine partnership. Just as Jesus asked the man possessed by a legion of false identities, *"What is your name?"* (Mark 5:9), so too must we ask ourselves: *Who told me this is who I am? And is it true?*

To excavate the false layers is not a denial of experience, but a refusal to allow pain to have the final word.

"Fear not, for I have redeemed you; I have called you by your name; you are Mine. "Isaiah 43:1.

Let this be our remembrance. Not the names of our past trauma or active performance. But the sacred name whispered from the wells of eternity. The name given to all by the Eternal Creator and God. Just ask in silence:

What names have I carried that no longer speak truth?

Who assigned those names; and why did I believe them?

What name might God be whispering over me even now?

Part 4.

The Excavation of Truth

To excavate truth is not to acquire something new, but to recover something eternal.

Truth is not invented; it is remembered. It is not constructed; it is revealed. Beneath the layers of cultural programming, religious conditioning, familial expectation, and the deep grooves of trauma, truth waits; not in a distant realm, but in the sacred center of the soul.

Like buried treasure beneath centuries of soil and stone, truth remains; untouched, incorruptible, luminous.

But excavation requires tools. And not all tools are made of steel or strategy. In the divine excavation of the soul, the tools are surrender, stillness, discernment, and courage.

This is not the work of intellectual striving. It is the gentle labor of love. The Spirit leads, the Word pierces, and the soul consents.

"Is not my word like fire," declares the Lord, "and like a hammer that breaks a rock in pieces?" Jeremiah 23:29

The Word of God is not merely a text; it is a force of restoration. It breaks apart the hardened layers. It pierces through inherited lies. It does not shame the false names; it reveals them. And in revealing, it frees.

But this process, while divine, is not painless.

The Tension of Excavation

> To dig down is to disturb.
> To reveal is to risk.
> To remember is to bleed.

The deeper we go, the more we encounter resistance. Not because truth is absent; but because lies have taken root. These lies are not always malicious; they are often born from fear. "Be strong." "Don't feel." "Be perfect." "Fit in." "Don't question." These phrases are not just words; we internalize them as operating systems.

The Subtle Tyranny of Silent Scripts

These lies are not always malicious; they are often born from fear. But once birthed, fear does not remain passive. It grows. It weaves into habits, language, culture, and identity. It becomes the silent tyrant in the back of the mind, whispering not just *what* to do; but *who* to be.

We are not merely resisting thoughts; we are dismantling scripts. Operating systems passed down by wounded generations, broken institutions, corrupted powers.

Each phrase sounds simple. Even helpful. But behind them, a dangerous molding takes place.

"Be strong."

At face value, strength is a virtue. But this version of strength is a distortion. It does not mean resilience with wisdom; it means suppression without healing.

We are taught: "Don't cry. Don't break. Don't show pain." But in reality, admitting weakness is the first doorway to true strength. Paul himself said:

"For when I am weak, then I am strong." (2 Corinthians 12:10)

True strength begins not in denial, but in surrender. It is the paradox of grace—that our most fragile moments are often the most sacred spaces for divine power to work.

"Don't feel."

This command is a slow death sentence to the soul. It may begin as a defense; blocking pain, hiding shame; but over time, it blocks joy, connection, even the voice of God. We are not machines. We are made in the image of a feeling Creator; One who weeps, rejoices, and burns with compassion.

"Jesus wept." John 11:35

To feel is to live. And to live is to risk. But without feeling, without emotions, we are being numbed into compliance; docile to deception.

"Be perfect."

This is the cruel mirage. A race with no finish line. A ladder with no top rung. Perfectionism does not produce excellence; it produces exhaustion, and shame.

But God never called us to be flawless. He called us to be faithful. Imperfections are not flaws in the divine design; they are invitations to humility and growth.

"The Lord is near to the brokenhearted and saves those who are crushed in spirit." (Psalm 34:18)

We are not called to pose as perfect, but to walk in the light; even with our cracks showing.

"Fit in."

Perhaps the most dangerous lie of all. Because to "fit in" is often to shrink down. To contort the soul. To trade authenticity for acceptance. But what is the cost of such compromise?

You may gain community; but lose your voice.
You may gain visibility; but lose your vision.
You may gain followers; but lose your soul.

This lie is the root of conformity; and conformity is the death of divine uniqueness. God never repeats a creation. If we are to honor the image of God within, we must *dare* to stand apart when truth demands it.

"Don't question."

Silencing questions is the gateway to control. To eliminate inquiry is to eliminate discernment. But Jesus welcomed questions. He asked them. He used them to awaken truth.

Without questioning, humanity is vulnerable to spiritual abuse, political manipulation, and ideological captivity. The Truth does not fear examination; it invites it.

"Come now, and let us reason together," says the Lord. Isaiah 1:18

To question is not rebellion; it is the beginning of revelation.

Breaking the Scripts, Becoming Whole

These phrases; these survival codes; may have helped us function for a time. But they cannot lead us to freedom. They were built for a sense of elusive protection, not transformation. And now, the Holy Spirit calls us to lay them down; not in anger or blame, but in love.

To break these scripts is to reclaim our soul.

We may still feel weak; but we are still worthy. We may not be perfect; but we are in process.

We may feel everything; but that it is okay it means we are alive. We may question deeply; but that means we are close to truth. We may not fit in; but we are already found.

This is the excavation. This is the work.

Not to destroy who we are; but to recover who we were before the world told us who we had to be.

But as we excavate, we begin to ask:

- Who gave me this story?
- Who benefits from me believing it?
- What divine truth is buried beneath this survival script?

And slowly, light begins to break through. We do not deconstruct truth; we deconstruct what was falsely built atop it.

Every soul is a temple. But not all temples are kept holy. Some have been overrun with thieves; voices of condemnation, systems of exploitation, expectations that sell us short of our divine design.

When Jesus entered the physical temple and overturned the tables (Matthew 21:12–13), He was not simply purging a building; He was modeling the spiritual process of restoration. The soul, too, must be cleared. The counterfeit must be cast out. What was corrupted must be cleansed.

"Do you not know that you are God's temple and that God's Spirit dwells in you?" (1 Corinthians 3:16). Truth is not merely something we believe; it is who we become when the inner temple is restored. This is the living soul's sacred excavation.

This is a sacred and divine holy work.

Part 5.

The Original Name; Reclaiming the Uncorrupted Identity

Before you were labeled, you were named. Before the world defined you, the Divine called you.

There exists a name; not of culture, creed, or convenience; but of truth. This sacred name was whispered into your being before the foundations of the earth were laid. It was written by the hand of God into the scroll of your soul.

This is the name the enemy works tirelessly to erase. Through systems, roles, wounds, and projections, we are renamed to fit molds and patterns not meant for us. The world benefits from our forgetfulness. Because a person who remembers their true name cannot be manipulated.

In the Scriptures, the significance of names is profound.

Abram became Abraham; "father of nations."
Jacob became Israel; "one who wrestles with God."
Saul became Paul; transformed from a zealot persecutor to a humble apostle.

Each transformation marked a return; not to a new identity, but to the divine calling originally etched into their being.

To reclaim your name is to reclaim your place. It is to stand, not as the world sees you, but as heaven knows you.

Isaiah 43:1 declares:
"Do not fear, for I have redeemed you; I have called you by name; you are Mine."

This is not metaphor. It is memory. A soul-deep reminder of the bond unbroken by time, sin, or shame.

But why is it so hard to remember this name? Because the world builds altars atop amnesia. Because forgetting keeps us docile, agreeable, and bound to roles that serve systems rather than purpose.

This section invites a sacred rebellion; not one of violence or outward resistance, but of remembrance. A holy confrontation with the labels that have replaced our divine essence.

The systems of this world; through fear, expectation, and survival; have taught us to answer to names that were never written in God's book of life.

You are not your job title.

The world may know you as a manager, technician, nurse, builder, or "just a parent."

But those are roles, not identities. When the job is stripped away, who remains? Beneath the performance and position is a soul crafted in the image of God; fearfully and wonderfully made; not for productivity, but for communion.

You are not the trauma you survived.

> Pain may have shaped part of your story, but it is not your name. Abuse, betrayal, illness, abandonment; these are chapters, not your identity.

> Real healing begins when we stop introducing ourselves by our wounds and start remembering the one who was never wounded; our true self, held in the heart of God before any harm occurred.

You are not the mask you wear to keep peace.

> Many wear smiles to survive. Some become the "helper," the "peacemaker," the "invisible one" so others remain comfortable.

> But God did not create you to disappear for the sake of others' comfort. The mask may keep temporary peace; but your authentic presence brings lasting transformation.

> You are not the story others wrote for you.

> Maybe your family called you "the failure," "the stubborn one," "the black sheep." Maybe religion told you that you were unworthy unless you conformed. But those narratives are not your scroll.

> God's Word calls you beloved, chosen, royal, redeemed. The story of your life is being rewritten with ink that cannot fade.

In a moment of sacred reflection pause ask yourself:

> What labels or titles am I still answering to that do not come from God?
>
> In what areas of my life have I confused survival roles with sacred identity?
>
> What would it mean for me to remember the name God whispered over me before the world taught me to forget?

A Profound Spiritual Insight

> This is not just healing; it is divine reclamation. This is not just self-help; it is the living soul's recovery.
>
> To reclaim your name is to return to your spiritual origin. It is to say with boldness: "I agree with Heaven's record over my life."
>
> You are the echo of divine intention. A breath-formed being with a name still resonating in the chambers of eternity.

To remember is to return. To return is to rise.

Part 6.

The Descent Is the Doorway; When Going Down Becomes Going Home

We have long been influenced and taught that the path to fulfillment, freedom, and divinity lies upward; toward the stars, toward the heavens, toward ideals that seem to exist way above and far beyond our messy human experiences.

But what if the real path forward is not a vertical ascent, but a sacred descent? What if the doorway to wholeness is not found in escaping the earth's gravity, but in entering more deeply into its womb?

We descend not to diminish, but to remember.
We go downward not to fail, but to find.
We yield to the inner pull not to collapse, but to finally rise rooted.

This is the divine paradox: The descent is not the end of the journey; it is the beginning of our return.

The Sacred Pattern of Descent in Scripture

We live in an age that glorifies ascent; higher platforms, higher status, higher spirituality.

Yet the divine pattern woven throughout Scripture is radically different: before there is exaltation, there is descent. Before there is glory, there is humility. Before there is resurrection, there is burial.

This is not incidental. It is intentional. And it holds a revelation that modern theology often bypasses: the way home is through the depths.

Descent as a Divine Pattern

From Genesis to Revelation, we see a consistent truth: every elevation begins with a descent.

> Moses was raised in Pharaoh's palace, yet before leading Israel to freedom, he descended into obscurity; a wilderness shepherd for 40 years.
>
> Joseph wore a coat of favor but found himself in a pit and prison before the palace. His descent was not a punishment but a preparation.
>
> Jonah descended into the depths of the sea, swallowed by a great fish, before proclaiming repentance to a nation.
>
> And then Jesus Christ; the One who descended farther than them all.

"What does 'He ascended' mean except that He also descended to the lower, earthly regions?

He who descended is the very One who ascended higher than all the heavens..." Ephesians 4:9-10

The Son of the Living God did not bypass the lowest places of existence; He entered them, death, darkness, the grave; not as a victim, but as a Conqueror, breaking chains, principalities and dominions.

A Mystery Hidden Since Genesis

In Eden, after humanity's fall, God stationed a flaming sword at the entrance to the Tree of Life (Genesis 3:24). Many see this as judgment alone, but what if it was also prophecy?

A signal that to regain access to life, one must pass through the fire; through death to self, through surrender of pride, through the consuming light of holiness.

That flaming sword guarded the way until Christ came. And how did He reclaim that path?

By descending; not ascending. By entering the place no one could escape; the realm of death itself; and breaking its dominion.

Christ's Descent; The Keys of Ultimate Authority

When Jesus declared:

"The gates of Hades will not prevail against My church." Matthew 16:18. He wasn't speaking theory. He was speaking a prophecy that He would fulfill days later.

In Revelation 1:18, the risen Christ proclaims:

"I am the Living One; I was dead, and now look, I am alive forever and ever! And I hold the keys of death and Hades."

Where did He take those keys? Not from heaven; but from Hades. He went into the heart of what humanity feared most and broke it open from the inside.

Why This Matters for Us

Christ's descent is not only history; it is our pattern. To return to wholeness, we too must descend; not into Hades, but into humility.

Into honesty. Into the hidden caverns of our own soul where false identities, buried wounds, and prideful illusions dwell.

The way forward is inward. The way home is downward. Not downward into despair, but into depth. Into roots. Into the place where our original name and purpose are waiting beneath the rubble.

The Prophetic Invitation

Descent is not failure. Descent is the sacred doorway back to Eden. When we surrender the masks, dismantle the false towers, and allow God to strip us of what was never ours to carry; we rediscover the narrow path that leads to life.

This is why Jesus said:

"Unless a grain of wheat falls to the ground and dies, it remains alone. But if it dies, it produces much fruit." John 12:24

Death to illusion is the beginning of life in truth. And the Spirit whispers still: Do not fear the descent.

For at its end, the roots of eternity await.

The Descent into Ourselves

This sacred journey isn't just about terrain; it's about territory within.

The Earth reflects what the soul remembers. Just as rivers carve canyons and roots plunge into the soil, so too must we allow our awareness to descend through layers of our inner being;

beyond ego, beyond intellect, beyond image; into the ancient ground where identity was first whispered into existence.

But to enter that sacred place, we must pass through the "narrow gate" of honesty.

"Enter through the narrow gate... but small is the gate and narrow the road that leads to life, and only a few find it." (Matthew 7:13–14)

The descent will ask for surrender. It will invite tears, silence, and shedding. But what we lose are not our true selves; they are the powerful but false garments we no longer need.

Real-Life Reflections of Descent

> A person who loses their job may feel they are falling; but often it is in the quiet of unemployment that they rediscover a buried calling.

> A marriage that shatters may feel like descent; but in its unraveling, hidden wounds come to light that now have a chance to be healed.

A season of burnout may feel like collapse; but in its ashes, the soul may finally cry for rest, renewal, and reconnection with what truly matters.

We are taught to fear descent. But in truth, it is often grace disguised as loss. For it is only when the outer scaffolding breaks away that the inner cathedral can be seen.

Descending with the Holy Spirit as Our Guide

We do not descend alone. As Jesus promised in John 16:13: "But when He, the Spirit of truth, comes, He will guide you into all the truth…"

The Holy Spirit does not simply lead us upward in ecstasy; but inward in intimacy. He descends with us into our tombs of forgotten dreams and buried pain. He enters the hidden caverns of our soul not to shame us; but to illuminate them.

And when His presence touches those forgotten places, resurrection begins.

Part 7.

When Roots Become Revelation; Living from the Depths

We live in a world obsessed with speed, surface, and spectacle. Growth is measured by visibility; by platforms and applause. Yet heaven measures differently.

For in the kingdom, the unseen is greater than the seen. The root matters more than the branch. Depth is the silent architect of height.

This is the paradox of spiritual life:
> Before fruit comes root.
> Before expansion comes grounding.
> Before glory comes descent.

The Power of Hidden Roots

No tree can reach toward the heavens without first anchoring into the earth. The deeper the root system, the greater the capacity to withstand storms. Shallow roots may sprout quickly, but they topple easily when winds rise.

The same it is with the soul. A life fixated on surface; image, status, spiritual performance; will look lush for a season, yet collapse in adversity.

But the soul that consents to hiddenness, that sinks deep into God through prayer, surrender, and self-honesty, becomes unshakable.

"Blessed is the one who trusts in the LORD, whose confidence is in Him. They will be like a tree planted by the water that sends out its roots by the stream.

It does not fear when heat comes; its leaves are always green. It has no worries in a year of drought and never fails to bear fruit." *(Jeremiah 17:7–8)*

Roots drink from an unseen river. Their life source is not the changing weather but the constant flow beneath the surface.

Roots and Revelation

Roots are not glamorous. They are buried, silent, unseen. But within their obscurity lies power. They do what leaves cannot: they draw nourishment, anchor the whole, and break through hard soil to find hidden streams.

In the same way, spiritual revelation is born in hidden places. It comes not in the glare of performance but in the quiet of prayer; not in striving for platforms but in surrender to Presence.

"So then, just as you received Christ Jesus as Lord, continue to live your lives in Him, rooted and built up in Him, strengthened in the faith as you were taught, and overflowing with thankfulness." *(Colossians 2:6–7)*

The world reverses this order; celebrating branches while neglecting roots. But the Spirit calls us to return to what sustains rather than what impresses.

Depth as Protection

When storms come; and they will; it is depth that determines survival. Shallow roots cannot hold weight. This is why Jesus warned of the seed on rocky ground:

"It sprang up quickly, because the soil was shallow. But when the sun came up, the plants were scorched, and they withered because they had no root." (Matthew 13:5–6)

In a culture of instant elevation and quick applause, shallow spirituality is a silent epidemic. Many rise fast but fall faster, because they mistook momentum for maturity. The antidote is descent. The remedy is depth.

Living From the Depths

To live rooted is to live differently. It is to choose depth over display, process over platform, authenticity over applause.

It is to allow the Spirit to dig beneath the surface of our lives; past pride, past fear, past the curated image; and sink us deep into Christ.

"I pray that you, being rooted and established in love, may have power, together with all the Lord's holy people, to grasp how wide and long and high and deep is the love of Christ." Ephesians 3:17–18

Love is the soil. Christ is the stream. Our calling is to root; not in opinions, not in trends, but in the eternal ground of God's love.

Practical Exercises for Rooting

1. The Hidden Hour (Silence Practice)

    Set aside one hour this week in complete silence before God. No agenda. No requests. Let this time remind you: fruitfulness flows from presence, not performance.

2. Name the Shallow Soil (Self-Inventory)

    Journal these questions:

    Where am I prioritizing branches over roots? Where am I performing for approval instead of abiding in love? What practices can draw me deeper into Christ?

3. Prayer of Rootedness

    Lord, uproot every illusion that keeps me shallow. Anchor me in Your love.
    Dig past my pride and fear until my roots drink from Your living water.
    Hide me where only You see, until my unseen life in You becomes my greatest strength.
    Amen.

Prophetic Whisper: Roots do not rush. Roots do not fear obscurity. Roots do their greatest work in secret. And so does grace.

The Spirit is calling a generation back to the depths; to the place where roots become revelation and stability births fruitfulness.

Part 8.

Unveiling the Hidden Wells; Drinking from the Eternal Streams

Life on the surface can feel barren. Seasons of drought; emotional, spiritual, relational; tempt us to believe that provision has dried up.

Yet heaven whispers a mystery: beneath the ground you walk on, living waters flow. The streams of divine life are never absent; they are simply hidden. And those who dare to dig; those who descend; will drink.

The Ancient Pattern of Wells

In Scripture, wells were more than water sources; they were symbols of sustenance, inheritance, and revelation:

> Hagar wept in the wilderness, believing her son would die of thirst. Yet "God opened her eyes, and she saw a well of water" (Genesis 21:19). The well was there all along; her despair simply blinded her to it.

> Isaac re-dug the wells his father Abraham had dug, restoring what the enemy had stopped up (Genesis 26:18). To reclaim inheritance, he had to uncover what was buried.

> Jesus, at Jacob's well, offered the Samaritan woman water beyond her imagination: "Whoever drinks of the water I give them will never thirst. Indeed, the water I give will become in them a spring of water welling up to eternal life" (John 4:14).

Do you see the pattern? The well is always near, but it must be revealed. And often the revelation comes in wilderness moments; when every other source has failed.

The Hidden Streams of the Spirit

Jesus declared:

> "Let anyone who is thirsty come to Me and drink. Whoever believes in Me, as Scripture has said, rivers of living water will flow from within them." John 7:37–38

Let's pay attention to the location: from within. The life you long for is not imported from an external source; it is unlocked from an internal one; the indwelling Spirit of the Living God. But why do so many live parched lives when a river runs through them? Because the living wells are discovered through digging.

Digging the Wells of the Soul

Wells are often covered by layers of earth; dust of distraction, debris of disappointment, stones of shame and fear. To access the flow, something must be broken. This is why the spiritual life requires intentional excavation:

> Prayer breaks the silence of neglect.
> Fasting clears the clutter of appetite.
> Worship pierces the hardness of heart.

Digging is disruptive; but it is holy work. It is the work that transforms drought into overflow.

Modern Illusions of Water

Our age offers countless mirages; technological streams, digital fountains, self-help cisterns; promising life yet leaving the soul dry.

Like Israel, we have "forsaken the fountain of living water and dug our own cisterns, broken cisterns that cannot hold water" (Jeremiah 2:13).

True water cannot be manufactured. It must be drawn; from Christ, the eternal well.

Living from the Hidden Wells

Those who drink from the hidden wells become unshakable in drought.

Their peace is not weather-dependent. Their joy is not market-dependent. Their hope is not headline-dependent. They are like the psalmist who said: "All my springs of joy are in You." (Psalm 87:7)

Practical Steps to Dig and Drink

1. Ask and Yield

   Begin each day with this simple prayer: "Holy Spirit, uncover the well within me. Let Your living water flow through every dry place in my soul."

2. Break the Surface; Silence & Prayer

   Take 15 minutes daily to sit before God with no agenda but presence. Silence is the shovel that breaks ground for the water to rise.

3. Remove the Stones; Confession & Release

What sins, fears, or lies are blocking the flow? Name them. Lay them at Christ's feet. Watch the water rise as shame is lifted.

4. Sing at the Well; Worship as Access

In Numbers 21:17, Israel sang: "Spring up, O well!" Worship is a prophetic act that calls the deep to rise.

Prophetic Prayer

Lord of Living Waters,
Today I choose to dig where You have planted me. Remove every stone of fear, every layer of shame, every debris of doubt. Let Your Spirit flow through me like a river in the desert. Make me a wellspring of life in a thirsty land. And let every dry place in me become a testimony of Your overflow.
Amen.

Where do I feel most "dry" in this season? What stones (fear, unforgiveness, pride) may be blocking the flow? Which practices will I commit to this week to uncover the well within?

Prophetic Whisper: The water you seek is not far away. It is nearer than breath. It is waiting beneath the ground of your surrender. The Spirit is saying: "Dig, and you will drink. Ask, and rivers will rise."

Part 9.

The Harmony of Depth and Height; True Ascent After True Descent

The human soul longs for elevation. We humans are dreaming of rising; above pain, above situations, above limitation, above the gravitational pull of life's struggles.

But here lies the mystery of the kingdom: true ascent is never achieved by bypassing descent. The height you seek is inseparably tied to the depth you embrace. This is the paradox the modern age resists:

We want the mountaintop without the valley.
We want resurrection without crucifixion.
We want glory without the grave.

But in God's sacred and divine economy, the way up is always the way down first.

The Divine Order

Paul wrote with piercing clarity:

"He who descended is the very one who ascended higher than all the heavens, in order to fill the whole universe." Ephesians 4:10

Christ's supreme elevation was preceded by His ultimate descent. From throne to manger. From majesty to mortality. From glory to Golgotha.

And in this mystery lies our model: we rise by yielding, we reign by bowing, we ascend by descending.

Depth Gives Birth to Height

Why does God insist on this pattern? Because height without depth is dangerous. A tree that grows tall with shallow roots becomes a casualty of storms. A tower without a foundation becomes rubble at the first tremor.

And a soul that seeks elevation without excavation risks collapse under the weight of influence and illusion.

Depth stabilizes height. Humility safeguards honor. Brokenness becomes the birthplace of blessing.

"Humble yourselves before the Lord, and He will lift you up." James 4:10

Ascending Without Losing the Ground

This is not about abandoning elevation; it is about sanctifying it. God is not against greatness; He redefines it.

He calls us to ascend, but with roots intact; anchored in His presence, nourished by His Spirit, guided by His truth.

Height is holy only when its strength comes from hiddenness. Elevation becomes dangerous when it detaches from the earth of surrender.

"Those who wait on the Lord shall renew their strength; they shall mount up with wings like eagles." Isaiah 40:31

Even eagles rise only after they learn to wait. Waiting is descent; soaring is ascent. Both are sacred.

Signs of False Elevation

Speed without depth; running ahead without roots.

Visibility without accountability; platforms that are bigger than character.

Performance without presence; living for applause instead of intimacy with God.

These are the towers of Babel disguised as blessings. And just like Babel, they lead to confusion and collapse.

True Ascent: What It Looks Like

Rising not for self, but for service.

Elevation as overflow, not ambition.

Influence as stewardship, not ownership.

The soul that has descended into humility becomes the safest carrier of heavenly heights. Such a life becomes a mountain of refuge for others; a place of shade, strength, and sustenance.

Prophetic Whisper:

The Spirit is saying:
"Do not fear the valley, for it is shaping your summit.
Do not despise the depths, for they are the womb of your wings.

Those who bow low will soar high; and their height will not break them, for their roots run deep."

Reflections; Echoes from the Depths

Every journey of our human life whispers its truth. This chapter has not given us a ladder but a shovel; not a map to the skies, but a call to the soil. For in the hidden silence of the depths, eternity hums.

We began by unmasking the illusion: that freedom lies in flight, that glory waits in escape. Yet heaven's paradox overturns the patterns of men; the way up is the way down first.

The ancients knew this. Their stories testify that wells do not rise on mountaintops; they spring forth in valleys, wildernesses, and waiting rooms of surrender.

Moses met God in obscurity before he climbed Sinai.

Joseph sat in the pit before he entered the palace.

Jonah prayed in the belly of descent before proclaiming mercy to a nation.

And Christ the Son of the Living God; Christ shattered the gates of death before wearing the crown of life.

Every ascent that lasts is birthed in a depth embraced. Depth stabilizes height. Roots guard wings. Wells sustain fruitfulness long after applause fades.

And here is the whisper for our time: Do not despise the deep. Do not resist the descent. For what feels like burial is often planting.

What feels like loss is often preparation for life beyond measure.

Pause. Breathe. Listen. The depths are not your enemy; they are your birthplace. The water you seek is not in the skies but beneath the ground you fear to touch. Dig. Yield. Drink.

For when the Spirit floods your roots, when the hidden well becomes a river, your ascent will not break you; it will bless nations.

Prophetic Benediction

May you go low, that you may rise unshaken.
May your roots run deeper than storms can reach.
May the hidden well spring up within you,
Until every dry place becomes a garden, and every wilderness sings with rivers.

For those who bow will soar. And those who descend will find the gates of Eden flung wide.

Chapter Two Summary

Reawakening the Inner Temple

Chapter Two invited the reader to a sacred descent; not into despair, but into the hidden sanctuary of the living soul. Beneath layers of labels, survival patterns, and false identities lies a living temple, waiting to be reawakened.

This temple was not built by human hands. It was formed in eternity and breathed into clay by the Creator Himself.

Yet in a world obsessed with outer image and upward striving, the living soul has become forgotten; misnamed, misused, or mistaken for something it is not.

But the living soul has never lost its name. It has only been buried. And through the pages of this chapter, we were invited to unearth it.

Through silence, truth, confrontation, and healing, we peeled back the layers to recover what was etched in us before the world told us who we should be.

This chapter in which we journeyed together was not just an exploration; it is an excavation. And in that sacred work, we begin to remember that:
We are temples of the Divine. We are not ascending; we are returning.

Remembering the Forgotten Name

The Living Soul; The Forgotten Sanctuary

We begin where we were first formed; not in visible places, but in the mystery of divine breath. The soul is not a concept, but a living cathedral woven by the hands of God. Forgotten in modern life, yet alive within, the soul whispers in silence and longing. Its sanctuary calls us inward, back to the divine blueprint. Not for escape, but for re-entry. The descent begins.

Beneath the Surface of Our Daily Identities

We wear names and roles; some chosen, most inherited. Beneath them is a deeper architecture. The soul is layered like an ancient city: memories, myths, masks. Excavation begins not with judgment, but with reverent curiosity.

What lies beneath what we've become? The digging is sacred. And necessary.

False Layers and Forgotten Names

Over time, false names are given: the pleaser, the strong one, the misfit, the saint, the failure. These are not our essence; they are adaptations; survival strategies dressed as identity.

But sediment becomes stone, and stone becomes foundation. Misnaming leads to mis-living. To be renamed by God is not a rebranding; it is a return to the original.

The Excavation of Truth

Excavating the soul is not a psychological exercise alone; it is a spiritual reawakening. The tools are not logic and labor, but silence, prayer, presence, and truth.

Excavation reveals not just what we have hidden, but what God has preserved. In the valley of dry bones, the breath of God calls even the forgotten parts of us to rise again.

Before we were wounded, we were named. Before we were praised or punished, we were known. Our true name is not spoken by men; it is etched in eternity. Scripture reminds us: "To the one who overcomes, I will give a white stone, with a new name..." Rev. 2:17. This is not fantasy. It is the foundation of divine identity.

The Descend is the Doorway

True transformation is not found in striving upward, but in returning inward. The descent is not punishment; it is the portal.

The lower we go, the truer we become. As roots must reach into darkness to bear fruit above, so must we enter our depths to awaken the temple within. The descent is not abandonment. It is invitation.

Our roots are not to be rejected. They are to be redeemed. The parts of us we were taught to bury; our pain, our questions, our history; can become revelation when surrendered to the light. What was hidden in the soil becomes nourishment for divine growth. Your ancient past is not your prison. It is your proving ground.

Within each soul is a well of living water, hidden beneath debris. Culture, trauma, shame; they clog the flow. But the well remains. Like Isaac re-digging the wells of his father, we too must uncover the water sources buried beneath cultural sediment and personal distortion. What flows from the soul is not manmade; it is eternal.

The goal is not simply to go deep or ascend high; but to live in harmony between the two. Spiritual maturity is not escape from earth, but alignment with heaven while walking in embodied truth.

The soul, once awakened, bridges realms. The deeper we go, the higher we rise; not in ego, but in divine embodiment.

Chapter Two is not merely a collection of truths; it is a return to the sanctuary of the living soul. It is the reawakening of what God has already placed within. The work is not glamorous, but glorious. Not loud, but lasting. The temple is not found on mountain tops, but in the quiet caverns of your own being.

You are not what you have been called. You are what you were created to be. The descent into the inner temple is the beginning of true ascent. What we uncover is not ruin, but revelation. What we find is not shame, but signature. The name given before time still waits to be spoken again.

"Fear not, for I have redeemed you. I have called you by name. You are Mine." Isaiah 43:1

Let this be your remembrance. Let the temple rise.

Chapter Three

The Unveiling

Becoming Who You Were Before the World Told You Who to Be

Having reawakened the inner temple and restored communion with the Divine within, the soul now approaches the sacred threshold of emergence.

The descent was not an end but a preparation; a gestation in the womb of mystery, where all divine life is conceived before it is revealed.

Now comes the moment of unveiling; not as a display, but as an embodiment; not as an arrival, but as a return to the image woven into being before the foundations of the world.

This unveiling is not a departure from humility but its fullest expression: the soul rising through surrender, shining not to be seen, but to illuminate.

For every true unveiling begins in stillness, where the hidden light of God breaks through the veil of human forgetfulness and declares again: *"You are My image. You are My breath. You are My beloved design."*

Every unveiling begins with fire. Not the fire that destroys, but the fire that purifies; not the flame of wrath, but the radiance of transformation.

The descent was the furnace in which illusion was melted away, where false identities dissolved, and only truth remained.

The living soul that descended into silence did not lose itself; it was refined, stripped of what was temporal so it could reveal what was eternal.

In this holy descent, we learned that surrender is not weakness, but wisdom. The Spirit does not lead us downward to diminish us but to distill us; separating the precious from the perishable, the true self from the shadow self. Even the gold of divine character is found only under the pressure of obscurity.

The Scriptures echo this rhythm: *"I have refined you, but not as silver; I have tested you in the furnace of affliction"* Isaiah 48:10.

Before revelation, there is always refinement. Before resurrection, there is always burial. Even the Son of Man descended into the depths of the earth before ascending to glory.

The soul's descent was never punishment; it was purification; the burning away of all that was not aligned with divine intention.

And now, emerging from that furnace, the soul begins to glow with the quiet brilliance of one who has seen truth and lived.

Why does the soul fear descent? Why does humanity tremble before silence, when silence is the birthplace of God's voice?

Because descent demands the relinquishment of control. It requires us to loosen our grip on the illusion of self-mastery and fall into divine mystery.

The ego fears the deep because it cannot perform there. There are no accolades in hiddenness, no applause in surrender. And yet, the Spirit draws us into these depths not to erase us, but to reveal the image of God untouched by time or trauma.

The earth itself testifies to this truth. Water, the source of all life, flows not from the sky, but from beneath. Gold and silver, treasures of civilizations, are drawn from the deep.

Seeds, holding the codes of creation, must first be buried in darkness before they rise. Roots stretch downward before branches reach upward.

The Spirit has written the story of redemption into creation itself: descent before ascension, darkness before dawn. And yet humanity, enamored with heights, continues to chase the stars while forgetting the sacred soil beneath their feet.

Could it be that our obsession with reaching upward is not about vision, but avoidance? That we chase the heavens to escape the pain buried within the earth of our being?

For true transformation never required flight, but courage; the courage to kneel in the dust, where divinity first breathed into man the breath of life.

There is a divine rhythm that governs all of life; a pulse of concealment and revelation, of dying and rising, of silence and sound.

The heaven itself dances to this rhythm: the moon waxes and wanes, the tides rise and fall, the seed hides and blooms. All creation preaches one truth; that hiddenness prepares for manifestation, and unveiling follows surrender.

Jesus Himself lived within this sacred rhythm. Thirty years of hiddenness preceded three years of revelation. Even His miracles emerged from moments of solitude, His public power drawn from sacred and private communion.

Before He spoke to crowds, He withdrew into mountains. Before He revealed glory, He embraced the cross. This is the rhythm of redemption; descent before resurrection, humility before exaltation, silence before song.

We resist this rhythm because we confuse hiddenness with absence, when in truth, hiddenness is the sanctuary of preparation.

But it is in those unseen seasons that the Holy Spirit refines character, roots identity, and cultivates purpose.

We are not forgotten in hiddenness; we are being formed for unveiling. The delay we dread is often divine gestation. The silence we fear is often sacred formation.

Look at creation again; even stars, those distant lights of wonder, are born in the wombs of darkness. Nebulas, vast clouds of dust and gas, conceal the birth of suns. The night sky, then, is not empty; it is pregnant with revelation.

So too, our own darkness is not absence but expectation; the place where divine potential is incubating until the time of unveiling.

And now, the veil begins to lift. The temple within, restored and rekindled, opens its gates, and light begins to flow outward. But this unveiling is not a performance; it is a participation in divine revelation. We do not emerge to impress; we emerge to embody.

The unveiling is not a reinvention; it is a return; a return to our original, undistorted essence, to the divine image breathed into our being before the world told us who to be. "You are My image. You are My breath. You are My beloved design."

These words echo across the ages, through prophets and poets, through wildernesses and wonders, through the silence of our own soul until they find a home in us again.

In this unveiling, the soul does not rise through striving, but through remembrance. This is not the ascent of ambition but the uprising of grace. We rise not to claim an identity but to reveal one; the one we carried since the dawn of creation.

To unveil is to stand once more in divine alignment, to live without pretense, without disguise, without the armor of survival. It is to breathe freely as a being who knows they are seen, known, and loved by God.

The unveiling is not for personal recognition but for restoration. It is not a coronation of ego but a communion of purpose; the alignment of inner transformation with outer expression. For when the soul awakens, it cannot remain silent. The light that has been kindled must shine, not to boast, but to bless.

We are not unveiled merely to be admired; we are unveiled to become conduits of divine life. The water drawn from the hidden well is meant to flow outward; healing, refreshing, and restoring. The treasure unearthed from the depths is meant to adorn the world with truth.

What was formed in the silence of prayer is meant to resound in the song of service.

To live unveiled is to embody what the Holy Spirit has revealed; to move through the world as a divine reflection of heaven.

In every conversation, every act of kindness, every choice to forgive, the unveiled soul manifests divine presence. This is the rhythm of embodiment: inner revelation expressed as outer compassion.

And so, the unveiling is not an end, but a beginning; the beginning of living as light in a world still shadowed by forgetfulness.

The unveiled life is a life of balance; grounded yet transcendent, humble yet radiant. It is not an escape from the human experience but its sanctification. The one who has descended and returned knows that heaven and earth are not enemies, but expressions of one divine harmony.

Living unveiled means walking through the world as a living sanctuary, carrying within the fragrance of divine remembrance. It means seeing the sacred in the ordinary, the eternal in the temporal. It means no longer striving to become, but simply being what God has already declared: "very good."

This unveiling marks the return of vision; to see beyond illusion, beyond division, beyond the false narratives of self and society.

It is the awakening of inner sight, the restoration of holy imagination that perceives creation as it truly is: one vast temple filled with divine presence.

The unveiled life is not louder, but clearer. It does not seek attention; it carries authority born of stillness. Its power lies not in performance, but in presence.

And now, the Spirit whispers again; not to the mind, but to the marrow of your being: *"Rise; not in your strength, not for your platform, not in mimicry of others; Rise in Me. Rise in Jesus Christ. Rise because the unveiling has begun."*

This rising is not upward in space, but inward in light. It is the ascension of awareness, the expansion of being, the alignment of heaven and earth within. To rise in Christ is to live unveiled; to become the revelation of His love in motion, the visible echo of invisible grace.

And so, the unveiling continues; not as a moment, but as a movement. Every breath, every word, every act of compassion becomes part of this divine emergence. The world does not need more noise; it needs living light-bearers; souls who have descended, remembered, and now arise in holy clarity.

For the true unveiling is not the end of descent, but its fulfillment; the revelation of what was hidden all along: Christ in you, the hope of glory Colossians 1:27.

Part 1

The Mirror Restored: Seeing Beyond the Shattered Image

The greatest tragedy of the fall was not merely the loss of Eden's garden. It was the distortion of the image; the image of God in humanity, once radiant, now obscured.

Before fig leaves and fear, before shame echoed in hiding, there was a pure and unbroken reflection. A mirror of divine essence. A face fashioned in glory. A soul crafted in sacred likeness.

But then, the fracture.

Sin did not just create distance from God; it created distortion within ourselves. What was once whole became fragmented. What once reflected heaven became shattered on the ground of human experience.

The mirror broke, not because God stopped seeing us rightly, but because we stopped seeing ourselves rightly.

And ever since, we've lived by the fragments. We live by fragments when: We define ourselves by what others call us. We anchor our value in our failure or success. We measure ourselves against cultural standards, generational scripts, or religious performance.

Fragments are deceptive. They contain a sliver of truth but magnify distortion. Like looking into a broken mirror, we see parts, but not the whole.

Some of us see only our flaws. Others see only their roles. Many see only what they were taught to see: unworthy, inadequate, or inferior.

We assemble an identity out of these jagged reflections, sharp edges and all. And in doing so, we hide from the face we were truly created to behold: our original design, the undistorted image in which we were formed.

"Let Us make man in Our image, according to Our likeness." Genesis 1:26

This was not poetic language. It was divine intentionality. You were made to reflect the nature, beauty, and wisdom of the Living God. Not partially. Fully. Not someday. From the very beginning.

But that reflection, through wounds and false mirrors, has been buried.

The Word as Mirror; The Restoration Begins

The Apostle James writes:

"Anyone who listens to the word but does not do what it says is like someone who looks at his face in a mirror and, after looking at himself, goes away and immediately forgets what he looks like." James 1:23–24

This is not merely a moral exhortation; it is a spiritual diagnosis. The Word of God is not just text;

it is a mirror held by eternity, revealing not who you've become under pressure, but who you've always been in purpose.

When we look into that mirror; into the unfiltered truth of Scripture and divine presence, we do not merely see our current state. We see our eternal identity. We behold the reflection of the One who made us, and in His gaze, we recognize our own.

But the world has offered us alternative mirrors:

> Social mirrors: that reflect worth based on followers and fame.
> Cultural mirrors: that assign value based on conformity or rebellion.
> Religious mirrors: that reduce holiness to rule-keeping rather than image-bearing.
> Trauma mirrors: cracked by past wounds, telling us we are too broken to be beloved.

And we have let these mirrors define us. We have adopted the reflection of a world still searching for itself, rather than standing in the mirror that remembers who we are.

Divine Identity Is Not Earned; It Is Recalled

What if the truth of who you are has never been lost; only forgotten? The Spirit is whispering again:

"Come back to the mirror. The one I showed you before the world named you. Look again; not until you see your wounds, but until My image swallows your illusion.

"You are not the fragments. You are the whole. You are not the fear. You are the flame. You are not the names they gave you. You are My name bearer."

In the Garden, humanity ran when shame took hold. Today, many still run; from the mirror, from the silence, from the presence that reminds us who we truly are. But restoration begins the moment we stop running; and start beholding.

Mirrors of This World vs. The Mirror of the Word

Let us take a moment and contrast two reflections:

The Living Word of God's mirror:

> You are forgiven and redeemed.
> You are beloved before you perform.
> You are a vessel formed in grace.
> You are fearfully and wonderfully made.
> You are known and called by name.

The World's Mirror:

> You are your failures.
> You are what you produce.
> You are too broken to be used.
> You must be perfect to be worthy.
> You are forgotten.

Let's remember these sacred words: One leads to striving, The other leads to stillness. One fosters shame, The other fosters sacred awakening.

The Image Restored Through Christ

The restoration of the mirror is not theoretical; it is personal. It is embodied in Christ.

"He is the image of the invisible God..." Colossians 1:15
"And we all... are being transformed into His image with ever-increasing glory." 2 Corinthians 3:18

Christ did not come to modify your fragments. He came to reveal your fullness. His life, death, and resurrection restore what was lost, not only access to God, but identity in God. Through Him, the mirror is mended. Through Him, the veil is lifted.

You are not merely saved from sin. You are restored into heaven's reflection.

The Consequences of Fragmented Reflection

Living without a restored mirror has real consequences. It:

Distorts how we see others, leading to comparison, judgment, or projection.

Distorts how we pray, approaching God as beggars rather than beloved.

Distorts how we lead, building influence around insecurity instead of wholeness.

Distorts how we love, offering affection from deficit rather than overflow.

False mirrors don't just affect your self-perception; they affect everything that flows from you.

Paul writes in 2 Corinthians 3:18:

> *"But we all, with unveiled face, beholding as in a mirror the glory of the Lord, are being transformed into the same image..."*

Transformation does not begin with trying harder. It begins with beholding deeper. We become what we behold. And we behold by stepping into the light of God's Word; not to analyze it, but to let it read us, restore us, and rename us.

Prophetic Meditation: Let's pause and go inward.

Take a moment of stillness; On a piece of paper, draw a line down the center.

1. On the left, write three false names you've carried: labels given by trauma, culture, or fear.

    > Unworthy. Too much. Always second best.

2. On the right, write three truths from Scripture that contradict those names.

    > Beloved. Chosen. Fearfully and wonderfully made.

3. Speak them aloud, slowly:

    "This is who I am. Not by merit, but by divine design." Repeat them until the truth rings louder than the lie. Until the mirror is no longer cracked; but clear.

The Call to Restoration

> You are not too far from wholeness. You are not too shattered to be restored. The mirror is not beyond repair; it is being mended by grace, piece by piece. And soon, you will not only see the face of God, but you will also see your own, radiant in His likeness. Now is the time to: Look again. Behold again. Remember again.
>
> And when you rise from that mirror, you will walk not in fragments, but in fullness.
>
> > You are not what they called you.
> > You are not what broke you.
> > You are what He breathed into existence.

Closing Benediction

> > "You are My image.
> > You are My breath.
> > You are My beloved design.
> > Come out from behind the broken mirror.
> > Step into the reflection that does not lie.
> > I have restored the mirror.
> > Look again; this time, see Me in you."
>
> Then speak them aloud: "This is who I am; not by merit, but by the grace of my Eternal Father and God."

Part 2.

The Breath Returns

> *"Then He breathed on them and said, 'Receive the Holy Spirit."* (John 20:22)

We live in a world obsessed with surface breakthroughs; where exposure is celebrated, where emotions are commodified, and where performance is often mistaken for transformation.

But true unveiling is not a public display; it is a sacred return. It is God breathing into the dust of our being once again, not to recreate a better version of who others expect us to be, but to restore us to the original blueprint He placed within us before time began.

> Exposure without breath is exploitation.
> Emotion without truth is manipulation.
> Identity without alignment is illusion.

"The unveiling is not simply an act of exposure; it is a reanimation. To become who you were created to be is not merely a psychological or emotional process; it is spiritual resurrection."

The above paragraph deserves a more profound expansion, especially in a generation where emotionalism is often mistaken for spirituality, and true transformation is rarely discerned through outward expressions alone.

Let's take a moment and together let's further explore and expand this profound message, offering clarity, scriptural depth, and real-life application that will help readers discern the true markers of spiritual resurrection versus counterfeit impressions.

Exposure vs. Reanimation

Exposure alone is not enough. Many today are "exposed"; their traumas unearthed, their emotions expressed, their stories shared.

But without divine breath, exposure can become exploitation, and vulnerability can be weaponized for applause rather than healing.

True unveiling is more than a show for public expression. It is the sacred act of God breathing new life into what was once dormant. And that breath transforms what we are, not just what we want or wish to say.

Transformation vs. Performance

In modern times, the word transformation has become strongly diluted. It is often confused with external behavior modification or emotional displays and physical feelings during gatherings.

But the Holy Scripture teaches us that true transformation (metamorphosis) is not a mere conformation to a diversified humanistic culture; but the renewal of the inner mind and heart by the Spirit of the Living God (Romans 12:2).

True resurrection doesn't need a spotlight; it often happens in silence, in deserts, in caves of isolation like Elijah's, or in the belly of the fish like Jonah's. It doesn't cry out, "Look at me!" but whispers, "I once was dead; but now I live."

Signs of Spiritual Resurrection

How can we tell the difference between emotional hype and Spirit-breathed resurrection?

Here are some real-life signs and markers that someone has truly encountered the Living Spirit of resurrection; not merely in word, but in essence:

1. A Deepened Hunger for Truth

    Not confirmation, but transformation. A longing for what is eternal, not what is entertaining.
    "Your word I have hidden in my heart, that I might not sin against You." (Psalm 119:11)

2. Peace in the Midst of Uncertainty

    Not the absence of storms, but the presence of anchored stillness.
    "You will keep him in perfect peace, whose mind is stayed on You." (Isaiah 26:3)

3. Death of the Need for Performance

    The resurrected soul no longer seeks validation through applause, titles, or platforms.
    "I have been crucified with Christ; it is no longer I who live..." (Galatians 2:20)

4. Obedience Without Observation

    True sons and daughters of the Spirit obey in secret. What they do in the unseen is more powerful than what others applaud in the visible.
    "But when you pray, go into your room... and your

Father who sees in secret will reward you openly."
(Matthew 6:6)

5. Fruit That Remains

Resurrection is marked not by flashes of glory, but by sustained fruit of the Spirit.
"By their fruit you will know them." (Matthew 7:16)

The Counterfeit:

Emotional Manipulation & Spiritual Hype

I remember one time in my preaching saying this phrase: "many are attaching themselves as being guided by the Holy Spirit, yet there is nothing more than physical emotions, self-exaltations, and mass manipulation."

This is a sobering reality:

- Tears can be real; and still not transformational.
- Shouts can be loud; and still void of the Spirit.
- Hands can be raised; and hearts can remain hidden.

Spiritual resurrection is not ecstasy; it is awakening. Not just feeling something new; but becoming someone new. It is not the height of the moment amidst a spontaneous emotion; but the depth of the root.

Would love to follow up with few Scriptural verses for Meditation and Reflection

John 20:22; *"He breathed on them and said, 'Receive the Holy Spirit.'"* Spiritual life is not taught; it is imparted.

Ezekiel 37:5; *"Surely I will cause breath to enter into you, and you shall live."* Divine breath precedes divine becoming.

Romans 8:11; *"If the Spirit of Him who raised Jesus from the dead dwells in you, He who raised Christ will also give life to your mortal bodies."*

Resurrection is not symbolic; it is transformational.

There is a powerful danger in mistaking trauma release for transformation. We must move beyond self-help and deeper into Spirit-help.

The modern world has turned confession into content, vulnerability into branding, and healing into merchandise. But without spiritual resurrection, we simply become more eloquent about our pain; never truly delivered from it.

And so, the Holy Spirit gently whispers:
"You were not called to remain cracked vessels patched with bandages of applause. You were meant to be rebuilt from the inside out, stone by stone, breath by breath."

Like Adam, formed from dust but lifeless until the breath of God entered him (Genesis 2:7), many today walk as formed but breathless.

Outwardly shaped by status, role, and success; but inwardly collapsed, panting for meaning.

Just as Ezekiel was commanded to prophesy breath into the valley of dry bones, this section speaks to those places in us that were shaped but never filled; areas where we exist, but do not live.

What is This Breath?

The breath that restores humanity is not just a shallow inspiration; it is the wind of divine remembrance.

It reawakens us to the truth that we are not becoming someone new under the cultural norms, but that we are returning to who we were before life's trauma, performance, and expectation buried us alive.

"Come from the four winds, O breath, and breathe on these slain, that they may live." Ezekiel 37:9

Breath returns, and with it:

Our Voice: once silenced, now rising.

Our Vision: once blurred, now clear.

Our Volition: once suppressed, now purposeful.

Real-Life Reflections: Where We Lost Our Breath

A child who was constantly criticized may grow up holding their breath; afraid that any expression will bring rejection.

A young adult pushed to succeed at all costs may forget how to breathe deeply, associating rest with failure.

A spiritual seeker burned by manipulation may unknowingly shut down the spiritual lungs, distrusting anything unseen.

These breathless spaces don't only affect our spirituality; they alter our posture, our nervous system, our creativity, our relationships. We perform, conform, and pretend... but we do not breathe.

When the Breath Returns

- Suddenly, tears flow without shame.
- Words emerge that were never spoken.
- The body stands taller; not in pride, but in remembered dignity.
- A name once forgotten is whispered again by the Holy Spirit:

"Beloved. Mine. Known."

The return of the breath is not always dramatic, but it is always divine. Sometimes it arrives in the middle of grief, sometimes in sacred silence, sometimes in the presence of a verse long forgotten. But when it comes, something begins to live again within us, and then we realize that true resurrection is more than feeling; It Is Becoming.

In an age where spiritual language is often co-opted by emotionalism and empty rituals, many declare they are "Spirit-led" without ever having undergone the death-and-resurrection process that marks true transformation.

To be led by the Spirit is not to perform spiritual acts but to be reborn by the breath of heaven; to emerge from the grave of false identity into the light of divine truth.

We must reclaim this sacred understanding: Resurrection is not a moment; it is a process. Not a hype; it is a holy hush, often marked by silence, true sacred surrender, and inner fire.

A Prophetic Whisper for the Unveiled Ones

"You did not awaken just to feel better.
You were resurrected to walk in truth.
You were unveiled not for attention, but for divine intention.
The breath that brought you back will sustain you, guide you, and move you.
Not by might. Not by power. But by My Spirit, says the Lord."

Part 3.

The Spirit of Exploration

There is a calling not only to ascend in the heavens, but to also explore the hidden chambers of the living soul. To uncover the utmost profound layers beneath our present self is to participate in a divine archaeology; not driven by curiosity, but by destiny.

You were not buried under pain, identity, or time as a life sentence; you were planted, with divine intention, awaiting the moment when the Spirit would awaken you to begin digging; within.

Just as the prophets were called to cry out in dry places, so too we are called to enter the caverns of our innermost being where the echoes of divine identity still whisper, "You are mine." But to hear this whisper, we must be willing to dig through the outside noise and its influence.

What Does a Sacred Exploration Require?

1. Courage to Confront

To explore the inner deep is to stir the past. Not to live in it, but to redeem it. *"And you shall know the truth, and the truth shall make you free." John 8:32*

The truth is often buried beneath years of suppression, false identity, trauma, and survival instinct. Like a miner searching for gold, the process requires courage and sacred endurance.

2. Honesty to Remove What Doesn't Belong

Not every stone was laid by divine hands. Some were placed by fear, others by societal molding, others by spiritual manipulation. *"Every plant that My heavenly Father has not planted will be pulled up by the roots." Matthew 15:1*

3. A Prophetic Eye to See the Blueprint

When exploring and excavating the deep, we must see not only what is; but also, what was meant to be. God doesn't restore us back to cultural ideals or religious molds; He restores us to our divine and original blueprint.

From Excavation to Revelation

Each buried truth, once uncovered, becomes a jewel in the foundation of your new identity in Christ Jesus. These truths are not decorative; they are architectural. They restore your frame.

They give form to your sacred calling. They allow the Holy Spirit to breathe into what once was forgotten under the duress of time.

"The hand of the Lord came upon me… and set me down in the midst of the valley; and it was full of bones." (Ezekiel 37:1)

Like Ezekiel, the Spirit brings us not only to glorious mountaintops but also to forgotten valleys; because in the dry bones, there is a prophecy waiting to be spoken. In the buried identity, there is a name waiting to be reclaimed.

At this moment I would like to present readers with few samples of our humanistic Real-Life Reflections of; Excavation in the Midst of Life:

A young woman, who always lived to please others, begins her journey of therapy and spiritual mentorship. For the first time, she uncovers that her "niceness" was actually a defense mechanism rooted in childhood rejection. Excavation begins; not to shame her, but to return her voice.

A successful businessman, always praised for being the "provider," breaks down in life after burnout. Through solitude, prayer, and spiritual counsel, he uncovers a deep fear of not being enough. Excavation tears down his false self and restores his humanity.

A lifelong churchgoer that has been always considered the "righteous one," suddenly feels numb in worship. Upon digging, he realizes he was living someone else's version of faith; never his own. In holy desperation, he begins the painful work of returning to his first love; Jesus Christ, not performance.

The Exploration of the Inner Deep Is Never Alone

You, dear reader, must know this unshakable truth: You are not alone in the excavation of your soul. You are not left with a solitary shovel in the dark, digging blind in the silence.

Even when the night feels heavy and the terrain seems unyielding, your Creator has never abandoned you.

He has watched over your life since before your first breath. His hands have carried you through the veils of forgetting, and His voice continues to whisper through the cracks of your conditioning.

"I will instruct you and teach you the way you should go; I will counsel you with My eye upon you." Psalm 32:8

From the beginning of time, the Holy Spirit has hovered; like in Genesis; brooding over the deep, waiting not to impose but to invite. The Holy Spirit does not crash in with noise and haste.

He hovers, whispers, broods, and guides with precision, like a sculptor who knows exactly where to strike the stone so as not to break, but to reveal what is hidden within.

"I will give you a new heart and put a new spirit within you, I will take the heart of stone out of your flesh and give you a heart of flesh. "Ezekiel 36:26

"And surely I am with you always, to the very end of the age." Matthew 28:20

This is not poetic sentiment alone; this is spiritual reality. You are seen. You are being accompanied. You are known. Even in the silence of descent, God is present; not as a distant deity, but as Emmanuel, God with us.

Guided Excavation vs. Isolated Effort

Too many embark on inner journeys as if self-help, performance, or productivity can redeem the soul. But true inner excavation is not self-driven; it is Spirit-led.

Here's what this looks like in real life:

In healing from trauma: The Holy Spirit gently reveals one buried layer at a time. Not all at once, lest we collapse under the weight of revelation. The presence of God is the safe container for your tears.

In confronting deception: When we have believed false truths about ourselves or others, the Spirit brings not shame, but clarity. He does not shame the blind; He opens their eyes.

In reclaiming identity: You may not know who you truly are yet, but the Spirit does. He is the great Midwife of your becoming. He breathes over dry bones, and He whispers life into buried truth.

Prophetic Insight: Why the World Offers Substitutes

The millennial question of the ages remains:
If true light exists, why does humanity still seek shadows?

Why do we exchange divine guidance for ideological noise, eternal presence for temporal influence, spiritual truth for doctrinal manipulation?

The answer is not only rebellion; it is distraction, distortion, and fear.

The world offers a thousand alternatives to the Voice of God; ideologies dressed as revelations, doctrines propped up as absolutes, movements masquerading as awakenings.

These are not neutral; they are designed to subjugate the soul, not to liberate it.

Humanity fears stillness, because in stillness the noise fades and the voice of God rises; and with it comes the demand to confront all that is false within.

"For the time will come when people will not endure sound doctrine, but having itching ears, they will accumulate for themselves teachers to suit their own passions." 2 Timothy 4:3

A Sacred Reminder to the Reader

You are not meant to journey by intellect alone, or emotion alone, or tradition alone. You are called to journey in Spirit and in Truth (John 4:24).

The excavation of your soul is not a burden; it is a return. A return to the Garden. A return to the Breath. A return to the original echo within you that still hears the Voice walking in the cool of the day.

The Holy Spirit is not just your companion; He is your guiding compass. Can you hear His Voice?

"You are not too late. You are not too lost. You are simply buried; so that you could be found by Me. Begin to dig, and I will meet you in the depth. For every buried breath, there is a sacred and divine wind waiting to awaken it."

Part 4.

The Resistance Before Resurrection

Resurrection never arrives uncontested. The moment genuine awakening dawns, the ecosystems that once thrived on our numbness rumble with anxiety.

Light always provokes darkness; not because darkness is equal in power, but because unveiled truth exposes everything built on deception.

"The light shines in the darkness, and the darkness has not overcome it." (John 1:5)

Why Resurrection Provokes

Whenever new life appears, three surface reactions often betray a deeper reality. First comes mockery or trivialization; half-smiles and comments meant to minimize your encounter, springing from hidden fears of losing control over old narratives.

Then, sometimes without warning, criticism arrives from unlikely sources; acquaintances or mentors who once applauded you become uneasy, because your freedom exposes agendas that relied on your silence.

Finally, a subtler warfare ensues temptations to return to old patterns whisper, "Nothing has changed; go back." This is not random. It is designed to re-chain what Christ just freed.

When Lazarus shuffled out of the tomb, the authorities immediately plotted to kill him (John 12:10–11). Why?

Because a breathing man who once was dead overturns every counterfeit system. Your mere aliveness carries the same disruptive power.

Resistance wears many masks.

External structures; workplaces, religious circles, social groups; may subtly punish the boundaries you now set.

Internal saboteurs; the inner critic, the orphan spirit, the imposter; whisper that safety still lies in the grave.

And there is atmospheric warfare: sudden heaviness, confusion, or fatigue that descends precisely when you take a new step of obedience.

Paul experienced this when a "great and effective door" opened; and "many adversaries" surfaced with it (1 Cor 16:9).

Navigating the Push-Back

What, then, do we do? Scripture offers four quiet but decisive practices.

First, embrace a shield of silence: moments of deliberate stillness (Ex 14:14) that starve the enemy of frantic reaction and create space for God's strategy.

Second, cultivate confession in trusted community (James 5:16); shared discernment turns isolation into intercession.

Third, wield declarations of identity; answer accusation with the words God spoke over His Son and over you (Luke 4:3–4).

And finally, honor rest-rituals: Sabbath pauses, unhurried sleep, rhythms that remind the soul God remains Sovereign even while we rest (Mark 4:38).

In returning and rest we are saved; in quietness and trust we find strength (Isa 30:15).

When Others Endure and Overcome

History and Scripture confirm this pattern. Nehemiah faced ridicule and false prophecy, yet finished the wall in fifty-two days.

Mary Magdalene pushed through disciples' disbelief to become the first apostolic herald of the risen Christ; and modern saints who leave toxic systems often endure public shaming, yet they remain focus and start planting refuge communities and mentor others into healthy freedom.

Each endured pressure; and rivers emerged where graves once lay.

Discernment for Your Journey

Where has your new obedience stirred unexpected push-back? Which inner voice tries hardest to drag you back to cold stone?

Ask the Holy Spirit if your response now is battle, rest, or holy stillness; for the Lord will be your confidence and will keep your foot from being caught (Prov 3:25–26).

Then in faith trust the Word: "He has clothed me with garments of Salvation." (Isaiah 61:10)

Prophetic Whisper

Stone rolls. Grave clothes fall. The tomb shouts in empty echo, but cannot reclaim what My breath has revived. Walk on. Even limping is victory when you are walking out of death.

Part 5.

The Overflow: From Roots to Rivers

Your inner excavation has reached water, and your resurrection has found breath. Yet the Spirit's goal is not merely that you be filled; it is that you become a conduit.

The life that surged upward in private now yearns to run outward in public, turning hidden wells into visible rivers.

Jesus promised the Samaritan woman, *"The water I give will become in them a spring of water welling up to eternal life" John 4:14*

Springs were never meant to stay capped; they press through soil until deserts bloom.

Prophet Ezekiel saw such a river flowing from beneath the Temple threshold; it was widest, deepest, and most life-giving the farther it travelled" Ezekiel 47:1-9

What God pours into you is designed to irrigate ground far beyond your own borders.

From Cup to Living Vessel

At first you sense the water as a cup; personal, intimate, enough for one parched soul.   Soon it becomes a fresh well, sustaining your household.

Stay faithful, and you discover a stream: creativity, generosity, counsel steadily blessing your wider circle.

Given time and obedience, a river bursts its banks, carrying provision to people and places your feet may never reach. Depth determines reach; hiddenness determines holiness.

Barriers that Narrow the Current

Still, rivers can be constricted. Fear of visibility whispers that public obedience will expose you. Scarcity thinking urges you to ration refreshment, as though the fountain might run dry.

Unresolved offense at times damns the flow; bitterness turns living water brackish. And false humility calls reluctance "meekness" when it is simply unbelief.

Isaiah's promise counters every barrier: *"You will be like a well-watered garden, like a spring whose waters never fail"* Isaiah 58:11

Practical Riverbeds

How, then, does the river run? Through encouragement offered in timely words; through hospitality; a table opened without agenda;

through creativity birthed in secret worship and released for public hope; through acts of justice and mercy that redirect resources toward the many that are overlooked.

Let's also remember Lydia's open house, Barnabas's affirming voice, David's hidden psalms, Isaiah's call to break oppression; all testify that rivers take many shapes yet share one source.

Portraits of Ordinary Rivers

Consider the retiree who prays, unseen, over every home on her street until neighbors begin knocking for prayer, reconciliation, and shared meals. Or the software engineer who hosts quiet, worship-saturated coding nights; colleagues feel peace, ask questions, and some find Christ; productivity rises, but more importantly, hearts awaken. Rivers on ordinary streets transforming ordinary deserts. Be a living Vessel in the Potter's Hand.

"You were never meant to be a reservoir. What I pour in must pour out. Fear not depletion; My rivers self-replenish. As you give, you grow; as you release, you expand. Let the banks widen, let the current run, for creation is waiting for the sound of your waters to flow."

The Test of a First-Fruits Flow

Before twenty-four hours pass, ask the Holy Spirit: "Who needs the water You have given me?"

Then act; send the encouragement, open your table, create the song, sow the gift. In your journal, note how joy rises as water leaves, and watch for unexpected replenishment.

Rivers never diminish by flowing; they carve new channels and deepen their own source within the inner divine.

You descended, not to disappear, but to discover.
You rooted, not to remain buried, but to rise unshaken.
You drank, not to hoard, but to become a river.

In the hush of hidden places the mirror was restored, the breath returned, and the Architect of your soul pressed a finger to ancient foundations and whispered, "Live." Tombs trembled. Resistance roared. Yet stone rolled, grave-clothes fell, and daylight kissed a face once shadowed by false names.

Now the world will taste the waters that surged up from depths no eye has seen.

And every step forward; whether bold stride or tender limp; echoes the anthem of resurrection: "I was buried to be planted, and I rise to bear fruit that remains."

So, walk on, unveiled one. Your sacred roots remember Eden. Your river remembers the Throne. And every desert you cross will bloom at the sound of your footsteps, for Life Himself walks within you.

I would like to close this chapter with a recap of our exploration and journey of inner excavation, in which we traveled deeper towards our roots, and I will leave you with these following Five-Part Imprint:

1. The Mirror Restored:

    God's Word is the true mirror, healing the fractured image and replacing every false label with heaven's original name.

2. The Breath Returns:

    Transformation is more than emotion; it is spiritual resurrection. The Holy Spirit re-animates dormant identity and fills lifeless places with living wind.

3. The Spirit of the Exploration:

    Inner archaeology is guided, never solitary. The Master Excavator uncovers buried truth with precision, redeeming past layers into present purpose.

4. The Resistance Before Resurrection:

    Awakening provokes opposition. External systems, internal saboteurs, and atmospheric warfare rise, yet practical strategies and divine presence secure the victorious path out of every tomb.

5. The Overflow: From Roots to Rivers:

    Hidden wells become public rivers. Depth becomes reach; private infilling becomes communal refreshment. The resurrected life is measured not by applause but by the deserts it turns green.

Remember these five pillars; let them steady your stride as we step into the next horizon.

Chapter Three Summary

The Unveiling: Becoming Who You Were Before the World Told You Who to Be

Let us take a moment to summarize this profound and prophetic chapter.

The Descent That Became Ascent

You descended, not to disappear, but to rediscover the divine code hidden in the dark.
You rooted; not to decay in silence, but to rise in immovable glory.

You drank from the hidden well; not to store living water, but to become a river that flows from secret places into broken lands.

In the hush of hiddenness, the Spirit restored your mirror. The breath that once filled dust returned. And the Architect of your being knelt in your ruins, pressed His hand to your ribs, and whispered,

"Live."

The tomb trembled. Resistance stirred. But the stone rolled. Graveclothes fell. False names evaporated. And daylight kissed the face of a soul unveiled.

The unveiling is not self-expression; it is divine emergence. You are not stepping forward to prove yourself. You are stepping into the light because your roots remembered Eden, and the river within you remembers the throne.

The Five Pillars of the Unveiling

To anchor the truths explored in this chapter, we name five key pillars, each a part of the divine unveiling process that restores identity and releases sacred impact.

1. The Mirror Restored

The greatest tragedy of the fall was not the loss of a location; it was the distortion of identity.
The image of God within humanity was fractured. Yet in Christ, the mirror is mended.

The Word is not just scripture; it is a mirror held by eternity, showing you not who life made you, but who God always saw. In this mirror, false names dissolve and your eternal reflection is restored.

"You are My image. You are My breath. You are My beloved design."

No social label, religious scar, or cultural distortion can define what Heaven has already named.

2. The Breath Returns

This journey is more than reflection; it is resurrection.

The breath that animated Adam is the same wind that filled the upper room and now fills your soul. What was dormant within you has not died; it was buried, awaiting awakening.

Resurrection is not a metaphor. It is a spiritual reality. The Spirit is not just your comforter. He is your oxygen.

He fills your lungs.
He stirs your bones.
He restores your voice.
And He prepares you to rise in divine rhythm, not human ambition.

The Journey Through Sacred Excavation

3. The Spirit of the Exploration

This unveiling is not a solo expedition. You are not left to dig blindly in your wounds.

The Holy Spirit is your Master Excavator, guiding, discerning, and revealing truth in layers. With gentle hands and holy precision, He unearths what shame buried, what trauma hid, and what time forgot.

You are not just healing; you are recovering design. This sacred archaeology of the soul reveals that your pain never canceled your purpose; it simply buried it until grace was ready to raise it.

4. The Resistance Before Resurrection

Every unveiling awakens opposition.

Just as resurrection triggered Roman resistance and religious uproar, your unveiling will provoke noise, external pressures, internal doubts, atmospheric warfare. But you are not left defenseless.

The cross was not the end.
The tomb was not a prison.
They were both thresholds.

And now, every time resistance rises, you carry within you the power to rise with it. Because Christ unveiled Himself from death, you can unveil yourself from distortion. Graveclothes may cling for a moment; but daylight is stronger.

The Overflow and Your Emergence

5. The Overflow; From Roots to Rivers

What was once hidden now becomes flow. The wells you uncovered in solitude become rivers of refreshment for others.

The truths you reclaimed in silence become songs for dry lands. You are not just restored to receive; you are unveiled to pour.

Your life becomes a vessel.
Your presence becomes a well.
Your story becomes a river.
And your deserts become gardens.

True resurrection is not proved by platform but by the deserts you turn green. The measure of unveiling is not applause, but overflow.

You are the bridge between concealed wells and public rivers. You carry the sound of Eden in your footsteps and the fragrance of resurrection in your shadow.

Reflection; The Journey Forward

Now, every step you take, whether a bold stride or a trembling limp, echoes with resurrection. You were buried not to be forgotten, but to be planted. And you rise now, bearing fruit that will remain.

Walk on, unveiled one. You carry Eden in your roots and the Throne in your river. Let deserts bloom at the sound of your soul's reawakening.

Forward Glimpse to Chapter Four: Sent Ones and Kingdom Blueprints

If Chapter Three unveiled who you are, then Chapter Four will reveal why you are sent.

You are not just restored; you are now released. From personal awakening to prophetic embodiment. From soul renovation to kingdom architecture.

You are a soul rebuilt not for hiding, but for heralding. The unveiling was not the end. It was the beginning of your divine assignment.

Let us rise together; sent ones, restored image-bearers, unveiled rivers of God.

Chapter Four

The Mantle in the Wilderness; The Mantle as a Sacred Trust

A mantle is never given lightly. It is not an ornament of honor, nor an achievement of ambition; it is a sacred trust, bestowed by God Himself to advance His eternal purposes on the earth.

Throughout Scripture and history alike, the mantle symbolizes divine responsibility; a weight of glory carried by imperfect vessels chosen not for their brilliance, but for their surrender.

When Elijah cast his mantle upon Elisha, it was not merely a prophetic gesture, or recognition; it was a transfer of stewardship. A mantle is never the possession of man; it belongs to God, who entrusts it to those proven in character, humility, and endurance. It carries the fragrance of heaven and the gravity of eternity.

To wear it carelessly is to risk misrepresenting the very nature of the Holy One who gives it.

Yet before the mantle can be worn, it must be *weighed*. Every divine calling carry both a weight and a witness. The *weight* is the invisible burden of accountability before God; the *witness* is the visible evidence of divine transformation that testifies through the life of the called.

This sacred balance ensures that authority flows from alignment, not ambition.

The mantle, therefore, is never operational at the moment of calling. It must pass through fire, the refining process of the wilderness; where the soul learns dependence, obedience, and trust.

In this holy testing ground, identity is purified, motives are sifted, and the foundation of endurance is laid. God does not entrust mantles to the unformed, for authority without transformation becomes manipulation, and gifting without grounding breeds destruction.

The wilderness is the divine classroom of every mantle-bearer. It is not a place of punishment, but of preparation. To the untrained heart, it may feel like exile; to the discerning spirit, it is evidence of divine trust.

For God only sends to the wilderness those He intends to use deeply.

Moses, who once walked the marble courts of Pharaoh, learned to hear the whisper of God in the stillness of the desert. David, anointed king, spent years in caves and solitude before he ever touched a throne. Even Jesus, the very Word made flesh, was led by the Spirit into the wilderness before He began His public ministry.

The wilderness strips away illusion. It dismantles the scaffolding of self-importance and teaches the soul to find joy in the absence of applause. It is here that one learns the rhythm of heaven: silence before speech, obscurity before visibility, refinement before release.

In this barren landscape, the soul meets itself. Pride is confronted, motives are revealed, and every false confidence is surrendered.

The wilderness is not about deprivation; it is about alignment. God hides those He loves until they can carry what He intends to reveal.

Those who rush through the wilderness misunderstand its purpose. For in the wilderness, God teaches the rhythm of reliance; the art of resting beneath the unseen hand of His providence.

It is here that the human heart learns to discern between calling and control, between divine direction and personal human drive.

The Process of Testing

Before a mantle is released, it must endure the process of testing, for no one is crowned who has not been crushed, and no one is entrusted who has not been examined in the fire of obscurity.

Scripture and experience both reveal that there are three arenas through which every true mantle is tested: against the eternal pattern, in the fire of hidden seasons, and in the face of subtle opposition.

1. Against the Eternal Pattern

Every divine work must align with heaven's blueprint. God does not endorse innovation that contradicts His eternal design.

Before a mantle operates in public authority, the vessel must conform to divine order in private life.

Moses was commanded to build the tabernacle "according to the pattern shown on the mountain."

Likewise, every servant of God must build their life, ministry, and purpose according to the pattern revealed in the secret place.

The eternal pattern demands holiness, humility, and obedience, not performance or popularity.

It is possible to display zeal without alignment, passion without purity. But such energy produces noise, not anointing. The eternal pattern ensures that the bearer of the mantle reflects the heart of the Giver, not the ambition of the vessel.

When one conforms to divine order inwardly, authority manifests naturally outwardly. Alignment precedes assignment.

The power of the mantle flows not from personality but from proximity to God.

2. In the Fire of Hidden Seasons

The second testing occurs in the fire of hiddenness; those long, quiet seasons when no one sees, no one applauds, and no one seems to remember the promise. These are the refining fires of the soul, burning away pride and performance until purity remains.

Hiddenness is not absence; it is incubation. It is in obscurity that the roots of true authority grow deep. Public ministry without private formation is a tree without roots, impressive for a moment but easily toppled by the winds of adversity.

In these hidden seasons, prayer becomes less about asking and more about abiding.

Worship ceases to be an act of emotion and becomes a posture of surrender. God's silence becomes the instrument of transformation.

The greatest work of the Spirit often occurs in the unseen chambers of the heart. The mantle that emerges from hiddenness carries an authority that does not depend on validation, because it was born in the solitude of divine intimacy.

The fire does not destroy the called; it defines them. Every trial, delay, and disappointment is a hammer shaping the vessel into a fit container for glory.

3. In the Face of Subtle Opposition

The third testing arises through subtle and often silent forms of opposition; the kind that creeps into the mind through misunderstanding, discouragement, or betrayal. These invisible pressures reveal the maturity of the living soul.

Elijah faced loneliness, Jeremiah endured mockery, and Paul experienced abandonment, yet each learned that divine companionship is not measured by human affirmation.

The mantle-bearer must learn to draw strength from communion with God, not the consensus of others.

Subtle opposition teaches discernment; the ability to recognize the difference between resistance meant to destroy and resistance meant to develop. Not every challenge is demonic; some are divine chisels, shaping character through contradiction.

It is in this testing that the mantle's bearer learns the art of perseverance: the quiet courage to continue without recognition, the steadfastness to love through rejection, and the humility to forgive without explanation. These are the fruits that make the witness credible.

The Tragedy of Premature Release

The most grievous danger in the journey of the mantle is premature release, when an untested vessel steps forward before the process of refinement is complete. The cost of sending an untested mantle is not measured in public failure alone; it reverberates through souls, communities, and generations.

Premature mantles misrepresent the image of Christ. The vessel may speak with passion but lacks purity of motive; they may operate in gifting but not in grace. The result is distortion, of truth, of witness, and of divine credibility.

When Saul ascended to kingship, his appointment was real, but his readiness to lead it was not completely formed. The throne revealed what the wilderness could have healed. In contrast, David waited. Though anointed, he refused to seize what God had not yet released. His restraint preserved both his crown and his character.

A mantle given too soon becomes a burden that crushes rather than crowns. God delays not to deny but to protect, both the vessel and the vision. Waiting is not wasted time; it is divine construction.

There is no shame in delay; the greater tragedy lies in running before being sent.

When God hides you, rejoice; for it means He values the purity of your purpose more than the immediacy of your performance. Patience is the heaven's proof of trustworthiness.

Biblical Continuity: From Genesis to Revelation

The principle of divine testing and trust weaves through all of Scripture. From Genesis to Revelation, God's pattern remains unbroken: Before He sends, He shapes. Before He releases, He refines. Before He crowns, He crucifies.

Joseph wore a dream long before he wore a robe. Moses carried destiny long before he carried tablets. Even Jesus Christ bore the cross before the crown.

In every story, authority is preceded by alignment, and manifestation by maturity.

The mantle is not the beginning; it is the *confirmation* of what has already been formed in secret obedience. True authority is never self-appointed.

It is recognized, not claimed; conferred, not constructed. It is the fruit of faithfulness in unseen places.

The mature soul understands that waiting is not punishment but partnership with divine timing. The place in the wilderness becomes a holy ground, and the process of anointing becomes sacred.

The Call to Patience, Process, and Preparation

This revelation is not a call to ambition but to alignment, to patience, process, and preparation. The wilderness is the forge of maturity; delay is the proof of design.

Do not seek a mantle; seek the shape that qualifies you for one. Do not chase visibility; pursue intimacy. Do not despise obscurity; it is heaven's womb.

The mantle is not a reward but a responsibility. It is not a symbol of spiritual hierarchy but a manifestation of surrendered trust. The one who carries the mantle carries the heart of God; compassionate, discerning, steadfast.

Value the wilderness. It is where wisdom replaces impulse, humility replaces pride, and purity replaces performance.

The wilderness teaches what the stage cannot: that power is not measured by applause but by obedience.

Discern the difference between counterfeit and premature callings. A counterfeit mantle mimics anointing without submission; a premature mantle moves before divine permission. Both lead to exhaustion, confusion, and collapse.

True authority, however, emerges from those who have been tested and trusted, those who have learned to bend before they are lifted, to listen before they lead, to love before they labor.

The wilderness is where mantles are not only earned but understood. It teaches that authority flows from intimacy and that the greatest calling is not to *do* for God but to *be* with Him.

Part 1.

The Eternal Pattern; Beyond the Outer Garment

The concept of a "mantle" in the Kingdom is often romanticized; wrapped in imagery of power, miracles, and spiritual authority.

Yet before the garment rests upon the shoulders of a vessel, it must pass through the fire of divine scrutiny. And that scrutiny begins with one plumb line alone: The Eternal Pattern.

To understand the weight of a mantle, we must not begin with the vessel but with the Author of the Pattern. Before ministries are launched, movements are named, and visions proclaimed, the foundation must be rooted in what existed before time began; a blueprint drawn in eternity by the Father, modeled in time by the Son, and sustained continually by the Holy Spirit.

This Pattern is not optional; it is the very essence of God's self-revelation. It is His signature, embedded in the structure of creation, covenant, and calling. It is invisible to the casual observer, but it governs all true spiritual operations.

The Source of the Pattern: Divine Unity and Eternal Purpose

"The Father's will is the eternal blueprint. The Son's ministry is its flawless expression. The Spirit's work is the living confirmation."

This triune cooperation is not merely theological; it is foundational for all divine action. The Father originates; the Son manifests; the Spirit animates. No true mantle can bypass this divine cooperation. Each Person of the Trinity testifies to the other. Each supports the Pattern, not by mutual agreement, but by indivisible essence.

To be called is not simply to serve a need, fill a role, or echo a trend; it is to be woven into the triune counsel of God's heart, to reflect His eternal intention on earth.

Any calling that seeks to operate independently of this flow is not from Heaven; it is human ingenuity with spiritual clothing.

This Pattern is the pre-fall design that governed Adam's communion with God, the framework that shaped Abraham's faith, the logic behind Moses' tabernacle, and the DNA embedded in Jesus' earthly ministry. It is the thread running through the prophets, fulfilled in Christ, and extended through His Body; the Church.

The Pattern as Plumb Line: The Non-Negotiable Standard

In building construction, a plumb line is used to ensure vertical precision. It doesn't adjust to the wall; it judges the wall's alignment. Likewise, the Eternal Pattern is not shaped by our desires, giftedness, or ministry goals. It judges the authenticity of all spiritual endeavors.

"None has ever deviated, for they are one in essence, truth, and purpose."

Abraham had to abandon the security of Ur to follow a blueprint he could not yet see.

Moses was forbidden from altering the design of the tabernacle: "See that you make everything according to the pattern shown you on the mountain". Exodus 25:40

David received the temple plans by the Spirit; yet was told he could not build it. 1 Chronicles 28:12

Jesus did "nothing on His own", but only what He saw the Father doing. John 5:19

The apostles "devoted themselves to the apostles' teaching"—not innovations, but alignment to what was handed down. Acts 2:42

Deviation, then, is not innovation; it is corruption. The Eternal Pattern guards the sanctity of the message by anchoring it in divine truth.

The Age of Counterfeits: Why the Pattern Matters Now

We live in a time of unprecedented access to spiritual language, prophetic expression, and charismatic fervor. Yet with abundance comes dilution. As movements rise proclaiming *fresh revelation*, the danger is not their zeal but their disconnection from the Pattern.

"Some may seem indeed that they are carrying a spark from Heaven, but if they cannot be traced in harmony with the eternal Pattern, they must be weighed, tested, and; if necessary; set aside."

Today, "mantles" are often marketed rather than measured. Conferences anoint without discernment. Platforms are built on charisma, not character. But no mantle can sustain weight that has not been tested against the Pattern. Anything born in the soul but wrapped in spiritual vocabulary is still a distortion.

The true test is not how *relevant, inspiring,* or *innovative* something sounds, but whether it echoes the voice of the Ancient of Days.

Jesus: The Manifested Pattern in the Flesh

Jesus Christ is not just our Savior; He is our template. He is the Pattern in bodily form.

"My teaching is not My own. It comes from Him who sent Me." John 7:16

"The Son can do nothing by Himself; He can only do what He sees His Father doing." John 5:19

Jesus operated with absolute dependence on the Father and yielded perfectly to the Spirit. In doing so, He demonstrated what alignment to the Pattern looks like; not performance, but obedience.

Even the Holy Spirit, often misunderstood as operating independently, "will not speak on His own; He will speak only what He hears." John 16:13

This reinforces the sacred order: nothing is released from Heaven that does not align with the triune unity.

Prophets and Apostles: Guardians of the Pattern

The ancient prophets were not innovators. They were messengers of alignment. Their cries were often not, "Here is something new," but "Return to the covenant."

Isaiah saw the Lord *high and lifted up*, and what followed was not a new vision, but a deeper consecration.

Jeremiah deeply wept because the people of God had broken pattern.

Ezekiel's visions, as wild as they seemed, were rooted in heavenly order.

Likewise, the apostles of Jesus Christ were not entrepreneurs; they were builders; constructing the Church on the foundation of Christ, "not with human wisdom, lest the cross be emptied of its power" 1 Corinthians 1:17

To carry a mantle today is not to invent, but to steward alignment.

False Alignment: The Dangers of Spiritual Plagiarism

One of the greatest tragedies in modern ministry is the mimicking of anointing without understanding alignment. Many want Elijah's mantle, but few endure Elijah's process. Many are claiming apostolic titles without apostolic fruit.

"Deviation from the Pattern, no matter how eloquent or emotionally stirring, is not divine and sacred revelation; it is distortion."

Spiritual plagiarism may impress crowds but offends Heaven. A gifted voice without alignment is a resounding gong. A revelation without order is noise. The mantle is not merely power; it is divine representation.

The Testing of the Mantle: A Call to Honor God's Order

To test a mantle is not to doubt a person; it is to honor God's order. It is not suspicion; it is stewardship. Just as gold is tested by fire, so must every calling be weighed against the Pattern.

"What is of Me will not fracture under the weight of scrutiny; it will shine brighter."

This quote reflects God's confidence in His own handiwork. True callings will endure examination. They are not fragile; they are forged. A mantle birthed in God will pass the test because it was born of eternal DNA.

The Pattern is not restriction; it is protection. "The Pattern is protection; it keeps the human messenger from becoming the message, and the gift from overshadowing the Giver."

Without alignment, messengers become idols, and messages become brands. Ministries centered around personalities fracture when personalities fail. But ministries rooted in the Pattern stand because they exalt Christ above charisma.

The Pattern reminds us:

> You are not the message; Jesus Christ is.
> You are not the power; the Holy Spirit is.
> You are not the sender; the Eternal Father is.

The Divine Whisper: Hidden to the proud, clear to the humble *"My pattern is not hidden to the humble, yet it is invisible to the proud."*

Pride blinds. It makes novelty seem more valuable than alignment. But humility opens the eyes of the spirit to eternal truths, not temporary trends.

This is why God often prepares vessels in wilderness seasons; places where noise is stripped, and clarity emerges. In stillness, the Pattern becomes visible. In obscurity, alignment is born.

Alignment in Practice: A Checklist for Discernment

How do we know if we are aligned with the Pattern?

Ask:

> Does this calling; echo the voice of Scripture?
> Does it promote the Name of Christ or my own?
> Is it birthed in prayer or in pressure?
> Is it confirmed by the Spirit or by popularity?
> Can it stand under divine scrutiny without fracturing?

If not, return. Repent. Realign.

A mantle tested and found aligned is a conduit of Heaven's authority. It brings healing without hype, clarity without confusion, and power without pride. It serves, not for personal gain, but for divine glory.

The Pattern is the anchor in the wilderness. It is the compass in confusion. It is the light in hidden seasons. To disregard it is to build on sand. To embrace it is to become unshakeable.

"Align with the Heavens Pattern, and you will never fear the day of testing."

Part 2.

The Fire of Hidden Seasons; The Invisible Furnace

There is a fire that does not consume but consecrates. It is not the fire of public miracles or spiritual warfare; it is the fire of silence, of divine delay, of waiting with no audience and no applause. It is the Fire of Hidden Seasons; God's crucible where mantles are not given, but forged.

To every true calling, there is a wilderness. It is the place where God's hand forms the vessel in secret before ever revealing it in power. Hidden seasons are not punishment; they are preparation. The fire is not for destruction; it is for distinction.

Before any mantle is placed upon a shoulder, it is first inscribed into the soul in secret. The fire does not burn us for failing; it burns off what cannot carry the weight of glory.

The Nature of Hiddenness: God's Holy Strategy

The hidden place is not an accident; it is a divine strategy. God never sends a vessel He has not first concealed.

- **Joseph** had dreams but was thrown into pits and prisons before the palace.
- **David** was anointed in private and returned to the sheepfold, then hunted for years before the throne.
- **Moses** spent 40 years in Midian after the palace before returning to Egypt.

- **Jesus** lived 30 years in obscurity before 3 years of ministry.

What do they share in common? God's delay was not denial; it was design.

"Before He sends, He shapes. Before He releases, He refines."

In a generation that celebrates visibility, hiddenness feels like failure. But in God's economy, it is the soil of eternal fruitfulness.

The Fire: What Burns in the Hidden Season

The fire of hidden seasons is not physical, it is internal. It burns off:

> Entitlement; The belief that calling means immediacy.
> Impatience; The refusal to wait on divine timing.
> Performance; The addiction to validation and applause.
> Ambition; The desire to be seen more than to be sent.

Hiddenness reveals what applause conceals. It shows us whether we love God's will, or just His platform. It is not the absence of activity; it is the presence of refinement.

In the fire, God burns away the outer man so that the inner man may carry His presence with integrity.

Obscurity as Ordination

The world ordains with ceremonies and recognition. God ordains with silence and solitude.

"He made His ways known to Moses, His acts to the people of Israel." Psalm 103:7

The people saw the acts; miracles, signs, and wonders. But Moses knew the ways, the heart behind the hand. Knowing God's ways is only possible in hiddenness. There, the voice of God is not drowned out by applause. It is refined to a whisper.

Obscurity is not a demotion; it is a divine enclosure, like the womb where life is formed. It is where identity is rooted, not in gifting, but in communion.

The Desert: Where Identity is Reconstructed

God will not entrust public power to those whose identity is rooted in visibility. In hidden seasons, the soul is stripped of false layers.

> You are not your ministry.
> You are not your gift.
> You are not your productivity.
> You are a son, a daughter, a vessel.

Only when you can be content with being His, not being known, are you ready to carry a mantle that won't crush you.

The desert is not barren; it is holy ground where self-dies, and Christ lives.

Hiddenness and the Voice of God

In hidden seasons, the voice of God becomes both subtler and stronger. He does not speak with fanfare but with fire.

"He was not in the wind, nor the earthquake, nor the fire, but in the still small voice." 1 Kings 19:11-12

Why does God whisper in hiddenness? Because He is close.

Hiddenness removes the noise so we can discern His tone. It teaches us to obey when no one is watching, trust when no one is applauding, and listen when no one is speaking.

The mantle is forged in this intimate discipline of obedience.

The Tension Between Promise and Process

God often gives a word long before He fulfills it; not to tease us, but to test us.

"Until the time that his word came to pass, the word of the Lord tested him." Psalm 105:19

Between promise and fulfillment is a gap. That gap is where mantles are forged.

Will you trust when the word seems dead?
Will you obey when the outcome is uncertain?
Will you stay faithful when no fruit is visible?

In hidden seasons, God teaches us that faithfulness is not seasonal; it is the foundation of authority.

The Internal Tests of the Hidden Season

Every hidden season carries specific tests, not to punish but to prepare:

The Test of Silence: When Heaven is quiet, will you still pray, worship, serve?

The Test of Delay: When the vision tarries, will you wait, or try to manufacture outcomes?

The Test of Rejection: When others don't see your calling, will you sulk or stay faithful?

The Test of Comparison: When others rise while you wait, will you bless them or envy them?

Each test removes another layer of self so that only Christ remains.

God Hides Those He Loves

Sometimes, we think God hides us because we are disqualified. In reality, He hides us because we are called.

"He took him aside from the crowd, privately..." Mark 7:33

Jesus often did His deepest works away from the crowd. The deeper the work, the more private the place.

God hides His treasures until the appointed time. Not to keep them from the world, but to preserve their purity until the world is ready to receive them.

When the Hidden Season Feels Like Death

Many hidden seasons feel like the death of the dream. The fire becomes so intense that we wonder if the calling was ever real. But God does not bury dreams to kill them; He plants them to resurrect them.

> Joseph had to be forgotten before he was remembered.
> Moses had to be broken before he was trusted.
> Jesus had to die before He could reign.

Hiddenness feels like death because it is. But it is death that leads to resurrection; the pattern of the Kingdom.

How to Steward the Hidden Season

If you find yourself in a hidden season, you are not lost; you are in divine training. Here's how to steward it:

Anchor in the Word: Let the Word shape your identity more than your calling does.

Embrace Obscurity: Serve in small places. Love the unseen. Wash feet where no one applauds.

Develop Depth, Not Image: Let your roots grow deeper than your reach.

Remain Postured in Worship: Worship is not a performance; it is an altar. Build one daily.

Listen and Journal: Record God's whispers. The words you receive in the wilderness will become the staff you lean on in your public ministry.

When the Season Shifts

Eventually, the hidden season ends; not when we demand it, but when we are ready.

"In the fullness of time, God sent forth His Son..." Galatians 4:4

God waits for fullness, not popularity. He waits until what He has formed in you can carry the weight of what He will release through you.

When the season shifts:

> Move without striving.
> Speak without proving.
> Lead without entitlement.

Those who emerge from hidden seasons do so with authority, not ambition. Their voice carries weight because it was forged in silence.

The Fire's Lasting Fruit

Hiddenness is not eternal, but its fruit is. It produces unshakable identity. It refines pure motives. It deepens communion. It anchors you in eternity.

The fire never leaves you the same. You come out not just gifted; but governed. Not just passionate; but pure. Not just available; but anointed.

If you are in a hidden season, you are not behind; you are in alignment. The wilderness is not the end of the calling; it is the womb of the mantle.

Let the fire do its work. Let the silence speak. Let the waiting build you. For when you emerge, you will not be one who simply holds a mantle, but one who has become a living witness to the Pattern, the Process, and the Presence.

Part 3

The Face of Subtle Opposition

Not all opposition comes with swords. Some come with smiles, with reasonable doubts, and with voices that sound spiritual; but carry no Spirit. For every obvious enemy, there are a thousand subtle ones, cloaked in flattery, half-truths, and even Scripture itself.

This is the battleground of subtle opposition; where the mantle is not attacked head-on, but slowly eroded through compromise, discouragement, isolation, and confusion.

If the fire of hidden seasons burns away the self, the face of subtle opposition tests what remains. It is the adversary's craft at its highest; to distort without detection.

The Nature of Subtle Opposition: Not Always External

When we think of opposition, we imagine external resistance; persecution, mockery, rejection. But subtle opposition often comes from within: Doubts that creep in at night. Fear of failure, dressed as humility. The need to be validated. The suggestion to "tone it down" or "wait a bit longer." Voices that say, "Did God really say...?"

Sound familiar? It is the serpent's whisper in Eden, still echoing today. "Now the serpent was more subtle than any beast of the field..." Genesis 3:1 Subtlety is Satan's ancient weapon; not to destroy immediately, but to misalign gradually.

The Mantle as a Target

The enemy does not fear giftedness; he fears anointed alignment. The moment a mantle begins to emerge; tested by the Pattern, refined in hidden fire; opposition arises. But now it comes disguised.

Why?

Because open attacks can awaken the warrior. But subtle opposition seeks to:

Weaken without warning.
Dull without damage.
Distract without noise.

The enemy does not need to defeat the mantle-bearer; just detour them.

The Weapons of Subtle Opposition

Here are the primary forms subtle opposition may take:
The Weapon of Delay Disguised as Wisdom

"Wait until everything is lined up."
"You need more confirmations."
"Maybe this is not the season."

While discernment is vital, there is a counterfeit wisdom that paralyzes with fear masked as maturity. Discernment moves in step with God. Fear masquerading as caution keeps us idle.

Subtle opposition makes inaction feel like wisdom.

The Trap of Comparison

> "Look at how far others are."
> "Your mantle doesn't look like theirs."
> "You must not be ready if you're still here."

Comparison shrinks the soul. It convinces you that what God is doing in you is not valid because it doesn't look like someone else's story.

Subtle opposition convinces you to question your assignment because it doesn't match someone else's highlight reel.

The Whisper of False Humility

> "Who do you think you are to carry this?"
> "You should let someone more experienced handle it."

This isn't humility. Its accusation wrapped in piety.

True humility says, "I am nothing without Him." False humility says, "Because I am nothing, He cannot use me."

Subtle opposition uses insecurity as a muzzle.

The Distraction of Good Things

Subtle opposition doesn't always tempt you with evil. Sometimes it offers good alternatives to your God-ordained calling:

Serving in places you were not assigned.
Taking on tasks you were not graced for.
Saying "yes" to ministry opportunities that dilute your oil. The good becomes the enemy of the God-ordained.

The Flattery of Misaligned Affirmation

Not all encouragement is from Heaven. Some compliments are designed to elevate your ego and bypass your process:

"You should be leading already!"
"They don't recognize your gift!"
"If I were you, I'd start my own thing."

The enemy flatters to provoke premature action. He wants you to seize a mantle you have not yet finished stewarding.

Biblical Portraits of Subtle Opposition

Joseph: Tested by Favor and Forgetfulness

Joseph faced overt betrayal; but subtle opposition came in the prison, when his gift was used but his name was forgotten.

"The chief cupbearer did not remember Joseph, but forgot him." Genesis 40:23

It was a subtle test: Would Joseph resent the silence? Would he strive? Or would he wait on God's timing?

Nehemiah: Distraction Disguised as Dialogue

"Come, let us meet together..." Nehemiah 6:2

Nehemiah's enemies didn't attack with swords. They invited him to talk. Four times they asked. The fifth time, they lied. Nehemiah's discernment was clear:

"I am doing a great work, and I cannot come down." (v. 3)

Subtle opposition seeks to bring you down by appearing reasonable.

Jesus: Temptation with a Twist

The enemy tempted Jesus not with sin, but with Scripture. *"It is written..."* Matthew 4:6. Satan quoted the Word but misapplied it. Jesus didn't just quote back; He rightly divided. Subtle opposition is not absence of Scripture; it is distortion of truth.

The Cost of Yielding to Subtle Opposition

Yielding does not always mean moral failure. Often, it looks like: Delay in stepping into divine timing. Distraction from your unique assignment. Disillusionment with your process. Division between you and trusted counsel. Depletion of spiritual energy by running in multiple directions.

Subtle opposition doesn't try to stop you all at once; it wants you exhausted, misaligned, and self-sabotaged.

How to overcome subtle opposition? By having a divine clarity of your calling. When you know what God said, you can silence every other voice. You can:

Revisit the word spoken over your life.

Record your convictions.
Return to the altar where He first called you.

Let clarity be your compass when voices grow confusing, by cultivate inner stillness. Stillness is not inaction; it is anchored listening.

Hidden seasons prepare you for this. In the swirl of options, stillness lets you discern divine timing.

Stillness protects the soul from emotional decisions, and will help you recognize the pattern. Subtle opposition often follows a pattern: Delay; Discouragement; Distraction; Detour

Discern the pattern, and interrupt it with prayer, fasting, and recalibration, surround yourself with true voices. Eliminate echo chambers. Surround yourself with:

Prophets who challenge, not flatter.
Friends who remind you of your identity.
Leaders who love your soul, not just your gift.

Sometimes the voice of God comes through trusted counsel, not angels. Guard the Gates: Eyes, Ears, and Emotions Subtle opposition often enters through what we feed on: Social media envy. Doctrines of mixture. Entertainment that dulls discernment. What you tolerate in secret will dominate in battle.

God does not remove subtle opposition immediately. Why? Because it reveals:

What still needs refining.
What fears still linger.
What ambitions still influence.

Every sound and whisper of opposition is a sacred opportunity to deepen dependence. Sometimes subtle opposition comes through people you trusted:

> A mentor who discouraged your next step.
> A friend who questioned your discernment.
> A leader who manipulated your loyalty.

Wounds from subtle opposition cut deeper because they are often relational, but healing comes when you: Forgive the vessel, and confront the spirit behind it. Bless the process, even when it breaks you. Stay calm, even when you're tempted to act in response.

What Emerges from the Battle

When you withstand subtle opposition: Your discernment sharpens. Your faith becomes unshakable. Your voice carries weight, because you didn't give in. Your mantle is now married to maturity.

The enemy fears those who passed through fire and still burn for Jesus.

The mantle is not just for power; it is for purity under pressure. Subtle opposition will come. But you are not called to survive it; you are called to overcome it in glory. Stand firm. Listen deeply. Walk carefully. Obey boldly.

For in the wilderness of subtle testing, God is forging a messenger who cannot be manipulated, distracted, or deceived. That messenger is you.

Part 4.

The Sacred Transfer

In the Kingdom of God, few moments carry as much weight as the transfer of a mantle. It is not merely the passing of a physical symbol like a cloak or the laying on of hands; it is a profound spiritual event where Heaven and Earth converge, signifying both the completion of one divine assignment and the birthing of another.

This powerful process that takes place it is more than just a symbolic ritual; it is the release of divine and spiritual weight

When Elijah's cloak fell upon Elisha (2 Kings 2:13–14), it was not just fabric that touched him; it was the impartation of prophetic weight, authority, and responsibility.

Similarly, when Moses laid hands on Joshua, Scripture reveals that Joshua was "filled with the spirit of wisdom" because of this sacred act (Deuteronomy 34:9).

"Then the LORD said to Moses, 'Take Joshua the son of Nun, a man in whom is the Spirit, and lay your hand on him. You shall give him some of your authority, so that all the congregation of the sons of Israel will obey him.'" Numbers 27:18–20

This shows that true mantle transfers are never just mere human ceremonies; they are spiritual transactions, that are initiated by Heaven and confirmed through obedience on Earth. While the physical act may be simple, the unseen shift in the spiritual realm is profound.

Every true transfer originates in the heart of the Everlasting Father and God. It is a divine decision made in eternity and revealed in time. Heaven determines who carries the mantle next, based on divine purpose, not human preference or politics.

Moses did not choose Joshua on his own; God named him directly (Numbers 27:18).

Jesus chose His disciples after nights of prayer, aligning His decisions with the Father's will (Luke 6:12–13).

This reminds us that a true mantle transfer is a sacred trust, not a human award.

When we see this dynamic through the spiritual eyes, it produces a sacred reverence and prevents the schemes of manipulation.

Though only a few may witness a transfer physically, Heaven itself watches. Hebrews 12:1 describes a "great cloud of witnesses" observing the unfolding story of redemption.

When Elijah was taken up in the whirlwind, it was not only Elisha who saw it; there were angels and heavenly witnesses that celebrated a seamless continuation of God's prophetic plan on Earth.

This means that every legitimate transfer carries an eternal record, witnessed by those who have gone before us. It is a reminder that our callings are part of a much larger Kingdom unfolding story.

A mantle transfer always signifies two realities happening at once:

Completion: One vessel has faithfully finished their season. Like Paul, they can declare, "I have fought the good fight, I have finished the race, I have kept the faith." (2 Timothy 4:7).

Commencement: Another vessel steps into their appointed time, carrying forward the mission while adding their unique obedience to it.

This dynamic ensures continuity in God's work. His Kingdom never suffers a vacuum; when one assignment closes, another begins.

For Leaders Passing the Mantle; Pray and discern Heaven's timing carefully. Do not cling to what God has completed, nor rush to release out of fear or fatigue.

Bless publicly what you have already affirmed privately. This act imparts both spiritual weight and public accountability.

For Receivers of the Mantle; Approach this sacred process with humility and holy fear. You are stepping into a legacy that is bigger than yourself.

Remember that the transfer is not the end of your preparation; it is the start of a new testing and refinement process. Carry the mantle as a trust, not as a trophy.

Receiving a mantle is not the end of preparation; it is the doorway into a deeper journey.

Many people mistake the moment of transfer for the culmination of their growth, but in truth, it is only the threshold realm of greater responsibility and refinement. I am reminded of my younger years, when I spent countless hours in martial arts training camps.

Many students trained with a singular focus; to reach the rank of black belt. To them, the black belt symbolized mastery, status, and arrival.

But one day, a wise teacher gathered us together and offered words I have never forgotten; You need to understand this truth.

Training hard to reach the black belt level is not the end goal. It is only the beginning. The day you tie that black belt around your waist is the day your true journey begins.

Until now, you have been preparing to stand at the starting line. From here, the real work, the real discipline, and the real battles commence."

That moment reshaped my perspective forever. In the same way, the mantle is like the black belt. It may feel like the peak of your calling; the sign that you have finally "arrived." Yet in Heaven's design, it is merely the initiation into a higher level of service, warfare, and refinement.

The years leading up to the transfer are years of training; but the years after that will define your true faith and maturity.

Let's remember these paragraphs:

Before the Mantle: You are in the training phase, sharpening skills, deepening character, and learning the foundations.

At the Transfer: This is the graduation ceremony, a recognition that you are ready to be entrusted with greater weight.

After the Transfer: The real proving begins. The mantle will stretch you, test you, and demand a level of surrender you never knew before, and because of that many are failing.

Just as a black belt must continue to train daily, pushing past physical and mental limits, the bearer of a mantle must continue to grow spiritually, emotionally, and relationally.

If the black belt is treated merely as a trophy to hang on the wall, its power is lost. If the mantle is worn for show, rather than carried as a trust, it becomes a hollow garment with no authority.

Part 5

The Receiving of the Mantle

A mantle is not merely given; it is received. And the true difference between being handed something and truly receiving it lies in the posture of the heart.

Heaven does not place mantles upon distracted souls or restless hands; it rests them upon those whose surrender has been proven in the hidden place.

The Spiritual Environment

The atmosphere in which a mantle is received is often one of obscurity rather than spotlight. God's call rarely comes with a parade; it comes in the quiet furrows of faithful work.

Elijah did not place his cloak on Elisha during a temple ceremony, but while Elisha was behind the plow, pushing through the dirt of everyday obedience (1 Kings 19:19).

Why? Because Heaven prefers to commission in the ordinary so that no man may boast in the flesh. The absence of public attention is not divine neglect; it is divine strategy.

Hiddenness Is Protection, Not Punishment

Seasons of obscurity shield you from premature exposure. Many cry out for elevation without realizing that early promotion can be a snare; without deep roots, the first gust of resistance can topple what God intends to grow into a towering tree.

"You are my hiding place; You preserve me from trouble; You surround me with songs of deliverance."; Psalm 32:7

Let's proceed further with few life applications:

Guard your private life;

If you are in a season where few see you, treat it as sacred ground. What you cultivate unseen will sustain you when seen.

Stop comparing seasons;

Others may be in their "public" phase while you are in your "hidden" phase. Both are equally ordained.

Evaluate your readiness; Ask yourself:

If God handed me the mantle today, would my inner life be able to carry its weight without cracking?

Faithfulness in the Ordinary

Elisha was not in a prayer meeting when Elijah found him; he was working the plow. God often looks for mantled leaders in the unglamorous spaces of diligence and responsibility.

"Whatever you do, work heartily, as for the Lord and not for men."; Colossians 3:23

Treat the mundane as training. Every single spreadsheet balanced, every room cleaned, every meal cooked with integrity is a rehearsal for handling kingdom assignments with excellence.

Serve where you are, not where you wish to be. The mantle often finds you faithful in one field before God sends you into another.

Cultivating the Atmosphere

Your spiritual environment is not just about where you are geographically, but what you are fostering spiritually.

Obscurity gives space to cultivate deep intimacy with God without the noise of the crowd.

"But when you pray, go into your room and shut the door and pray to your Father who is in secret."; Matthew 6:6

Build a prayer history with God. Journal your prayers, record your answered prayers, and track the whispers of the Spirit. This history will become your anchor when the mantle is tested.

Feed your inner man daily. Mantles rest on those who are nourished in the Word and saturated in prayer, not on those who are spiritually malnourished.

Protect your mind gates. Limit voices of distraction; whether media, toxic influences, or hyper-critical environments; so, you can hear the Holy Spirit clearly.

The Inner Posture

A mantle is never just a garment; it is weight. The sacred weight of responsibility, of anointing, of accountability before Heaven.

Before God entrusts it, He examines the vessel's inner posture; the unseen attitudes and motivations that will either sustain or sabotage the calling.

Humility Over Ambition

Ambition wants the mantle for recognition; humility receives it for service. Elisha did not chase Elijah across Israel shouting about his abilities and qualifications; he quietly followed, poured water on Elijah's hands, 2 Kings 3:11, and learned the ways of the Spirit before the mantle rested upon him.

"Humble yourselves before the Lord, and He will exalt you."; James 4:10

Check your motives. Ask yourself, Do I want the mantle so I can be seen, or so Christ can be seen through me?

Serve another's vision first. Before God gives you your own platform, He may require you to build faithfully in someone else's field.

Let honor find you. Resist self-promotion; God's timing is the only safe elevation.

The mantle will pull you into assignments beyond your comfort zone. Inner posture means having a heart ready to say *yes* when it's easier to say *later*.

"Enlarge the place of your tent; stretch out the curtains of your dwellings, do not spare."; Isaiah 54:2

Embrace the discomfort. Growth rarely feels like rest; it often feels like stretching muscles you didn't know you had.

Say yes in faith. Some mantles come with instructions you won't fully understand until you begin walking them out.

Expect resistance from within. Your own fears and insecurities will try to negotiate with the call; answer them with obedience, not delay.

The mantle magnifies whatever is in your heart. If bitterness, offense, or hidden sin lingers, the weight of the mantle will press it to the surface.

"Blessed are the pure in heart, for they shall see God."; Matthew 5:8

Allow deep cleansing now. Let the Holy Spirit address wounds, unforgiveness, or pride before they become stumbling blocks in public ministry.

Keep short accounts. Practice confession and repentance quickly so your spiritual pipeline stays unclogged.

Filter your intake. The purity of what you consume; whether teachings, media, or social conversations; shapes the purity of what flows out.

The Testing Grounds

Before the mantle rests fully, God will often take the vessel through proving seasons; these seasons are sometimes long, often misunderstood,

and almost always uncomfortable. These testing grounds are not a delay to your destiny; they are the preparation that ensures you can carry the weight without collapsing.

Before David wore the crown, he tended sheep in obscurity, defending them from lions and bears (1 Samuel 17:34–37). Faithfulness in the hidden pastures will became the foundation for authority in the palace.

What we can learn from King David? To:

Guard the small assignments. How you handle "insignificant" tasks proves how you will handle the visible ones.

Resist resentment. Many mantles are lost in the heart long before they are placed on the shoulders; bitterness in obscurity erodes readiness for promotion.

Celebrate the field season. Recognize that the field is where your spiritual muscles are built and your dependence on God deepens.

Because God will often allow opportunities for compromise to surface; not to trap you, but to reveal the strength (or weakness) of your moral foundation.

"The integrity of the upright guides them, but the crookedness of the treacherous destroys them." Proverbs 11:3

Let's close any hidden doors now, because the secret sin will crack under the weight of the mantle.

Let's choose truth over the convenience of life, knowing that integrity may cost relationships, opportunities, or comfort, but it secures the true anointing of Heaven.

Let's remember, eyes are always watching. The unseen audience of Heaven is more important than the visible crowd on earth.

The mantle is not for sprinters; it's for those who endure to the end. Elijah tested Elisha's persistence three times, telling him to stay behind (2 Kings 2:2, 4, 6). Each time Elisha refused, proving he could endure inconvenience, fatigue, and delayed reward.

God's mantles are delivered at appointed times; never a moment too soon, and never a moment too late. Moses waited forty years on the backside of the desert; David was anointed as a boy but did not wear the crown until years of testing refined his heart.

Premature mantling can destroy both the message and the messenger. But when the time is right, what was once a private burden will become a public trust, and no opposition will be able to ever overturn it.

Refuse premature exits. Many are quitting right before the breakthrough, mistaking testing for abandonment.

Strengthen your endurance disciplines. Prayer, fasting, and Word immersion are the fuel that keeps you moving when emotions fade. See delay as divine filtering. Testing seasons separate those who are curious from those who are committed.

Positioned for the Mantle

The divine mantle is not placed upon the unprepared; it rests upon those whom Heaven has shaped in secret. The spiritual environment determines the soil in which the seed of calling will germinate; hidden fields, not crowded platforms.

The inner posture ensures that when the cloak brushes your shoulders, you wear it in humility rather than pride, letting it rest as God intended instead of forcing it into your own design.

And the testing grounds forge the resilience, purity, and endurance that keep the mantle from becoming a burden you cannot carry. In every case, the process is not meant to humiliate, delay, or discard you; it is meant to anchor you so deeply in the Giver that no amount of warfare, praise, or criticism can separate you from the assignment.

Many rush to be seen in the garment, but few are willing to be formed to bear it. The call of Heaven is not merely to wear the mantle; it is to become the kind of vessel that the mantle will not crush.

Part 6.

The Weight of Recognition

The moment a mantle is transferred is sacred, but the journey that follows can be even more challenging. For while Heaven has already affirmed what has been placed upon you, the world will now begin to watch, interpret, and respond.

This section explores the profound difference between Heavenly recognition and human validation, the evidence of a true mantle, and the dangers of misinterpretation when others see the outward signs of what God has done inwardly.

Heavenly Recognition vs. Human Validation

When Jesus was baptized, He experienced one of the most powerful moments of affirmation recorded in Scripture. The heavens opened, the Spirit descended like a dove, and the Father's voice declared:

"This is My beloved Son, in whom I am well pleased." Matthew 3:17

This was Heaven's recognition; pure, perfect, and complete. It came before Jesus had performed any miracles or preached to crowds. His divine identity was affirmed not by what He had done, but by who He was.

But notice what happened immediately after this divine moment: *"Then Jesus was led by the Spirit into the wilderness to be tempted by the devil."* Matthew 4:1

The first stop after Heaven's affirmation was not a public ministry stage or a celebration. It was the wilderness, where His identity would be tested in silence and struggle.

The Wilderness as the Crucible

The wilderness is the place where the mantle is proven. It is hot, dry, and isolating. There are no crowds cheering, no applause to affirm you, no platforms to validate you. It is just you, the Spirit, and the adversary whispering lies.

This is where many contemporary leaders falter. They receive a mantle; or even just a taste of spiritual gifting; and instead of being led into the wilderness, they run to the stage. They expect immediate visibility and applause, unaware that without wilderness refinement, the very power they carry can become a snare.

Jesus endured forty days of testing because before His ministry could expand outward, His identity had to be unshakable inwardly.

> Satan tempted Him to perform for validation: "If you are the Son of God, turn these stones into bread."
> He tempted Him to seek earthly recognition: offering Him all the kingdoms of the world in exchange for compromise.
> He tempted Him to test the Father's faithfulness, demanding dramatic signs to prove His identity.

Each temptation mirrored the traps leaders face today: pride, power, and performance.

The Modern Parallel

Many modern preachers, prophets, and leaders fail because they mistake human applause for divine approval.

When recognition comes too soon, it fuels pride and the desire to control. Crowds can shout "Hosanna!" one day and "Crucify!" the next. Without wilderness testing, a leader's sense of self-worth becomes tied to public opinion rather than God's eternal voice.

> When they crave applause, they become performers rather than servants.
>
> When they cling to titles, they begin manipulating others to maintain control.
>
> When they fear rejection, they compromise truth to keep people happy.

The tragedy is that while they may still wear the mantle outwardly, its true power fades inwardly. The mantle becomes a garment of performance rather than a cloak of authority.

Lessons from Jesus' Example

Jesus emerged from the wilderness "in the power of the Spirit" (Luke 4:14). His divine authority was undeniable because it had been forged in a sacred hiddenness that became proven under pressure.

He didn't need the crowd to validate Him because the Father's voice had already defined Him.

Life Application:

> Expect the wilderness. If you have received a mantle, prepare for testing rather than public applause.
>
> Silence the need for external validation. Let God's voice be enough.
>
> Recognize pride's subtle creep. Pride often begins not in rebellion but in reliance on the crowd's approval.
>
> Guard the mantle. The wilderness protects you from mishandling what God has entrusted to you.

The Evidence of a True Mantle

A mantle is not proven by titles, charisma, or the size of one's following. Its authenticity is revealed through heavenly evidence; signs and fruit that cannot be manufactured by human skill or manipulation. Just as Elisha's first act after receiving Elijah's mantle was to part the waters of the Jordan, so too will every genuine mantle manifest undeniable proof of its divine origin.

> "Then he took the mantle of Elijah that had fallen from him, and struck the water, and said, 'Where is the Lord God of Elijah?' And when he also had struck the water, it was divided this way and that; and Elisha crossed over. Now when the sons of the prophets... saw him, they said, 'The spirit of Elijah rests on Elisha.' (2 Kings 2:14-15)

This passage shows us that the evidence was not Elisha's announcement of his calling, but the visible manifestation of God's power through his obedience.

True mantles carry heavenly weight, causing the spiritual atmosphere to shift when the mantle bearer acts in alignment with God's will.

This authority is not loud or dramatic; it is recognized even by unseen powers.

> In Acts 19:15, demons recognized Paul's authority because he carried an authentic mantle: "Jesus I know, and Paul I know; but who are you?"

> This is why counterfeit leaders, like the seven sons of Sceva, were exposed; they tried to wield authority they did not truly possess.

Spiritual authority flows from intimacy with God, not position or platform. Test your actions: Do they bring true transformation, or only temporary excitement?

If resistance increases, don't panic, because true authority is often challenged by darkness before it is revealed.

A genuine mantle carries a stream of divine wisdom that goes beyond natural intelligence.

> Joseph interpreted Pharaoh's dream and offered a strategy that saved nations (Genesis 41:38-40).

> Solomon's mantle of wisdom was evidenced when even a difficult case between two mothers revealed Heaven's insight (1 Kings 3:16-28).

This kind of wisdom is not about clever words or intellectual debate; it is heavenly solutions for earthly problems.

When faced with complex challenges, seek the Spirit's guidance before leaning on human logic. Allow others to see God's wisdom through your decisions, giving Him glory for the outcome. Recognize that with greater wisdom comes greater responsibility to steward it well.

Jesus gave the ultimate test for authenticity:

"You will know them by their fruits." Matthew 7:16

True mantles always produce Kingdom fruit: lives are being transformed, true justice advanced, healing released, and communities renewed. This fruit may not always be immediately visible, but over time, it reveals whether a work is birthed by God or by human ambition.

True Signs of Kingdom fruit often include:

> Changed lives: People grow in holiness, humility, and love for God.
>
> Communal blessing: Families, churches, or communities experience peace and restoration.
>
> Multiplication of disciples: The mantle bearer raises up others rather than hoarding influence.

We need to evaluate the long-term fruit of our ministry, not just short-term excitement. We need to be aware of platforms that often produces hype but lacks a lasting transformation, and we need to be able to celebrate small beginnings, knowing that at times the fruit often grows slowly but steadily.

Elisha's question; *"Where is the Lord God of Elijah?";* was not doubt, but expectation.

When the waters parted, it became clear that the same God who empowered Elijah was now working through Elisha. Similarly, others will recognize a true mantle not because of your words, but because they see the hand of God at work in ways that no human effort could achieve.

Life Application:

> Stop trying to convince people of your calling; let obedience speak louder than explanations.
>
> Understand that recognition may take time; Elisha's authority was revealed gradually as he continued to walk in faithfulness.
>
> Stay focused on your assignment, not on proving yourself to critics.

The Danger of Misrecognition

When a mantle is visible, it draws attention, and then people begin to see the outward signs of authority, but they often misinterpret what they are witnessing.

This misrecognition can be just as dangerous as outright opposition, because it doesn't come with hostility, but with misplaced expectations, flattery, and idolatry that can derail both the mantle bearer and those who follow them.

The crowd rarely understands the true nature of a mantle. They see miracles, wisdom, or authority and assume it exists for their personal agendas. Even Jesus faced this challenge.

> *"Jesus, knowing that they intended to come and make Him king by force, withdrew again to a mountain by Himself." John 6:15*

After feeding the five thousand, the people wanted to crown Jesus as a political ruler. Their expectations were earthly, while His mission was heavenly. If He had yielded to their vision, the cross would have been abandoned, and salvation lost.

Not every open door is from God. Some so-called opportunities are traps dressed as blessings. Learn to say "no" when people try to define your mission for you. Seek the Eternal God's voice over the crowd's demands, even when they mean well.

Flattery is more dangerous than strong criticism because it feels good and this feeling can void the mantle carrier of the reality of its surroundings.

People are many times tempting to elevate the mantle bearer rather than honoring the Eternal One who gave the mantle. Over time, this can feed pride and create an unhealthy dependence on human praise.

> Herod faced this in Acts 12:22-23 when the crowd shouted, "The voice of a god, not of a man!" Instead of redirecting the glory to God, he accepted their praise; and judgment fell immediately.

Modern leaders face the same danger. Platforms, social media, and titles can turn servants into performers if flattery is not resisted.

How can you resist flattery? By regularly remind yourself: "I am just a vessel, not the source." By surrounding yourself with people who will speak truth, not just compliments. By redirect every word of praise back to God publicly and privately.

The ultimate danger of misrecognition is when people begin to worship the vessel instead of the Giver. This leads to spiritual dependency on a person rather than intimacy with God.

Paul addressed this in 1 Corinthians 3:4-7 when some believers claimed, "I follow Paul," while others said, "I follow Apollos." Paul rebuked this division, reminding them that he and Apollos were merely servants; God alone caused the growth.

As a leader, always point people upward, not inward. As a follower, remember to honor those who carry mantles but keep your ultimate trust in Christ. Beware of the spiritual celebrity culture; it weakens the Church's collective discernment.

Respect people but trust in the Everlasting Father and God, remain hidden in Christ. Why?

Because the best active defense against misrecognition is to stay humble and to remain hidden in Christ. Even as visibility increases, cultivate a private life that no one else sees.

Jesus often withdrew to solitary places to pray '. Luke 5:16, ensuring that His relationship with the Father remained central.

Maintain disciplines of secrecy: fasting, prayer, and giving that no one knows about (Matthew 6:3-6). Protect times of solitude where you can hear God's voice without outside noise. Resist the urge to announce every spiritual experience or revelation.

Closing Reflection; Anchored in Heaven's Voice

The journey of carrying a mantle is not only about receiving it, but about stewarding it well once the world begins to notice.

First, let's remember that we are called to seek Heavenly recognition over human validation.

Just as Jesus was affirmed by the Father before entering the wilderness, so must we root our identity in God's voice alone, resisting the temptation to build our worth on applause or popularity. The wilderness is not punishment; it is protection.

Second, the evidence of a true mantle will always emerge over time. Like Elisha parting the waters, spiritual authority, divine wisdom, and lasting Kingdom fruit will reveal what cannot be manufactured by human hands. There is no need to strive for proof; obedience will speak louder than words.

Finally, we must guard against the danger of misrecognition. Crowds will misunderstand, flatter, or even idolize the vessel. Their misplaced expectations can derail both the leader and the mission if not handled with humility and clarity.

The safest place for any mantle bearer is hidden in Christ, where glory is continually redirected back to God.

As these truths converge, we realize that recognition is both a blessing and a burden. It provides confirmation but also invites testing.

The weight of recognition is not meant to crush us, but to keep us tethered to the One who gave the mantle.

Every mantle tells a story. It begins in secret, woven by the hands of the Father even before time began. It is revealed through wilderness fire, where false identities will burn away and a true purpose emerges. It is proven through obedience, forged in battles seen and unseen. And in the fullness of time, it is released; not as a trophy for display, but as a trust for generations yet to come.

The journey of the mantle is never about one person. It is a sacred thread woven through history, connecting past, present, and future. Elijah's cloak did not die with him; it rested on Elisha, whose obedience birthed miracles for a new era.

The same Spirit that raised Christ from the dead now clothes His people with power, not for fame, but for faithfulness.

"Not by might, nor by power, but by My Spirit, says the Lord of hosts." Zechariah 4:6

As you walk forward, remember: The wilderness will come before the crowds, and this is God's mercy. The testing will come before the sending, and this is God's preparation. The recognition will come last, and even then, it is only a shadow of Heaven's unseen applause.

Lay down your striving. Surrender your titles. Let the weight of the mantle rest fully on the shoulders of Christ, who alone carries the government of Heaven. Isaiah 9:6.

You are a steward, not the source. A vessel, not the voice. And yet, through you, His Kingdom will come; and His Supreme Will be done on Earth as it is in Heaven.

Prophetic Whisper

"Do not fear being unseen, nor be intoxicated by being seen.
The same voice that called you in secret will sustain you in public.
When they misunderstand you, the One who called you will vindicate you.
When they exalt you, remain humble and encapsulated by the love of the Eternal One that loved you with an everlasting love
Stay close to Him, and your mantle will remain pure, shining as a beacon reflection of the Kingdom of God, rather than your own name."

I humble declare:

"Lord, my identity is in You alone. I surrender every voice but Yours."

Chapter Four Summary

The Mantle in the Wilderness

Chapter Four walks us through the divine journey of the mantle; from its preexistence in the eternal counsel of God, through testing, opposition, transfer, reception, and ultimately to public recognition.

This chapter unpacks not just the symbolic weight of a mantle, but the profound spiritual cost, process, and purpose behind every true calling.

It challenges the reader to stop romanticizing ministry influence and instead surrender to God's ancient, hidden, and holy formation.

Each of the six parts of this chapter is a stage in the consecration of a vessel, showing us that before anyone is sent with power, they must first be shaped in secret.

The Eternal Pattern

Before a mantle is ever placed, it must be measured against Heaven's blueprint. This eternal pattern: revealed through the unity of the Father, Son, and Holy Spirit, serves as the plumb line by which all callings, visions, and mantles must be aligned.

The first test is not public; it is internal alignment to the unchanging nature of God. What deviates from the Pattern, no matter how gifted or impressive, is a distortion.

The Fire of Hidden Seasons

True mantles are not born on platforms but in obscure furnaces; seasons of divine silence, delay, and seeming invisibility. These hidden times refine the soul, burning away pride, performance, and premature ambition. Here, identity is rooted not in what we do, but in who we are in Christ. God hides those He loves; not to punish them, but to prepare them for what their calling demands.

The Face of Subtle Opposition

Once the fire has done its work, the next test comes, not with open conflict, but with covert resistance. This is the realm of distraction, flattery, false counsel, delayed obedience, and comparison.

Subtle opposition does not aim to destroy but to dilute, detour, or derail the messenger. Discernment becomes critical. Without it, one may unknowingly forfeit the purity of their assignment while thinking they are still "doing God's work."

The Sacred Transfer

A mantle is never self-assumed; it is transferred. And that transfer happens in sacred, often hidden moments, orchestrated by divine timing and validated by those who have walked with God.

Elijah and Elisha illustrate this dynamic: hunger must meet honor, and succession must be rooted in servanthood, not ambition.

Sacred transfers require both generations to walk in humility, honor, and spiritual obedience.

The Receiving of the Mantle

Receiving the mantle is not about catching a cloak; it is about catching a burden. What is passed down is not a performance, but a portion of God's heart.

It requires readiness, consecration, and the willingness to carry what others carried with tears, blood, and worship. This stage affirms the transition from being prepared privately to stepping into public assignment, though still under the Lordship of Christ.

The Weight of Recognition

When a mantle is received and rightly stewarded, the final movement is public recognition, not for fame, but for function. This is when Heaven affirms and people bear witness to the authority carried.

However, this moment is dangerous if the previous stages were skipped. Without the Pattern, fire, testing, transfer, and preparation, recognition becomes a curse, not a commission.

Recognition is not the goal; it is the confirmation of God's craftsmanship in the wilderness. Those who emerge from the process don't boast; they weep, worship, and walk lightly, knowing the mantle is not about them, but about the One who gave it.

The wilderness is not wasted; it is woven into the very mantle we are called to carry.

Every mantle that carries Heaven's authority must first walk through Heaven's wilderness.

The Heaven's Pattern aligns us. The fire refines us. The subtle opposition matures us. The transfer humbles us. The receiving consecrates us. The recognition confirms us.

May every reader of this chapter come to understand: the call is holy, the process is painful, but the result is a mantle forged in eternity, refined in obscurity, tested in conflict, and revealed in due season. Let us not seek mantles. Let us seek the Man behind the mantle.

"Align with The Heaven's Pattern, and you will never fear the day of testing."

Chapter Five

The Descendance

From Carriers to Gatekeepers; Descending into Sacred Foundations

There is a holy gravity in the spirit realm; a divine invitation not to rise higher, but to go deeper. After the wind and fire of mantling, after the sacred weight of calling descends from Heaven, there comes a pause.

A silence. A spiritual shift. It is not the call to ascend further, but to descend into the hidden places.

Chapter Four left us clothed in the mantle; Chapter Five beckons us into the foundations beneath it. For what use is the garment of glory if it has no altar to rest upon? What meaning has an anointing that has not yet been rooted? It is here that the Spirit whispers, not "How far will you go?" but "How deep will you yield?"

"Descendance" is not a common theological term, but in the spirit, it defines a sacred movement that follows every mantle. It is the call not to expand outward, but to be drawn inward. Not to perform, but to be purified. Not to be lifted, but to be lowered into the deep wells of divine counsel. This is not regression, not collapse, not retreat.

It is holy deepening; a yielding into original intent, sacred altars, and ancient gates.

The question of this descent is not; What are you carrying? but" Where are you rooted?" So often we seek to carry mantles like flags, waving them before men and enemies alike.

But a mantle without a foundation is like a banner with no fortress. It flies proudly until the wind turns against it. But when a mantle finds its altar; its buried altar, it becomes an enduring flame that no wind can extinguish.

This is the invitation of The Descendance: not to lose ground, but to find depth; not to be known, but to be hidden in the One who knows all things.

In the economy of Heaven, the strength of any call is not in its visible expression but in its invisible foundation. You do not see a tree's roots, yet they determine its height. You do not see a building's foundation, yet it bears its weight. Likewise, in the spirit, every true mantle demands:

A foundation deeper than applause.
An altar older than your assignment.
A gate hidden beneath the surface of your soul.

"Where is the altar beneath your altar?"; This question becomes the thunder beneath this chapter's silence. In an age obsessed with platforms, God is searching for depth-dwellers; those who will not only walk in power but guard the gates beneath the earth, the thresholds where Heaven meets hiddenness.

Before God builds towers, He digs trenches. Before He sends prophets, He buries seeds. Before He releases glory, He shapes humility.

Every anointing that will stand before kings must first kneel before the unseen. Every voice that will shake nations must first be silenced by divine stillness. The weight of eternity requires depth, not display.

The mantle is not the final proof of maturity; it is the beginning of stewardship. To be a carrier is to wear; to be a gatekeeper is to guard.

And in this era, God is raising not performers of the Spirit but protectors of the sacred. Gatekeepers are not entertainers of revelation; they are guardians of dimension.

Carriers rejoice in moments of anointing; gatekeepers dwell at thresholds, ensuring that what flows from heaven remains unpolluted as it enters the earth.

They are watchers between worlds. They have walked through silence, pain, and the stripping of self. They have learned the language of thresholds; the stillness before movement, the whisper before the wind.

These are the ones who know that not all power is divine, not all fire is pure. They have descended into the architecture of God's counsel; places where calling is not expressed but buried, awaiting resurrection.

Their authority is born from proximity, not platform. They carry keys, not crowns.

To become a gatekeeper is to understand that access is not privilege but responsibility. The deeper one descends, the more one guards. For revelation that is not protected becomes revelation that is perverted.

And so, God trains His gatekeepers not through recognition but through refinement. They stand not on stages, but at thresholds; unseen, uncelebrated, yet absolutely essential to the flow of heaven's order.

"What if the sacred is not always above, but beneath?" What if the true portal does not demand elevation, but excavation?

In my dream, the very dream that birthed this book, the mountain did not beckon upward. It instantly opened downward. What I saw was not an ascent, but an unveiling from below, the earth itself opening into light. It was not a call to climb, but a call to enter.

This dream shattered the old paradigm. It revealed a prophetic architecture: God is no longer drawing His people to visible summits but to hidden sanctuaries.

The new high place is not the platform but the prayer room, not the crowd but the cave, not the visible fire but the buried flame.

It is a spiritual inversion; the revelation that descent is the new ascent. *As Christ descended into the lower parts of the earth before He ascended. Ephesians 4:9–10.;* so too we must follow.

Heaven's pattern has always been paradoxical: the way up is down. The greatest glory of all, is born in the greatest humility.

What if the mountain itself is a mirror of the living soul; its summit our ambitions, its depths our altars? What if God is not asking us to climb higher but to open deeper?

The light that changes the world is not that which shines from the summit, but that which burns unseen beneath it.

The true gate is not the public one that applause opens, but the hidden gate that only surrender unlocks. It lies beneath ambition, beneath gifting, beneath even zeal. It is buried in three sacred chambers:

The True Secret Place; where communion replaces performance, where intimacy outweighs impact. Here the voice of God becomes the breath that sustains.

The Honest Place; where the soul stops pretending. Where motives, wounds, and longings are laid bare before divine light. Truth is not punished here; it is purified.

The Surrendered Place; where one gives up control, choosing trust over strategy, presence over progress. This is where mantles become anchored, and movements become eternal.

To descend is to find these gates; thresholds beneath thresholds. This is not mysticism but blueprint. The enduring mantles of history were not preserved by public success but by private surrender.

A mantle is not merely a symbol of power; it is a covenant of purpose. And every covenant must be sealed in foundations or it will fracture in storms.

The ancients climbed mountains to encounter God. Moses on Sinai. Elijah on Horeb. Even Lord Jesus Christ on Tabor. But in this revelation, the mountain opened a portal at its base; heaven concealed in the earth's womb.

It was a holy reversal; the Spirit teaching that sometimes, to find heaven, we must go beneath what looks spiritual and into what feels hidden.

This is not about climbing; it is about entering. The way in, is not up; it is through. Through obedience, through humility, through surrender to stillness, through the narrow gate that requires the shedding of self. *Here, ego dies and glory dwells. Here, vision ceases to be ambition and becomes alignment.*

The portal of descent is not a punishment; it is preservation. God hides what is holy until it is holy enough to handle. He buries purpose so that it will not be stolen by pride. He hides revelation not from us, but for us, waiting until the vessel can contain it without corruption.

Why does God call us downward after the mantle? Because what He is building is not a moment of influence but a foundation of inheritance. He is not constructing a ministry; He is cultivating a lineage.

The descent is generational in scope. What you anchor today will carry those who come tomorrow.

He is searching for fathers and mothers who are not swayed by the tides of trend. Intercessors who do not flinch when altars quake. Voices that do not echo culture but release eternal sound.

The descent is not isolation; it is transformation. It is where the scepter is forged, where the living scroll is inscribed, where the groaning of nations becomes audible in the spirit.

The descent births the intercessors of eternity; those who bear the burdens of the age in silence and prayer.

When you descend, you do not leave the heights behind; you bring the light with you into the depths. The deeper the descent, the brighter the illumination. God's glory is not limited to the heavens; it fills the earth, even its hidden chambers. It is here that purpose becomes eternal; where what is born in silence shakes the nations.

We are being reoriented. The call of this chapter is not to chase more fire or favor, but to listen beneath your mantle. To return to the altar under your own assignment. To descend into the hollowed-out places where He alone speaks; our Holy Father and Eternal Creator.

This is the movement of this age; from noise into nuance, from function into formation, from visibility into vision. The greatest revelation is not in what is seen, but in what is concealed.

God is inviting a generation not to perform His Word but to embody it; not to climb toward glory but to carry it inwardly into the depths of being.

Heaven is shifting the axis of anointing. The question of tomorrow's leaders will not be "How high did you rise?" but "How deep did you root?" Not "How loud did you speak?" but "How still did you listen?"

The mantle of this generation will not rest upon those who desire spotlight, but upon those who choose solitude. They will be called" keepers of the inward gate", guardians of sacred foundations, architects of altars beneath altars.

Their ministry will not echo noise but release resonance; the deep sound of heaven vibrating through human vessels.

This is The Descendance; the holy movement downward. It is the mystery of becoming smaller; that you might contain more. It is the revelation that what falls into the earth does not die; it multiplies.

The mantle that is buried in obedience will rise in unshakable glory.

Do not fear the descent; it is your consecration. Do not resist the silence; it is your shaping. Do not despise the depth; it is your inheritance. The foundations of heaven are not laid on heights but in hearts surrendered to the gravity of grace and mercy.

And in the stillness beneath all striving, the Spirit whispers once more: *"Go deeper still. Guard what is sacred. Root what is eternal. For the gates you open in humility will become the doors through which heaven enters earth."*

The Descendance is not the end of ascension; it is its fulfillment. The deeper you go, the higher His glory rises within you. For in the kingdom of heaven, only those who descend shall truly ascend.

Part 1.

The Mountains as Thresholds

The Sacred Geography of Encounter

Mountains have always stood as metaphors of majesty. Yet in the divine narrative, they are not just landforms, they are liminal places: thresholds between realms, realms between times, doors between dimensions. Every mountain in Scripture isn't just an elevation; it is a transition.

God never wastes topography. He uses it to mark sacred moments. And so, when we speak of mountains in this chapter, we are not admiring landscapes; we are discerning landmarks of revelation. To understand what it means to descend into foundation, we must first re-examine the mythology of ascent.

The Myth of Ascent and the Theology of Thresholds

In modern spiritual culture, ascent is everything.

> Climb higher.
> Reach further.
> Break through.
> Go to "the next level."

But true spiritual growth often rewrites the metaphor. God is not only found at the top of mountains; He is waiting at their base, inside their caves, whispering at their roots.

"Let's take a few moments to delve further together into the powerful stories of the mountains where Earth kissed Heaven and eternity breaks into time."

Mount Sinai; The Furnace of Instruction and Covenant

Mount Sinai is the birthplace of national identity for Israel, and a true prophetic illustration of divine initiation. Here, on Mount Sinai, fire descended, not to consume, but to instruct. Heavy smoke, thunder, and trumpet blasts did not signal judgment; they marked invitation. God Himself stepped onto the mountain to speak, shape, and seal.

"Mount Sinai was covered with smoke, because the Lord descended on it in fire." Exodus 19:18

Yet what many overlook is that before Moses ascended to receive commandments, he removed his sandals at a burning bush, at the base of the mountain.

The summit holds instruction. The base holds invitation. The bush burned but was not consumed. This speaks of divine fire that purifies without destroying, a symbol of the mantled vessel in formation.

"Encounters at the summit begin with reverence at the base. The removal of sandals precedes the receiving of stone tablets." Sinai's blueprint for threshold navigation: Awe before ascent. Instructions through encounters. Law rooted in intimacy. It is a holy reminder: Before revelation thunders; humility whispers.

Mount Zion; The Chosen Hill of Presence

Where Sinai booms with spectacle, Zion whispers with permanence. Zion is not the tallest mountain, but it is the most desired:

"For the LORD has chosen Zion; He has desired it for His dwelling: 'This is My resting place forever.'" Psalm 132:13-14

Zion doesn't intimidate; it invites. It doesn't impress; it inhabits. It is here that the Ark found its home, David built his kingdom, and the Psalms were birthed. Unlike Sinai's flash, Zion offers consistency. It speaks of dwelling over display.

"Destiny is not always dramatic. Sometimes it is rooted, consistent, and chosen by grace."

Zion's Revelation:

God doesn't always choose the highest place, but the right place. Presence is not based on spectacle, but selection. It teaches us to value the unseen favor of being chosen, rather than the seen spectacle of being visible.

Mount Tabor; The Summit of Transfiguration

On Mount Tabor, Jesus is transfigured. It is the culmination of divine unveiling. Here, the narrative reaches a crescendo:

His face shone like the sun. His garments gleamed with glory. Moses and Elijah appeared, bearing witness.

And then Heaven speaks: *"This is My beloved Son... Listen to Him." Matthew 17:5*

This mountain carries the most intimate unveiling of Christ's divinity to that point. But it is not public. It is not for the crowds. It is for three disciples; those He trusted. This shows us that glory is not for performance; it's for proximity.

Moses "the Law" and Elijah "the Prophets" yield to Jesus the Living Word. Heaven reorients its focus, not on tradition or power, but relationship.

"Do not merely marvel at the manifestation; listen to the voice of the Beloved."

Tabor speaks not only of unveiling but of audibility; you don't just see glory; you hear the Beloved. Olympus and Kailash; Mythologies and the Echo of Archetype

Even in pagan lore, mountains symbolize divine domains: Mount Olympus; The throne of Greek gods. Mount Kailash; The seat of Lord Shiva in Tibetan tradition.

These myths, though theologically errant, echo a universal truth: Humanity knows that the divine meets us at the heights.

"Mountains are not simply geological. They are symbolic of the soul's yearning for the divine." Every culture's mountain myth reveals something embedded in us: A hunger for transcendence. A powerful longing to break gravity. A hope to touch the invisible.

These myths tell us what theology confirms: We were made to encounter God. In all the examples, biblical and mythic; the mountain is more than terrain. It is a mirror: A mirror of yearning. A mirror of transformation. A mirror of movement between flesh and spirit.

What we must see now is that these are not destinations; they are thresholds. "Some are invited to receive instruction "Sinai". Some are called to dwell in intimacy "Zion". Others are chosen to behold the glory "Tabor"."

Each mountain is not a monument; it is a moment. A moment where God interrupts time with eternity. This is where everything shifts.

"What if the next level of intimacy with God requires not a step upward… but a step inward and downward?"

The mountain in my dream opened a portal at its base. This prophetic picture dismantles centuries of climbing theology.

Here's what it reveals:

> Revelation doesn't require altitude. It requires accessibility.
> The goal is not to ascend higher, but to enter deeper.
> Thresholds are not always at the summit; they are at the foundation.

This is more than poetic. It is prophetic architecture. It reconfigures our interior compass. God is not waiting on the mountaintop; He is opening the gate within the ground beneath our feet.

The Dangers of Summit Theology

In modern spirituality, many are chasing elevation:

>Bigger platforms.
>Higher anointings.
>Greater visibility.

But summit obsession can:

>Replace surrender with ambition.
>Mistaking gifting for maturity.
>Confuse altitude with authority.

"Have I confused elevation with revelation? This is a clarifying question. God is not impressed with height; He is seeking depth-dwellers.

Spiritual Lessons from the Mountains

Let's distill each into a spiritual posture:

Mount Sinai: Instructions and Covenant. Reverence and Humility.

Mount Zion: Presence and Rest. Consistency and Surrender

Mount Tabor: Glory and Sonship. Proximity and Intimacy.

Mount Olympus/Kailash: Human Yearning. Recognition of Deep Longing.

Each threshold requires a different response; but all invites us into a deeper descent, not a greater climb. If we truly believe God is opening foundations; not peaks; then we must:

Lay down climbing.
Take up entering.
Descend into our inner altar.

This means letting go of:

The performance mentality.
The comparison with other "summits."
The addiction to being seen.

God's whisper is clear: "Heaven is not obsessed with how high you climb. It's focused on how deep you listen."

Let the Mountains Speak

"What if the next threshold is not a door ahead of you; but a gate beneath your feet?" You are being invited to: Reframe your theology of growth. Rediscover sacred geography. Reimagine what it means to encounter.

Let Sinai speak. Let Zion dwell. Let Tabor transfigure. Let Olympus echo. Let Kailash long. Let the thresholds of encounter become divine portals of your transformation; not by climbing higher, but by kneeling lower.

Part 2.

The Foundation Holds the Mystery

A Sacred Discovery on the Path of Descent; The Illusion of Ascent and the Sacred Descent

We are taught to rise. Upward is success. Elevation is enlightenment. From the Tower of Babel to modern skyscrapers, humanity's obsession with height reflects a misplaced spiritual compass. Yet the soul's journey does not merely ascend; it descends.

In Escaping Earth, the revelation is subversive: the mountain does not demand your climb, it invites your entering. The true escape is not through elevation but by returning; into the depths, into the origin, into the foundation. This is the holy inversion. The sacred paradox.

To descend is not to regress; it is to remember. To remember is to realign. To realign is to return to the foundation.

Descent as Divine Architecture

Spiritual traditions across cultures whisper of this mystery. In the Hebrew scriptures, altars were built on stone, covenants etched in rock. Psalm 11:3 cries out: "If the foundations be destroyed, what can the righteous do?"

The foundation is not merely structure; it is a sacred covenant. Not merely just a base; but new beginning.

God builds from below. Eden, too, had rivers flowing from it; not downward from the heavens, but upward from its springs.

In Ezekiel's vision, the glory returns not from the sky, but from the East gate; the place of dawn, the place of roots. The architecture of the divine begins in soil.

In my dream-vision, the helicopter does not rise. It descends; into the mountain's womb. This image shatters our instinct. It mocks the escape fantasy. The machine of flight becomes the vessel of entry. Earth, often viewed as exile, is reintroduced as sanctuary.

This is not the escape from Earth, but the escape into Earth's womb. The descent is a remembrance of who Earth is.

The helicopter's descent into the belly of the mountain is an echo of Christ's descent into Hades; into the forgotten, the bound, the buried. Only there could liberation begin.

Mountains have always been sacred spaces; Mount Sinai, Mount Zion, Mount Tabor. Yet the revelation is not merely atop the peak. It is within.

The belly of the mountain speaks of primordial truth. It is the place of lava, fire, pressure; the foundation of tectonics. Beneath the stone is memory.

Foundations hold the memory of what was spoken before walls were raised. They hold the intention of what was dreamed before form was shaped.

To enter the belly or the sacred womb of the Earth, is to access the unspoken word, the unshaped light, the pre-material promise.

Foundations as Living Altars

In ancient practice, altars were not built high. They were laid low; in earth, in stone, in silence. The foundation is where altars breathe.

In spiritual practice, we often seek the spectacular; the fire from heaven, the cloud of glory, the voice from above. But the deepest fire is not in the sky. It is in the embers of the foundation. In the still-burning coals beneath.

To build without foundation is to erect a shell. To lay the foundation is to lay presence. In returning to the foundational altar, we don't just remember what was; we re-sanctify the space.

The Mystery Hidden in Plain Sight

Foundations are hidden; not because they are secret, but because we don't look down.

We look up, out, ahead. But rarely beneath. The mystery is not obscure; it is embedded. Beneath our feet, beneath our fears, beneath our stories.

The deepest truths are not far, but buried. Awaiting excavation. Mystery, in this sacred journey, is not esoteric. It is relational. It waits for intimacy, not intellect. The foundation holds the mystery because it holds the trust of the architect.

Why the Foundations Were Forgotten

In this age of surfaces, we mistake exposure for depth. We build high without digging deep. We call acceleration progress, and visibility value. Foundations are forgotten because they do not flatter. They do not produce quickly. They demand patience, obscurity, quiet.

To dwell in the foundation is to accept the hidden life. But what if this is the truer life? The hidden seed in the soil. The root beneath the flower. The still voice under the thunder. What if the foundation is the original Eden?

The Unseen Places of Encounter

Moses met God on the mountain; but he first met Him in the bush, at ground level. Jesus preached from hillsides; but his first revelation came not in the temple, but in the womb.

All true encounters begin low; in caves, in deserts, in stables. The foundation is the geography of encounter. Not because God cannot speak from high; but because we cannot truly listen until we are low. Descent prepares the ear. Descent humbles the heart. Descent opens the eyes that ascendancy blinds.

The Foundations as Collective Memory

Every civilization carries a foundation myth; a beginning, a story of descent. Not ascent.

The Hebrews: a garden and a river.
The Mayans: the underworld and resurrection.
The Greeks: chaos before cosmos.
The Egyptians: the mound rising from the waters.

The foundation is not only spiritual; it is collective. Cultural. Cosmic. We have forgotten our foundations because we have forgotten our stories. To return to the foundation is to remember who we are; not merely individually, but together.

The Returning to the Root; A sacred practice to engage the foundation is not metaphor alone; it is practice.

We must: Slow down; Excavation requires stillness. Listen; The foundation speaks in tremors, not shouts. Touch earth; Literal grounding reawakens inner ground. Pray low; Knees remind the soul it is not the summit that sanctifies, but surrender. Unlearn; Foundations cannot be built upon assumptions.

This is not romantic. It is rigorous. But it is the way. Presence does not dwell in performance. It settles in substance. The foundation is the place where presence can rest. Not the mere flash of manifestation, but the weight of dwelling.

God did not walk on the roof of the tabernacle. He rested between the cherubim, on the mercy seat; upon the foundation of covenant and blood. Mystery is not the absence of clarity. Mystery is the fullness of presence.

We, too, have foundations. In our psyche. Our past. Our soul-architecture. Most of us live within spiritual penthouses built on emotional ruins.

To descend is to do the work. To find the wound that shaped us. To revisit the words, we believed. To touch the silence beneath the noise.

It is therapy. It is prayer. It is the living soul-excavation. And it is sacred. We cannot soar unless we have somewhere to return.

From Escape to Embrace; Escaping Earth is not a flight from reality. It is an invitation to embrace it; fully, deeply, downward. The Earth is not exile. Earth is altar. Earth is womb. Earth is a sacred and eternal foundation.

In embracing Earth, we embrace our full humanity; and thus open the gateway to divinity.

The Gate is Below

In most mythologies, the gate to the otherworld is underground. The Celtic sidhe. The Greek Hades. The Mesopotamian underworld. The Jewish Sheol. This is not hell. It is not punishment.

It is transformation. The underworld is the place of shedding, of testing, of becoming. The gate is not punishment; it is process. To escape Earth, we must enter her gate. Which means to kneel. To descend. To weep. To remember.

The Mystery Reclaimed

Mystery is not confusion. It is depth. It is the sense that something real lives beneath what is seen. To reclaim mystery is to reclaim reverence.

And reverence begins in the foundation. We do not need more revelation; what we truly need is re-foundation.

Prophetic Blueprint: Foundation as Template

The mountain opening like a portal in my vision is not an anomaly; it is archetype. Prophets have always been drawn to the foundation. Jeremiah speaks of plucking up before building. Isaiah speaks of the cornerstone in Zion.

Christ himself is called the "stone the builders rejected"; yet He became the foundation. And Christ the true foundation is the eternal divine blueprint for wholeness. Until we return there, we build in vain.

In the paradox of heaven's physics, descent *is* ascent. The deeper the root, the higher the fruit. The lower the humility, the greater the authority.

The more hidden the sacrifice, the more lasting the legacy. This is not motivational; It is mystical. The gate is beneath. The glory is within.

In the journey of Escaping Earth, we come full circle; not to leave Earth, but to re-encounter her as first Earth; as the garden, the altar, the origin.

The foundation is not simply what supports. It is what speaks. It is the memory of Eden. The tremor of the first Word. The seed of resurrection.

To descend is to live again. To return to the foundation is to begin anew; not with naivety, but with sacred knowing.

So, we descend, not to escape, but to enter. And we find, not abandonment, but the Presence waiting.

Part 3.

Return to The Sacred Core

A Sacred Discovery through Darkness, Depth, and Divine Encounter

The Sacred Spiral: Descent Before Ascent

Across time, space, and scripture, the pattern is unmistakable: descent precedes revelation.

Joseph: From favored son to pit-dweller, to prison, to palace ruler.
Jonah: From prophet on the run to prophet reborn; from storm to the belly of the fish to Nineveh.
Christ: From Cross to tomb, from tomb to throne.

This spiral is not symbolic only; it is sacred architecture. It is encoded into the cosmos, into DNA, into the mythic story embedded in every soul.

Before light, there is concealment.
Before voice, there is silence.
Before flight, there is falling.
Modern Delusion: Skipping the Depth

Contemporary spirituality mascaraed as religious piety, often trades depth for the emotions of an instant dopamine effect. It offers:

Enlightenment without endurance.
Awakening without wounding.
Escape without excavation.

But this is not transformation. It is bypass. The living soul is not a hot air balloon; it is a seed. And a seed must fall. It must break. It must be buried. Jesus did not skip the tomb. He sanctified it.

The Sacred Core: Where Light is Conceived

In the womb of the Earth, something ancient lives. The Sacred Core is not metaphor; it is memory. It is the place beneath all masks, layers, stories, trauma, striving. It is the fire at the center, the still-point in the spiral, the voice in the silence.

To descend into the Sacred Core is to return; not to where you've never been, but where you've always been held. The Kingdom of Heaven is not built above; it is buried within (Matthew 13:44). It is a sacred treasure hidden in a field, not displayed in the sky. You are the field.

The treasure is not external. It is entombed in you. Burial is not the end: It is the Beginning. In divine logic, burial is not death; it is germination. We are taught to fear the dark. But it is in darkness that:

> Babies are formed.
> Seeds sprout.
> Stars are born.

What if the dark is not void but womb? The Sacred Core is the dark that births light. To embrace it is to surrender to divine timing, divine pacing, divine pressure.

Pressure is not punishment; it is precision. Diamonds are formed below. Oil is pressed below. Wine is fermented below.

Anointing, clarity, brilliance; they are always the result of what happens in the deep, in the hidden, in the buried. To escape Earth is not to flee pressure; but to be re-formed by it. To be crushed and still chosen. To be hidden and still holy.

The threshold of descent carries: Initiation, not exile. Every descent is an invitation into initiation. The cave is not your grave; It is your classroom. The valley is not your failure; It is your training and transformation. The belly of the fish is not a process of rejection; It is redirection.

God does not waste the descent. He inhabits it. To be in the Sacred Core is not to be forsaken, it is to be forged. Every sacred lineage carries this rite of passage: Abraham went down into Egypt. Moses was hidden in the desert. David was exiled before he was enthroned. Elijah fled to the cave. Jesus entered Sheol.

And all of them emerged; not the same but transformed. Why? Because in the sacred geography, the Sacred Core is truly an Inward Gate. The geography of the soul is not linear. It spirals, coils, contracts. The gate is not always before you, it may really be beneath you.

This is the great reversal of sacred journeying: We seek outward answers; the Sacred Core calls us inward. We crave elevation; the Sacred Core draws us down. We want fast answers; The Sacred Core teaches slow unfolding.

The descent is not deviation; it is design, and this divine design helps us to discern between the False Light and the True Flame.

Not all light is holy. There is a counterfeit light, glitter without gravity, charisma without character, ascension without altar. But the flame in the Sacred Core does not flicker. It does not boast. It burns slowly. Purely. Deeply.

It is the bush that burns but is not consumed. It is the coal that touched Isaiah's lips. It is the fire that Christ kindled in the hearts of the disciples on the Emmaus road. You cannot find this flame unless you go down, encapsulated by the Power of the Sound in the Silence.

In the Sacred Core, noise ceases. Not because there is no sound; but because the soul becomes still enough to hear the true vibration. Elijah found God not in the wind, quake, or fire, but in the whisper. The silence.

This is why the descent feels like void, but you are not abandoned; you are being retuned.

You are learning to hear what ego cannot. To hear the hum of holy.

When the descent begins, it feels like disorientation. The soul says: Where is the light? Why am I buried? What did I do wrong?

But here is the secret: You are not lost; you are entering into a new season. You are not punished; you are positioned. You are not dying; you are deepening.

The Sacred Core is not for those who perform. It is for those who yield. And every sacred realm has its own guardians, not as punishers, but as protectors.

The Sacred Core is protected by trials, tests, thresholds:

> Fear
> Doubt
> Silence
> Loneliness
> Darkness

These are not enemies. They are sentinels. They ask, "Do you really want to see them?" To pass them is not to fight, but to trust. Not to conquer, but to surrender.

Treasure in the Earthly Vessel

The apostle Paul declares: "We have this treasure in jars of clay." Not jars of gold. Not temples of glass. Clay. Earth. Fragile, flawed, formed. This is the mystery of incarnation: that the divine chooses the dust.

To enter the Sacred Core is to honor your vessel, not in shame, but in awe. Your body is not an obstacle; it is the altar. And when you prostrate down at the foundation of this altar the process of transfiguration starts from within.

When Jesus was transfigured, it was not light descending from heaven. It was light emerging from within Him.

The Sacred Core is where transfiguration begins. Not when conditions change. Not when you are seen. Not when you escape. But when the inner flame ignites, undistracted by the world's applause.

When you are so rooted, so buried in God, that glory rises like sap from your soul. In descent, you lose what is not essential. You shed names, titles, roles, projections.

And then, in the core, the Holy One whispers the name only He knows; the name written before time. This is the name no crowd can chant. It is the name that remembers you. The descent into the Sacred Core is the undoing that leads to unveiling. You are not who you thought. You are more.

And when the descent is complete and the treasure embraced, you do not emerge to conquer; you emerge to carry. Not to dominate, but to bless.

Moses returned from Sinai not to command, but to serve. Christ left the tomb not to boast, but to gather. The Sacred Core does not inflate the ego; it crushes it into compassion. You emerge not with a mission, but as a mirror, and you start to reflect what you have seen in the depths.

True descent opens the sacred gate that will give you access to walk on the pathway that leads you into divine union.

And so many times we forget that true union is not achieved, but it is being revealed. And true divine revelation happens when there is nothing else left to prove.

In the Sacred Core, the false self dissolves. The ache for approval melts. The mask falls. And there you are naked, known, and not alone.

God was always there. He did not descend to meet you; you descended to remember Him.

Because the Sacred Core is not just a temporary destination. It is divine recognition, and this recognition will help you start living from the Sacred Core. And to live from the Sacred Core is to carry depth into the surface world. It means: Speaking less but saying more. Acting slower, but truer. Shining gently, but with weight.

The world does not need more noise. It needs more rootedness. You are not called to escape Earth, but to embody Heaven within the Earth. To live from the Core is to become a sanctuary in motion.

Truly the journey into the Sacred Core is not a detour; it is the return. It is the prodigal coming home, not to a house, but to the heart.

To descend is to find: That darkness is not your enemy. That burial is not your end. That silence is not God's absence; but it is to discover that the treasure was not above, beyond, or later. It was always here.

Waiting. Buried. Holy.

Part 4:

Gates Hidden in Plain Sight

The Sacred Thresholds of the Ordinary

The Paradox of Hiddenness

We seek the divine in the dramatic, cathedrals, visions, mountaintops. But the gate of heaven is not always wrapped in thunder or glory. It is often wrapped in dust.

Jacob did not find the gate in a temple but in the wilderness. A barren place, a stone pillow, a fugitive heart; and yet, this was the gate of heaven.

The truth is this: sacred gates are not hidden because they are far. They are hidden because they are familiar. We overlook them because we do not expect the holy to whisper in the ordinary.

Many times, in our life the Gate is where you are. "Surely the Lord is in this place, and I did not know it…" Genesis 28:16. This is not just surprised, but truly it is a sacred confession.

Jacob's awareness shifted, and suddenly the ground beneath him shimmered with presence. The same stones that formed his bed became part of an altar. The gate did not arrive. It was revealed. This is the nature of holy gates: They do not need to be summoned. They need to be seen. The sacred is not missing; it is misrecognized.

Throughout the Scripture, mundane places become portals when hearts awaken: A bush becomes holy ground. A fishing boat becomes a pulpit. A jail cell becomes a sanctuary. A cross becomes a throne.

God is not waiting for you to arrive somewhere else. He is waiting for you to see and meet you right where you already are. The gate is not a location. It is a recognition.

If gates are hidden in plain sight, what causes them to open? The answer is not effort; it is awareness. The keys to unlocking hidden gates are: Stillness: The gate does not respond to striving. Surrender: It opens to the yielded. Reverence: Mystery unveils itself to those who honor it. Listening: Not hearing to reply but listening to receive.

You cannot barge into the holy. You are invited. You cannot force the gate. But you can posture yourself to perceive it, if you are a seeker of truth.

The seeker is not defined by how far they travel but by how deeply they notice. The true seeker asks not just "Where is the gate?" but "What in me is asleep to it?" Because hidden gates require not only open eyes, but open hearts. To seek rightly is to live in a state of ongoing revelation; to expect that any moment may become a threshold.

Celtic Christianity called these hidden gates "thin places." Places where the veil between heaven and earth is barely perceptible. But what if the veil is always thin, and we simply live too fast, too loud, too distracted to notice?

What if thinness is not a property of place, but a posture of soul? When we slow... soften... sense...Then every place becomes thin. Then every moment can become a gate.

Gates in the Wilderness

The wilderness is often misjudged as void. In reality, it is a threshold. Moses' burning bush appeared in the wilderness. Jesus' testing and anointing came in the wilderness. Hagar heard God's voice in the wilderness.

Gates hide in the places we are most tempted to curse. Loneliness. Disorientation. Exile. But these are not endings. They are entrances. Wilderness is not absence; it is womb.

In Luke 24, two disciples walk toward Emmaus, defeated. The resurrected Christ joins them; but they don't recognize Him. Only when He breaks bread do they see. The gate was with them the whole journey.

Revelation came through a familiar gesture; not through a sermon or miracle, but in the process of breaking the bread. This is the lesson: The divine is clothed in the familiar, waiting to be revealed. You may already be walking with the Presence and do not know it.

If we understand that the Earth is indeed a living threshold, then we will come to the sacred recognition that we are here not to escape Earth, but we are indeed placed on earthly landscape paramount to be able to rediscover Earth's original sacredness.

Gates are not in the stars; they are in the soil, and the Earth is not merely a backdrop, but it is an active participant in the divine story. Earth bears gates in: Cracks in the canyon wall. Patterns of tree bark. Silence between wind gusts. The ache of memory in a familiar room.

The land holds memory. The land holds mystery. The land holds the altar, and the altar is not a raised stage; it is a holy moment. Every time we stop to honor the present moment, we build an altar.

When we pause before eating, we bless the gate. When we breathe deeply in grief, we open the gate. When we thank the moment, we want to rush past, we sanctify the threshold.

The mundane becomes mystical through mindfulness. Altars are not places. They are postures. And these moments of postures are the ones where the seeker stops climbing.

The seekers climb because they think the divine is up there. But gates open when the seeker descends into stillness, humility, and inner knowing. Jacob did not build a tower to meet God. He laid his head on a rock. He rested. And in resting, the gate opened. This is not a gate of ambition. It is a gate of intimacy.

We need to learn that Divine gates rarely come with fanfare. There is no grand opening, no flashing neon light. Just a shift. A shimmer. A knowing.

Encounters are invitations, not invasions. You are always free to walk past.

The gate is polite. Subtle. Patient. To walk through the gate requires attention.

But here comes the reality of the danger of overlooking the gate. And we have so many examples when many people, even in the Scripture, missed the gate: The innkeeper in Bethlehem did not see the child as a gate. The rich man walked past Lazarus. The Pharisees stood in the presence of God and were blind to Him.

The danger is not that God is silent. It is that we are kept busily distracted. The sacred does not scream; it patiently waits.

Recognizing a hidden gate is not a mystical accident. It is a spiritual discipline. It requires:

Daily pausing. Stillness reveals.
Asking questions. What is sacred here?
Blessing small things. Gratitude opens portals.
Listening beneath words. Spirit speaks softly.

This is not escapism. It is engagement. To live as one who sees gates is to walk Earth like a priest in a living temple. We often think gates are escape routes. But the most sacred gates lead deeper in. Into the self. Into memory. Into healing. Into God.

These are not exits but entrances to the soul's interior castle. You may enter a gate thinking you're escaping grief; and find you're entering healing. The gate does not remove the pain. It transforms it.

Those who see gates are called to become gates. To hold space for others. To cultivate presence so profound that others pass through you and find themselves on holy ground. You become a living invitation: A calm presence in chaos. A wise voice in confusion. A kind gesture in hardness.

You do not just show them the gate. You are also inviting them to the gate. Ultimately, all gates point to one true and eternal Gate, Jesus Christ. He declared, "I am the gate." John 10:9

He is the threshold between seen and unseen, time and eternity, flesh and spirit. He is not merely the destination. He is the door. And He hides in plain sight:

In the stranger on the road.
In the prisoner.
In the poor.
In bread and wine.

To recognize Christ is to see the gate everywhere. In this moment, you may be closer to a sacred threshold than you know. Right now, sitting at your desk, sipping your drink, scrolling these words, you may be at the edge of revelation.

Do not wait for a mountaintop. Do not delay for a more dramatic moment. Pause. Listen. Bless the ground.

For surely, the Lord is in this place. And this… is none other than the gate of heaven.

Part 5.

Stones, Caverns, and Hidden Altars

A Sacred Descent into Subterranean Revelation

The Portal Beneath the Stone

The sacred dream of the mountain portal is not fiction; it is memory. Etched into scripture, myth, and the architecture of the soul, the theme echoes:

A stone rolled away not to let a dead man out, but to reveal eternal life.
A cavern holding not just echoes, but the voice of God.
A hidden altar beneath a threshing floor, unseen until it became the cornerstone of a temple.

These are not just moments; they are metaphors for the deepest journey: What is buried is not lost. What is hidden is not absent.

Let us begin with the Resurrection Stone. When the stone was rolled away from Christ's tomb, something cosmic happened. Not just the resurrection of one man; but the reversal of the world's trajectory.

A grave became a gateway. The place of burial became the birthplace of new creation. This is the mystery: God hides life inside death; he hides hope inside surrender. Eternity inside stone. The tomb became a temple.

Caverns: Where Silence Speaks

Elijah's cave on Mount Horeb is another holy descent. Elijah expected God in fire, wind, and quake. But the voice came in stillness. The cavern did not echo noise; it filtered it out.

Only in silence could Elijah hear what spectacle would drown. This is the paradox of the cavern: it is not hollow; it is hallowed. Silence is not the absence of presence; it is the womb of revelation.

Hidden Altars Beneath Everyday Life

When David bought Araunah's threshing floor, he did not know it sat atop an ancient altar. Later, that spot became the foundation of Solomon's temple. The altar was not built in a holy place; it made the place holy.

This is the truth of hidden altars:

> They are beneath our routines.
> Beneath our grief.
> Beneath our thresholds.

And they are waiting, not for construction, but for recognition. We often associate low places with failure, loss, punishment. But scripture teaches that low places host holy things.

> Jesus was born in a lowly stable.
> He knelt to wash feet.
> He descended into the grave.

God is not afraid of depth. He consecrates it. Your lowest point may hold your highest calling.

Archetypal Echoes Across Cultures

These motifs are not unique to the Bible:

> The Greek oracle of Delphi spoke from a cavern.
> The Egyptian underworld was where souls were tested and transformed.
> The Norse Yggdrasil tree had roots reaching into the underworld, guarded by serpents of wisdom and death.
> The Mayan cenotes were gateways to Xibalba; both feared and revered.

The spiritual ancestors knew that true depth births wisdom. The Earth is not just ground, it is gateway. Beneath every visible threshold, there is an invisible one.

We may think we've "arrived"; only to discover a deeper invitation. Every breakthrough conceals another burial. Every revelation opens another mystery. Like peeling back layers of stone, the soul discovers:

> There is always more beneath.
> The portal lies *under* the expected.
> Sacredness sinks deeper than sight.

The journey into caverns is not a mere geographic descent; it is personal. Your heart contains caverns carved by: Loss. Love. Silence. Story.

Sometimes we fear what we will find if we go deeply inward. But God does not avoid these places; He inhabits them. In your inner cavern, the still small voice still speaks.

The Language of Stone

Stones in scripture are never passive:

> Jacob's stone became a pillow, then an altar.
> Moses struck the rock and water flowed.
> The Ten Commandments were etched in stone.
> Jesus is the "cornerstone the builders rejected."

Stones speak. They remember. They endure. To touch stone is to touch memory. The ancient. The unshaken. To enter the stony place is to meet what cannot be moved.

Altars in Unexpected Places

Altars do not have to be ornate. In fact, the most potent altars are:

> Hidden in caves.
> Built from ordinary stone.
> Placed where grief or glory once broke open a heart.

Your tears can become the water of consecration. Your wrestling can become an offering. Altars rise where the soul surrenders. To find the hidden altar, we must excavate. Not with shovels, but with; Memory: What pain did we bury? Attention: What holy moments have we ignored? Wonder: What space have we misjudged as barren?

Excavation is a sacred act. It is the return to what we covered in fear, shame, or distraction. God is not asking you to build from scratch. He is asking you to uncover what He already laid on the eternal foundation.

In ancient tabernacle tradition, the fire on the altar was meant never to go out. Even when the people wandered, the fire was to remain.

Even now, under your life's harden surface, beneath your busyness, pain, doubt, there is a coal glowing. A sacred spark waiting for breath. You do not need to light the fire. You need to unearth it.

The Invitation of Stillness

Caverns do not rush. Stones do not speak loudly. Altars do not chase attention. To meet them, we must:

> Slow down.
> Kneel low.
> Remove our shoes.
> Let silence stretch long enough for the living soul to soften.

The hidden and sacred revelation responds to reverence, not recognition. The stone the builders rejected became the cornerstone. Why? God builds differently than we do. He does not discard what is cracked, buried, forgotten. He chooses it.

You may feel like rubble, but He sees a foundation. Your cavern may feel empty, but He hears echo as prayer. You are not disqualified. You are prepared.

If altars were obvious, we'd rush to them casually. But the sacred veils itself until we are ready.

Hiddenness is mercy. It invites transformation, not merely an emotional transaction.

The altar does not serve our convenience; it requires our reverend change. That's why it hides beneath threshing floors, within caverns, behind rolled stones. So only those who are hungry, who dig, those who descend; may be able to find it.

In ancient cities, gates were often hewn into rock walls. Carved. Chiseled. Hammered into being. Thresholds do not always appear gently. Sometimes, they are created through:

> Years of pressure.
> Cycles of grief.
> Unanswered prayers.

Your cavern may not be punished; it may be passage. Your pressure may not be cruelty; it may be carving. You are becoming a doorway.

In the end, altars are not just places. They are people. When your life carries the fire, when you remember the silence, honors the hidden; you become an altar. A place of meeting. A space of sacredness.

A threshold where others encounter God not because of what you say, but because of how you burn. The stony parts of your life are not curses. They are consecrated.

You do not need to ascend a ladder to meet the divine. You need only descend into the forgotten, the buried, the real.

And you only need to remember that:

> The stone rolled away.

The cavern echoing Presence.

The altar is beneath the floor.

Because they are not just stories from long ago. They are active, sacred and divine invitations for now, yes even now.

Stop.

Listen.

Dig.

Dear reader, know that you are nearer to the sacred than you imagined. You are standing on the threshold of the hidden altar. And please remember that heaven still speaks from the cave.

Part 6.

Rediscovering the Mountain Within

A Sacred Homecoming to the Inner Summit

The True Mountain Is Within

The mountain has always held allure; its majesty, its height, its symbolism. But the climb was never about geography. It was always about the living soul. Why? Because truth be told, you are the mountain.

Not because you are immovable; but because you are sacred space. Not because you stand tall; but because you host mystery in your depths. The journey of the Descendance has not led us away from the Earth, nor toward the heavens; but into the hidden holy space within.

In life we were taught to seek higher:

> Higher experiences.
> Higher status.
> Higher revelations.

But in this sacred reversal, the invitation is not to ascend, but to awaken. The summit is not above you; it is inside you. Like Moses who met God on Sinai, we too are invited to host holy fire, but not on stone peaks. In human hearts.

The true tabernacle is not built with hands. It is carved in spirit. And "The Spirit stirs beneath the surface of our ordinary lives". Not in ecstasies. Not in escape. But in the mundane:

> In the morning silence before the world awakes.
> In the ache that doesn't go away.
> In the breath between anxious thoughts.

The Spirit does not demand spectacle. It longs for space. It speaks from within; not from without. You do not need to climb to hear. You need only to descend into stillness.

Every previous part of this chapter has pointed to external thresholds:

> Mountains.
> Caverns.
> Stones.
> Altars.

Now, the mystery sharpens: these were mirrors of your inner world. You host the mountain. You carry the cavern. You contain the altar.

And at your foundation lies a gate. Not a gate to another just world; but to the Real World, the unshakable kingdom within.

The ego wants to build. It says, "Let me earn this, make this, climb this." But the soul whispers: "You do not need to build the gate. You need to behold it." And beholding is not passive. It is deeper than action, it is a sacred and divine alignment.

When we behold the gate within:

We begin to trust presence over performance.
We stop striving and start surrendering.
We stop searching for God and begin seeing with God.

The gate is opened through reverent noticing. And sacred revelation does not always come through peak moments. Often it is found in foundations; especially in those places in our story we've overlooked, buried, or rushed past:

Childhood memories we never re-visited.
Deep griefs we never grieved.
Silent years we labeled wasted.

But the sacred foundation holds not just pain; it holds presence. You don't need to go back in fear. You return in reverence. To reclaim what you thought was lost. To behold what was always holy.

You are not being asked to rise. Not yet. You are being asked to return.

To return to:

That still place beneath your striving.
That sacred truth you've avoided.
That voice that's never stopped whispering your name.

This is not regression. It is homecoming. You are not regressing. You are remembering. And remembering, you are re-membered; put back together in sacred order.

We've also heard it many times said that the mountain is the place where heaven touches earth. But what if that geography is internal? What if heaven and earth meet:

> In the tear you finally let fall?
> In the embrace you finally receive?
> In the silence you stop running from?

You are the meeting point. You are the sacred overlap. "Close your eyes... There is an opening in the rock. A veil in the stone". This image is more than metaphor. It is the mystical center of you, the place of Holy of Holies within.

The veil is not to be torn by violence. It is lifted by love. And behind it? Presence. Not in judgment, but in joy. Not in demands, but in embrace.

You are not being asked to prove yourself; you are being asked to meet yourself. And in the rediscovering process you find God waiting on you.

When the soul says yes to this descent, this return; something beautiful happens. The mountain rises. Not externally, but internally. Not in posture, but in presence. You begin to live with sincere and true groundedness, gravity, and grace.

You begin to:

> Speak from depth.
> Walk with rootedness.
> Carry silence without fear.

This is the paradox: You descend... and the mountain rises in you. And to live as a mountain is not to be immovable, but to be anchored. It is to become: A place where others find rest. A space that hosts divine presence. A soul that does not shake when the world trembles.

You become an altar without needing others permission or recognition. You become a gate without needing to be seen. You become a living meeting place between Spirit and Earth.

Dear readers, this final part of Chapter Five ends not with instructions, but invitation: Where have I believed that revelation only comes through climbing or achieving? Have I overlooked the foundations in my life that hold divine meaning? Is there a place I've been afraid to descend into, a memory, a silence, a sacred truth?

These are not questions to be rushed. They are keys to your own hidden gate. Dare to pause. To feel. To breathe. The gate opens slowly. And only to those who honor the ground they stand on.

Benediction: You Are the Sanctuary

> You are not outside the sacred.
> You are not behind the veil.
> You are not disqualified from the fire.
> You are the sanctuary.
> You are the veil parting.
> You are the mountain awakening.
> So lay down your striving.
> Behold the gate.
> Let the Presence meet you at your rediscovered foundations. The descendance is complete.

And the rise has already begun.

Chapter Five Summary

The Descendance

Mountains, Foundations, and the Inward Gateways

Overview

In Chapter Five: The Descendance, the journey deepens inward. We are no longer climbing; we are descending. But this descent is not a fall from grace; it is a return to sacred ground.

This chapter unveils a hidden architecture beneath the spiritual terrain: a mountain that does not rise but opens; altars that are not built but found; gates not seen, but revealed.

Across six powerful parts, we are called not to escape Earth, but to re-enter her depths; and rediscover the divine beneath our very feet.

The Mountains as Thresholds

We begin with a holy disruption: the mountain is not calling us up; it is calling us in. The traditional model of ascent is inverted, revealing that escape is not elevation, but *entry*. The mountain becomes a living portal; not to flee Earth, but to encounter her mystery at the root.

This is the sacred descent: a gateway opens *within* the belly of the Earth, and with it, the soul is summoned into deeper presence.

The Foundation Holds the Mystery

Here, the hidden dimension of foundation is revealed as essential and sacred. Foundations are often ignored because they are unseen; but in this divine order, they are where the holy dwells. The helicopter vision descending into the core of the mountain mirrors the soul's inward journey. The foundation is not just structural; it is relational, intentional, and revelatory. It holds what was spoken before the world was shaped. To descend is to remember. Remembering is to realign.

Descent into the Sacred Core

The descent continues into the Sacred Core, the place of hidden treasure, pressure, silence, and transformation. We are reminded that all sacred transformation begins in darkness: Christ in the tomb, Jonah in the belly, Joseph in the pit. This is the pattern of divine becoming. In these depths, the fire burns differently.

The Sacred Core is not loud. It whispers. And its voice is only heard by those who embrace the descent as initiation, not exile. The core reveals that death is not the end, it is the womb of transfiguration.

Gates Hidden in Plain Sight

Now the revelation shifts: the gates of heaven are not far off or hidden in elite sanctuaries; they are right where you are. We walk among holy portals every day, blind to them because they appear too ordinary.

Like Jacob at Bethel, we wake to realize: *"Surely the Lord is in this place, and I did not know it."* These places are everywhere around us, but they can be only perceived by stillness, surrender, and reverence.

The seeker is not one who climbs, but one who notices. You may be standing on the gateway, even now.

Stones, Caverns, and Hidden Altars

This part uncovers the holy geography beneath our feet; stones that speak, caverns that echo Presence, and altars buried beneath everyday life.

The story of the stone rolled from Christ's tomb, Elijah's cave, and David's hidden altar beneath a threshing floor all reveal the same truth: what is buried is not forgotten; it is consecrated.

The low places, the silent, stony, shadowed places; are where God builds his most enduring altars. This is the holy work of excavation: to uncover the flame already burning beneath the rubble.

Rediscovering the Mountain Within

The final part returns us not to external geography, but to interior sacredness. The mountain we sought was never "out there." It has always been within us. The gate at your foundation is not to be built, but to be *beheld*.

You are the temple. You are the altar. You are the mountain. And the invitation now is not to rise, but to awaken.

This is the final paradox of descendance: the deeper we go, the higher we rise. Revelation is not above; it is within.

Themes & Symbols

Descent as Revelation: Spiritual maturity is not upward movement but sacred deepening.
Foundation as Presence: What lies beneath is not shameful, but holy.
Gates and Thresholds: Access to the divine is everywhere when we learn to see.
Caverns and Silence: Stillness reveals more than spectacle.
Beholding vs. Building: The sacred is not to be constructed but uncovered.
The Mountain Within: The final revelation: you are the meeting place of heaven and earth.

This chapter invites the seeker to: Pause instead of press. Descend instead of striving. Listen instead of performing. Behold instead of build. Excavate instead of escape. It is not a chapter of climax, but of communion. Not of reaching, but of returning.

Chapter Five closes with a sacred reversal fully realized: we are not escaping Earth; we are entering her mystery. We are not climbing toward God; we are remembering that He already dwells at our inner foundation. The gates are not ahead; they are beneath. And the mountain is not to be conquered; it is to be claimed from within. The descent is not downward. It is inward. And from within... we rise.

Chapter Six

The 5 Cascades of Revelation – When Dreams Become Maps

There are dreams that arrive like a whisper, and others that descend like a divine storm; rearranging the inner landscape of the soul.

What follows is not a study but a sacred remembrance of one such encounter: the night vision of the five cascades, the revelation that flowed not from heaven to earth but from within the very mountain of being.

It was not a climb upward but a journey inward. Not a reaching beyond, but a descent into the living depths where revelation breathes.

This chapter," The 5 Cascades of Revelation – When Dreams Become Maps", unfolds what I saw and what I became within it.

Each cascade revealed a dimension of awakening; five divine progressions of encounter, purification, remembrance, embodiment, and return.

Each flowed with its own rhythm, yet all were one continuous river; the same Spirit manifesting in layers of grace. Let the imagery wash over you as language gives way to living understanding.

It began with sound; not thunder, but the hum of creation itself stirring beneath the surface. The first cascade broke through like light splitting the dark: fierce, pure, and tender. Its purpose was not to reveal knowledge but to awaken wonder.

Awe is the first movement of revelation; the breath that resurrects the living soul from numbness.

We live in a world that anesthetizes wonder. Familiarity becomes blindness, and routine becomes religion.

The first cascade shatters this paralysis. It pours through the hardened crust of indifference and awakens sensitivity to divine nearness. I felt it rush over me like the first wind of Eden; that ancient breath that said; Behold, all is alive.

In the flow of awe, nothing is ordinary. Every atom tremble with presence. Revelation begins not when we understand but when we stand undone.

The soul's awakening is not an ascent of intellect but a trembling before mystery. Awe fractures arrogance; it reopens perception. In this first cascade, the Spirit whispered, "Begin not by reaching, but by beholding."

Awe is the gate. To be awed is to remember you were made for more than comprehension; you were made for communion. The first cascade invites the seeker not to analyze God, but to encounter Him.

It is the shattering of numbness, the rediscovery of wonder, the sacred permission to begin again.

The next flow came like a river of molten clarity. It did not comfort; it confronted. This was the refining cascade; the one that strips away the illusions that masquerade as truth. Its water was transparent yet fierce, revealing everything it touched.

To confront illusion is to face the falseness we have befriended: the masks we wear, the motives we defend, the stories we tell ourselves about who we are. This cascade was not cruel; it was merciful. Its mercy was fire. It revealed that illusion is not destroyed by argument but dissolved by exposure to light.

As the river passed over me, reflections shattered. I saw the false securities built around reputation, fear, and ambition dissolve like dust in rain. The Spirit whispered, "What you call protection is often a prison. Let the flow refine." The more I yielded, the more transparent my being became. The water of truth never condemns; it cleanses. It frees not by punishing but by unveiling.

This cascade teaches that revelation requires surrender to reality. It unmasks self-deception and invites the soul to stand unclothed before divine eyes.

The refining flow does not destroy identity; it restores authenticity. It burns away performance until only presence remains.

What emerges is not shame, but freedom; the naked honesty of a heart that no longer fears to be seen.

As I moved deeper, the sound softened. The roar of confrontation became a melody; a rhythm of stillness. The third cascade flowed like liquid light, luminous and quiet, whispering secrets older than words.

It was not a torrent of information but a communion of knowing. Here, revelation became remembrance.

This is the cascade of hidden wisdom; not knowledge acquired, but truth recalled. Beneath the noise of striving, there exists a sacred memory written into the living soul. Every drop of this water carried resonance with eternity: "You once knew this. You have always known this."

In the flow of hidden wisdom, silence teaches more than speech. Dreams, symbols, and divine impressions become languages of remembrance.

This is the river of inner scripture, where revelation is not learned but reawakened. It calls the soul to listen to what creation already sings.

This wisdom is not given to the curious but to the

surrendered. It cannot be forced; it must be received. It rises like mist when the noise subsides.

To drink from this cascade is to rediscover the origin of thought; the divine blueprint within.

The Spirit whispered, "The truth you seek is not distant; it is dormant."

The third cascade transforms seekers into listeners, learners into lovers. It restores the rhythm of divine memory beneath the static of survival. In its light, knowledge becomes communion, and every revelation becomes an echo of a greater remembrance: the sound of Eden stirring again.

When I entered the fourth cascade, I felt time slow, as if eternity itself were inhaling. The water here was not loud or forceful; it was alive with stillness. It glowed from within, surrounding me with a peace that transcended comprehension. The Spirit said, "Here you no longer watch the river; you become part of it."

This is the cascade of embodiment; where revelation ceases to be external and becomes incarnate. What the soul has seen, it now must live. Presence no longer visits; it abides.

This is the holy transformation where being replaces doing, where the seeker becomes what they have beheld.

To embody presence is to consent to transparency; to allow the divine to dwell unresisted. It is not achieved through effort but through surrender.

The ego loosens its grip, and the self becomes a vessel through which eternity breathes. You do not merely reflect the light; you become luminous with it.

Here, the words of Christ echo: "The Father and I are one." This is not a statement of separation overcome but of awareness restored. The fourth cascade is the fulfillment of the previous flows; awe, truth, and wisdom converging into oneness.

The river no longer teaches; it transforms. To abide here is to live as revelation, not merely to carry it.

Embodying presence means walking through the world as a living altar, each breath a prayer, each word a wave, each silence a sanctuary. The river has become flesh, and flesh now flows like a river of grace.

The final cascade did not descend; it expanded. It flowed outward, radiant and uncontainable. Its waters sparkled with golden hues, reflecting every color of the previous flows yet now united in harmony.

This was the flow of return, the radiant commission of those who have descended and emerged transformed.

Here revelation takes its truest form; not as possession, but as transmission. The one who has encountered and embodied the divine does not hoard light but becomes its vessel.

The fifth cascade pours outward through those who have learned to flow. Their lives become living rivers that heal, restore, and awaken others.

Returning with radiance is not about returning to where you were, but returning as who you've become. The world remains the same, but you no longer move through it the same way.

You carry the frequency of heaven within earthly frames. You speak, and atmospheres shift. You walk, and burdens lift. You forgive, and chains fall away.

This cascade commissions without command. It sends forth without striving. It is not ambition that moves you, but love; the current of divine compassion now embodied in motion. Revelation finds completion not when it is understood, but when it is shared.

When Dreams Become Maps

The five cascades are not merely stages of revelation but states of being. Together they chart the inward geography of divine encounter; from awakening to radiance, from awe to embodiment.

They teach that dreams are not escapist illusions; they are invitations into reality's deeper architecture.

Revelation is not vertical ascent but inward immersion. The mountain you entered was never external; it was the landscape of your own living soul.

Each cascade is both descent and elevation, each flow a deeper surrender. To dream is to remember the eternal dialogue between Creator and creation.

The purpose of revelation is not to escape earth but to sanctify it. To awaken awe in a sleeping world. To confront illusion with living truth. To remember wisdom older than time. To embody divine presence amid chaos. And finally, to return radiant, carrying heaven within humanity.

This is the map the dream left behind; not of places, but of postures. It is not an instruction to climb higher but an invitation to live deeper.

For in the end, revelation is not something you receive; it is something you become.

And when all the cascades have poured through, and the river has become one with you, the Spirit whispers again; soft as light, strong as eternity: "Flow; For the world thirsts for what you have become."

Part 1.

Entering the Hidden Realm

The Descent into the Dream's Revelation

There are realms that are surrounding our humanity not charted on maps. There are sacred thresholds that are not marked by stone gates, only revealed by silence, surrender, and the stirring of the Holy Spirit within.

In the night, a vision came; not wrapped in metaphor, but vibrating with the clarity of revelation.

> I did not rise.
> I did not ascend.
> I entered.

At the base of a mountain, a portal opened, not upward into the clouds, but inward into the very body of the earth. It called not to the climber, but to the one willing to descend. And I went in, not with striving, but with awe. And what I beheld inside defied natural comprehension.

The Cascades of Revelation

Inside the belly of that mountain flowed not lava, nor darkness, nor stone; but water; living, luminous, and unceasing. There I saw five waterfalls cascaded in succession, each flowing into the next. Each one of them was more thunderous, more radiant, more overwhelming than the one before.

They did not fall from the sky. They rose from within; like breath, like prophecy, like a heartbeat hidden in the mountain's chest.

These cascades were no ordinary falls. These were cascades of truth, each having a dimension of revelation.

And I knew, standing before them, that this was not a vision for entertainment. It was a calling.
An invitation. A map.

Revelation Begins in Descent

To enter this realm is not to escape Earth. It is to see what Earth contains when seen through awakened eyes. It is to abandon the obsession with outward ascent and return to the chambers beneath the surface; the secret architecture that undergirds all truth.

The mountain, which in previous chapters cracked open its belly and revealed its altars, now shows its rivers. This is not water for washing alone. It is water for awakening.

Each cascade is not a piece of knowledge; it is a stage of transformation.

Each one is a revelatory current designed to move you, shape you, baptize you into a new way of being.

The Mountain Portal That Found Me

I did not seek this place. The hidden realm found me; at the base of everything. At the end of striving. At the point where descent became devotion. There was no ladder. No thunder. No angelic announcement.

There was only openness; a veil torn in stone, and a knowing that I was standing before something eternal. I was truly witnessing something out of this world. This was not symbolic grandeur. It was divine architecture.

I felt small but not insignificant. I felt overwhelmed; but not afraid. The weight of revelation was not crushing; it was commissioning.

Awe Was the First Language

Before I understood anything, I beheld everything. The first sound was not teaching. It was thundering. The first sensation was not comprehension. It was immersion.

The hidden realm does not offer information. It invites you to feel the truth before you define it. It was as though the veil between this world and the eternal had become a pathway; and I was allowed in, not because I was ready, but because I had surrendered. And here, in this place, language itself bent under the weight of wonder.

Cycles Within the Mountain

Each waterfall was not separate. They were connected. One led to the next, yet not by force, but by flow. There were no steps. No ropes. No guidebooks. Only water. Only revelation. Only the gravity of grace pulling all things deeper.

This was not a climb. This was a circular unveiling, each cascade, both a completion and a beginning. They were thresholds, not destinations. You do not conquer them. You pass through them.

This hidden realm is not exclusive to one dream or one person. It is alive. It exists beyond the veil of noise.

And those who dare to quiet their spirit, to stand at the base of the mountain rather than rush to its peak, may find that the portal is still open.

You don't have to force it. You don't have to earn it. You only have to enter. With reverence. With humility. With a heart ready to be changed.

The Five Falls Await

The five cascades I saw in my night vision are not external phenomena; they are living invitations within the spirit:

Awakening Awe; the shattering of numbness

Confronting Illusion; the stripping away of falsehood

Receiving Hidden Wisdom; the memory of ancient knowing

Embodying Presence; the fusion of revelation and incarnation

Returning with Radiance; the commissioning into the world as a vessel of truth

Each one has a dimension. Each one a descent. Each one a sacred door.

This is not just a chapter to read; it is a terrain to enter. You are not climbing toward God. You are entering God's revelation; alive, fluid, and roaring with purpose.

Reflection Invitation

Close your eyes. Feel the mist on your face. Hear the echo of the falls.

Where in your life is a portal waiting to be seen?
Have you confused stillness for stagnation?
Have you dismissed awe as emotionalism?
Have you refused to descend, hoping instead to escape?
Stand at the base of your own mountain.
Let the veil open.

    The hidden realm has always been there.

        Waiting For You.

Part 2.

Revelation Comes in Layers

The Dimensional Descent of Knowing

Truth rarely comes like lightning. It comes like divine and sacred rain; layered, rhythmic, and transformative over time.

We often imagine revelation as a singular burst; one moment, one vision, one unveiling. But in the realm of sacred architecture, revelation moves not as a line, but as a cascade. Each flow builds upon the last. Each wave prepares the heart for what only the next layer can carry.

What I saw in the dream; the five waterfalls flowing from within the mountain; was not a symbolic display. It was a divine blueprint, carrying a divine message.

Each waterfall was a layer of transformation. Each one deeper. Each one fuller. Each one flowing out of the last, not breaking it, but expanding it.

Revelation Is Not Linear. It's Dimensional.

Human reasoning often demands linearity: step one, then two, then three, and so on... But divine revelation is dimensional.

> It folds in upon itself.
> It revisits old truths with new light.
> It repeats the sound of heaven at deeper octaves.

To the uninitiated, this can feel like confusion. But to the one who listens, it is like hearing a song's chorus become a majestic cathedral. God does not reveal to inform. He reveals to transform.

And transformation does not come in a straight line. It descends through layers of surrender.

Cascades flow with grace, not force. Because of that you cannot climb revelation. You can only receive it. Each waterfall I beheld in the dream did not crash down as violence; it poured like an invitation. There was force, yes. But it was the force of truth washing over illusion. There was depth, but it did not demand; it called.

This is the movement of grace: Not to push you ahead of your readiness, but to flow into you exactly at the capacity your living soul can carry. This is why the five cascades cannot be rushed.

They must be walked through. They are not chronological. They are thresholds of interior space, revealed majestically within the mountain.

Five as Sacred Pattern

Why five?

The Spirit revealed it wasn't random. It was encoded into the very design of divine expression.

The Five Books of Moses

Each book unfolds a greater understanding of covenant, wilderness, law, presence, and promise.

The Five Wounds of Christ

Hands, feet, side; a portal of suffering that opened the path to resurrection. Five openings of surrender.

The Five Senses

The gates of earthly perception. When awakened, they become pathways of transcendence. From tasting to knowing. From seeing to beholding.

Five is the number of:

Grace; unearned flow.
Passage; movement from one realm to another.
Wholeness in transition; not perfection, but sacred evolution.

These cascades are not to be observed. They are to be entered to be refreshed and renewed.

Capacity Must Be Formed

You cannot receive what you are not prepared to hold. The first cascade awakens awe. But the second shatters illusion. This is the pattern of all true revelation:

> It *awakens*.
> It *confronts*.
> It *empties*.
> It *fills*.
> It *sends*.

Each stage is not separate from the others. They are interdependent flows. The more you surrender, the more you can hold.

The more you let go, the more becomes possible. This is why truth comes in layers; because the soul must be formed to carry fire.

Beware the Idol of Instant Knowing

We live in a world addicted to speed. But revelation cannot be microwaved. What comes too quickly is often not truth; but illusion cloaked in emotional noise.

True revelation is not merely understood; it is lived into. It arrives in layers of encounter:

Sometimes with fire.
Sometimes with silence.
Sometimes with questions that won't leave you alone for years.

But always; always with love.

The Spiral of Sacred Descent

Revelation is not a ladder. It is a spiral staircase. You return to the same place; but from a deeper vantage. You hear the same verse; but now it speaks in thunder. You revisit an old truth; but now it's not just in your mind, it's in your marrow. This is the sacred spiral.

This is what the five cascades embody: A descent that deepens, a return that refines.

Entering the Waters, Not Just Watching Them

It is tempting to stand back. To observe the waterfalls. To be moved by their beauty. To feel their mist. But this journey is not about watching. It is about entering. You must let the waters touch you. Let them drown the lies. Let them awaken the wisdom hidden in your bones. Let them carve new capacity in you.

Reflection Invitation

> Are you rushing to understand, or allowing yourself to be undone?
> Have you mistaken revelation for information, when it is actually transformation?
> Can you name the current cascade you're standing beneath?

> Close your eyes. Listen. You are not falling behind.

You are being formed. Let the layers wash over you. Let the old peel back. Let your soul become river-shaped. For revelation does not land like a stone. It flows like water. And you were made to flow with it.

Part 3

The First Cascade – Awakening Awe

The Shattering of Numbness, The Invitation to Begin

Before truth teaches, it touches. Before revelation informs, it surrounds you. Before anything can be received, something must be felt: Awe.

This is where the descent truly begins; not with answers, but with astonishment. Not with clarity, but with a trembling recognition that you are standing before something greater than you imagined.

This is the first cascade: Where the veil begins to thin. Where the sacred reveals itself not in words, but in wonder. Where the presence of the Eternal is not understood, but encountered. You are not yet changed; but you are no longer asleep.

The Roar of Unfiltered Wonder

In the dream, the first waterfall was immense; thundering, luminous, alive. It didn't speak; it roared. Not to frighten, but to awaken. This cascade did not offer any theology. It didn't explain anything. It simply surrounded and encapsulated my soul.

I stood in its spray, undone. Dwarfed by the magnitude of what I was beholding. And in that holy overwhelm, I realized: Revelation begins not with understanding; but with awe.

The first cascade doesn't give you language. It takes your language away. It doesn't begin with clarity. It begins with the cracking open of awareness.

The Undoing of Numbness

Modern life is saturated with noise but starved of wonder. We scroll, we skim, we survive. We become calloused by repetition, dulled by distraction, sedated by cynicism.

But awe breaks through numbness like light through a sealed tomb. It does not whisper. It does not wait. It shakes you. Not to damage, but to awaken. Not to impress, but to reveal what's always been there.

To encounter awe is to be disrupted in the best way. It reroutes your logic. It pauses your striving. It commands your reverence.

Moses saw the bush burning and turned aside. Isaiah beheld the throne and cried, "Woe is me!" John fell as though dead when he saw the Risen Christ.

Awe is not entertainment. It is the divine disrupting the illusion of control. Awe is often not born in the spectacular, but in the familiar re-seen.

A rock that suddenly burns.
A voice that thunders in silence.
A moment that glows with eternity.

Awe takes what you thought you understood and wraps it in mystery. The first cascade does not show you something new; It shows you something true, that you were too asleep to see before.

But the truth of the matter is that truly the Awe it is just a key, not a destination. And many are making the mistake and are stopping at their Awe moment, or others are starting to make and build a monument at the place where they encounter their Awe.

Why?

Because they mistake the initial unveiling for the whole journey.

But awe moment is not the revelation. It is the doorway to it. It is the knocking at your heart.
The echo that pulls you deeper. The wind that turns your soul to face the mountain. To stand in awe is not to arrive. It is to begin.

Awe does not fill you with information; it empties you of indifference. Only when the heart is pierced can the soul begin to receive.

The first cascade washes away assumptions. It loosens the grip of control. It softens the shell of familiarity. You are not yet changed; but you are now reachable. Awe has broken the crust of comfort. And the deeper work can begin.

In the first cascade, familiar texts become alive.

> *"Holy, holy, holy..."* is no longer a chant; it is a thunderclap in your spirit.

> *"Let there be light..."* reverberates like a song sung inside your bones.

Awe does not just affect what you see. It transforms how you see everything. Your living soul becomes a lens; washed clean, widened, ready.

To be in awe is to enter the cloud of unknowing. Not because God is far; but because He is near in a way that shatters categories. The mystery is not darkness; it is sacred weight. It is the sacred pressing into your present. The first cascade is the removal of casualness.

It is the remembrance that God is not an idea. He is a presence; He is the eternal Holy Father and Creator of All. And when He draws near, nothing remains untouched.

Reflection Invitation

> When was the last time you were undone by something holy?
> Have you grown numb in your spirituality; living with language, but not presence?
> Is there space in your life to be disrupted by awe?

Close your eyes.

> Hear the thunder.
> Feel the mist.
> Let the awe wash over you; not as emotion, but as sacred invitation.
> You are standing at the gate.
> And the gate is open.
> Do not rush past.
> Let awe do its work.

Part 4.

The Second Cascade – Confronting Illusion

The Refining Flow of Truth That Unmasks the False

To descend further is to surrender deeper. The awe of the first cascade opens the eyes. But at the second, you must allow the water to reach the hidden places.

And this current does not caress. It strips away the old. It tears through illusion. It peels away false constructs. It reveals what you were never meant to carry; beliefs, masks, roles, narratives. This is not cruelty. It is mercy by truth.

Unlike the thunderous awe of the first cascade, the second flows with sharp clarity. It doesn't dazzle; it divides. Here, the water begins to separate shadow from light, myth from memory, attachment from identity.

And it begins with one painful yet sacred question: What is not real in you?

This question is not about shame. It is about freedom. The truth does not shame; it shakes loose the illusion that wants to keep you still bound. This is the moment when awe gives way to honesty. You begin to see:

The masks you've worn to belong.
The lies you've believed to survive.
The stories you've inherited without questioning.

And perhaps more painful still: You see the truth you knew all along, but avoided.

This cascade does not scream, or shouts loud; it reveals. And in its revealing, it asks: Are you willing to let go?

The Fire Within the Water

The second cascade is not fire and brimstone. It is a gentle, relentless fire within the water; refining, not condemning.

You feel the current pass through your soul, and you know; This is not just water. It is holy fire in liquid form. It does not destroy you. It destroys what cannot follow you forward.

This is where the illusion begins to unravel completely. The fantasy of escaping Earth, escaping suffering, escaping responsibility; it dissolves.

Then you start to realize that:

> The mountain was never meant to be climbed.
> The gate was never out there.
> The escape was never about leaving; it was about returning to what's true.

And to return to what's true, you must confront what is false.

This moment echoes through scripture:

Jacob, wrestling the angel, is asked: *"What is your name?"*; not because God didn't know, but because Jacob needed to face the identity he had hidden behind.

Isaiah, in the throne room, cries out: *"I am a man of unclean lips…"*; not because of guilt, but because the presence stripped away every illusion.

Peter, after the miraculous catch, falls to his knees, *"Depart from me, Lord…"* because truth had pierced his false self.

Revelation does not coddle the ego. It frees the soul.

The current of this second cascade is not personal; it is precise. It knows what must fall away.

Old religious conditioning. Emotional armor. The compulsive needs to be always right. The fear-based theology that kept you safe but small.

Here, the self you thought you were; begins to dissolve in the truth of who you were always becoming. And yes; it may feel like dying. Because something is dying. But only so something greater can start living within.

You cannot fight the current of truth. You can only let it carry you. The more you resist, the more it exposes your resistance. The more you release, the more it reveals your hidden wholeness beneath the fracture. Letting go is not losing. Letting go is passing through.

From Illusion to Intimacy

This cascade does not just strip away. It prepares your spirit, soul, body and mind. By confronting illusion, it clears the channel for true intimacy with God. You are not left naked and ashamed. You are left real and ready.

Only what was false has died. Only what was heavy has been carried away.

And now; You are ready to receive what can only be poured into emptied hands.

Reflection Invitation

What illusions have I built my life on that are now beginning to crumble? Have I confused safety with truth? Is there something in me resisting the current that is trying to free me?

Close your eyes.

Feel the water; steady, alive, unyielding.
It is not your enemy.
It is your liberation.
Let it flow.
Let it confront.
Let it carry away what no longer serves your becoming.
The next cascade is nearby.
And your soul is ready.

Part 5.

The Third Cascade – Receiving Hidden Wisdom

The Sacred Remembering Beneath the Noise

There comes a moment in the descent when all striving ceases. You are no longer reaching. You are simply open to capture and be captured.

Stripped of illusion, you are not empty; you are ready. And this is when it begins. Not with a trumpet. Not with a scroll descending from heaven. But with a whisper. A knowing. A resonance.

This is the third cascade.

It does not crash like the first. It does not confront like the second. It flows in silence. And in that silence, something ancient begins to awaken. And then something powerfully divine happens.

You begin to remember.

This is not the acquisition of new facts. It is the recovery of forgotten truth. You are not learning something new; you are remembering what was inscribed from the beginning of time within you.

As if something buried deep within your bones recognizes the sound of wisdom as it flows. It bypasses logic. It moves through memory. It stirs the part of you that was woven before time.

Here, you begin to realize: What is true has never been far; only hidden beneath noise. Here wisdom flows where words once failed. At this stage, revelation is not loud; it is not external, it is deeply within the hidden chambers of your whole being.

It moves within:

> In the quiet thought you didn't expect.
> In the image that lingers without explanation.
> In the tears that rise for no apparent reason.
> In the sudden knowing you cannot source but cannot deny.

The third cascade is not information; it is impartation. You don't carry it like a doctrine, or like an ideology that has been birthed with defect because of people's confused imaginations. You carry it like a womb, that carries the breath of life.

This is where the veil becomes translucent, and the mirror of divine remembrance starts to reflect the truest you. Here is where you begin to see yourself differently.

Not through the lens of what was stripped away. But through the lens of what was always true beneath the surface, revealing that:

> You are not your mistake.
> You are not your survival strategies.
> You are not your performance.
> You are a vessel of memory.
> You are a steward of light.

And now the wisdom hidden in your depths begins to rise; like spring water through the cracks of once-hardened ground, and the Earth starts whispering within you.

Why?

Because the wisdom you receive here is not abstract. It is deeply rooted. It is as if the Earth itself begins to speak; not in sentences, but in knowing.

Trees no longer just stand. They witness.
Water does not just move. It remembers.
Silence no longer feels empty. It echoes.

This is the moment where creation ceases to be scenery and becomes a sacred scroll. You begin to read the Earth as revelation. Because now, your inner terrain has been made clear enough to recognize the sacred woven through everything that encapsulates your being in its reality.

This cascade carries the wisdom long buried beneath the noise of the world, the truths that have been long silenced by:

Busyness
Religion
Shame
Distrust

But now, with the ego disarmed and illusions dissolved, the deeper current flows. You begin to hear, not louder, but truer:

The voice that spoke before your wounds.
The calling that sang before your career.
The truth that still speaks underneath all the theology.

You realize it and capture its sounds proclaiming: I was not made to discover wisdom. I was made to become a vessel for it, a carrier of it. And because of this realization also called awakening, you do not take notes, you do not start debating; You absorb, you listen and you start receiving what only the living soul can carry.

This is where:

The stories become parables.
The parables become symbols.
The symbols become revelation.
And revelation becomes remembrance.

And then something powerful starts happening: What was spoken in your early years but misunderstood...What was whispered in dreams but ignored...What was long buried under "being responsible"...It returns. It doesn't demand belief. It simply invites recognition.

"You've known Me before," says the Voice behind the veil. And you answer not with certainty, but with awe-full yes.

Let's pause a moment through the reflection of few scriptural echoes

Mary sat at Jesus' feet; not to be taught, but to absorb mystery.

Daniel saw visions and was troubled; not because they were wrong, but because they were deep. Jesus, full of grace and truth, often said, *"Let those who have ears, hear..."*; for not all hearing is listening.

The third cascade flows where your living soul is no longer trying to understand; but willing to become understanding itself.

Sincere reflections:

> What truth has been whispering to me beneath the surface?
> Am I open to receiving what cannot be explained but only absorbed?
> What wisdom have I silenced in myself because it didn't sound like the voices around me?

Meditate few moments, close your eyes. Let the river run through you; not loudly, but deeply.

Remember:

You are not searching anymore. You are remembering. You are returning. You are receiving what you've carried all along.

Part 6.

The Fourth Cascade – Embodying Presence

Becoming What You Have Beheld

There is a moment in every sacred journey when revelation shifts form. It no longer arrives as something that has been influenced from the external, and it no longer feels like something that was received.

Why?

Because the revelation it begins to live inside you. You are no longer just the witness. You are now the embodiment.

This is the fourth cascade; where truth and presence converge inside your being and begin to move through you.

The living soul was not made to just collect and capture truths; It was made to carry them, and in order to be able to carry the revelation; it has to be incarnated within the depths of your soul.

How?

By opening and nurturing the ground foundation of you being, to let the truth grow roots in your bones. To let truth rise in your walk, your tone, your posture. This is not mimicry. It is not performance. It is a process of transformation so deep that the line between Spirit and Vessel begins to blur.

Then the revelations no longer sound like an echo from the heavens, but are divine rediscovered echoes from the eternity that were etched within the fabric of your essence

This cascade does not roar like the first. It does not confront like the second. It does not whisper like the third. It breathes. You begin to notice:

The way you speak changes.
The way you see others softens.
The way you move through space becomes sacred.
The breath in your lungs feels full of fire, but not of noise.

This is not the birth of doctrine. It is the birth of a Holy Presence. Not just around you. In you. As you. This is the threshold where you realize that you are becoming the altar.

You are not meant to simply approach altars. You are meant to become one. Wherever you walk, the ground becomes holy. Not because of ego, but because of embodied reverence. People begin to feel something different around you.

Not charisma; but consecration. You are now the space and the altar where the divine can dwell. Not just visit. Dwell.

The old life moved from obligation. This new life moves from overflow, and you start living from inside out, reflecting your inner transformation in your external manifestation.

Your decisions flow from inner alignment. Your voice carries the cadence of stillness. Your actions begin to mirror the heartbeat of the unseen. This is not human perfection. This is a sacred and divine Holy Presence. You are not striving to reflect truth. Truth has taken residence in you; and now it reflects itself through you.

What you once experienced in glimpses; You now carry in gestures. The tone of your words. The patience of your silence. The clarity of your no. The tenderness of your yes.

You're no longer searching for the sacred. You are now living from it. It doesn't come in flashes anymore. It flows in your everyday movements. You don't quote presence. You become it.

Few scriptural Echoes of Embodiment

- **Jesus**, the Word made flesh, walked among us full of grace and truth, not as an idea, but as embodied revelation.
- **Paul** wrote, "It is no longer I who live, but Christ who lives in me."
- **Mary** did not only carry the Word; she gave it a body.

Embodiment is not reserved for the divine. It is the call of every living soul who surrenders to the eternal flow of living waters.

To embody Presence is not to glow with spiritual superiority. It is to carry: Gentleness that doesn't collapse. Strength that doesn't dominate. Wisdom that doesn't need applause. Fire that doesn't consume but warms.

You are no longer reacting to life from trauma. You are now responding from Presence. This is sacred maturity. Not how much you know. But how much you carry in stillness.

At this cascade, you no longer seek proof of your encounter, because the path you choose to move forward is not any longer an outward journey.

Your life becomes the evidence now, and even if no one understands it, you know what you carry. You are not becoming a preacher. You are becoming a living flame. You are not escaping Earth. You are now walking upon it as one who hosts the eternal within the temporal.

Reflection Invitation

> Where in your life is truth asking to become movement?
> What part of you has known, but not yet embodied?
> Are you willing to let Presence take up full residence in you?

Close your eyes. Feel the sacred current of the fourth cascade. It does not overwhelm. It inhabits. Let it take shape in you. Let your breath become altar. Let your life become Presence.

Part 7.

The Fifth Cascade – Returning with Radiance

The Commission to Carry What You've Become

There comes a moment after the descent when you must rise. But not in escape. Not in ego.
Not to return to the noise unchanged. You rise with the power of the revelation inside you. You return; not as the seeker, but as the steward.

This is the fifth cascade; not an outpouring upon you, but a pouring through you. It does not push you away from Earth. It plants you deeper into it.

The final cascade is not a reversal. It is a release. You do not leave the realm; You bring it with you, because you are part of it, and the realm now is part of you.

And because the realm is part of you, you do not exit the mountain empty-handed. You carry the mountain's sacred revelation within every fabric of your manifested essence.

Where once you sought portals, you now understand: "You no longer seek the gate. You are becoming one." And this is not a burden. It is a divine transfiguration.

You do not glow because of what you saw. You glow because of who you've become.

Like Moses descending Sinai...
Like Jesus returning from the wilderness...
Like Paul after the third heaven...

There is always a moment where heaven-vision must become earth-mission. This final cascade flows with the mystery of commissioning.

Not with titles.
Not with applause.
But with authority rooted in presence.

The authority of the one who has passed through fire and water and emerged; not untouched, but transformed.

Now you start to carry what you once sought, and the river you search for the refreshment of your living soul, is no longer behind you, or out of your reach, because now the river starts flowing from within you and through you.

It flows now:

Through your words.
Through your touch.
Through your silence.
Through your eyes.

Wherever you go, a current moves with you; not of personality, but of presence. You are no longer just affected by the realm. You are now its emissary. You have been marked by descent.
You have been lit by remembrance. You are now a living vessel of sacred flow.

The radiance that reflects from you after the mountain encounter it is not loud. It does not need a stage. It does not seek attention. It does not perform. Why? Because sacred radiance is the true definition of quiet power.

It is the invisible river in the desert. The oil on the priest's beard. The light in the eye of the healed. It says nothing; but at the same time, it says everything.

You walk into a room, and things shift; not because you're powerful, but because you are aligned. And when you are aligned through you comes forth the echoes, reflection and the radiance of the returning Ones.

Scripture is full of radiance-bearers: Moses, whose face shone after speaking with God, had to veil himself. Stephen, whose face was like that of an angel while being stoned, because his gaze was full of heaven. Mary, whose quiet yes became the entrance of the Word into the world.

Radiance is not what you show. It is what you carry without trying, and this is the truest meaning of *Escaping Earth Manuscript*: Not departure, but descent so full, so complete, that you emerge transformed.

You are not leaving this world behind. You are stepping into it with sacred clarity. You do not curse the ground. You water it. You do not avoid the systems. You carry presence within them. You do not seek light. You become a window for it.

The world doesn't need more voices, but what the world needs it is to be encapsulated by the One True and

Everlasting Voice, that will produce forth a sacred radiance through the aligned ones.

And the fifth cascade reveals the hidden assignment: You are not called to impress. You are called to illuminate. To be:

> The one who listens longer.
> The one who sees deeper.
> The one who remembers the real story behind every mask.
> The one who walks slow because they carry glory.

Reflection Invitation

> What have I received that I now must carry?
> Where am I being sent—not in ambition, but in presence?
> Can I live as one who no longer seeks portals... because I am becoming one?

Close your eyes. Feel the final cascade; quiet, steady, radiant.

It does not push; It commissions.

It does not exalt; It sends.

And it speaks:

"You have passed through awe, through illusion, through remembrance, through embodiment. Now... go and flow."

Part 8.

A River Through You

Living as the Flow of Revelation

You have descended. You have been undone, re-formed, lit from within. And now you stand; not outside the sacred realm; but as a vessel through which that realm flows.

The five cascades in this prophetic and profound dream were not simply experiences.

> They were activations.
> They were alignments.
> They were anointings.

And now; They are not behind you. They are within you. You do not walk away from revelation.
You walk in the revelation.

You have passed through:

> Awe: The arrest of wonder
> Illusion: The stripping of falsehood
> Remembrance: The receiving of hidden wisdom
> Embodiment: The becoming of presence
> Radiance: The return with divine light

And now you are no longer the same. You are no longer looking for the waterfall. You are the place where water now flows. Revelation is no longer something you remember. It is now something you release.

The cascade has become a river, and you no longer move from waterfall to waterfall. You now carry a continuous stream. It flows in your speech. It rises in your silence. It weaves through your presence. And the world, thirsty, distracted, and desperate, doesn't need more performers, but does in truth needs rivers that refreshes humanity.

Let's pause for a sacred moment and remember the living words of our Lord and Savior Jesus Christ: "Whoever believes in Me... rivers of living water will flow from within them." John 7:38

Dear reader, you are that river, and because you overflow within, now the revelation lives in active motion.

The danger of profound spiritual experience is to make it a monument. But rivers do not stay still. They flow. You must not turn your descent into a museum or into a monument.

You must let it move through you: Into your workplace. Into your family. Into your art, your voice, your presence.

The cascades were not for escape. They were for engagement. Now, every moment is a place where heaven can pour through you, because you became a living portal.

You were once the seeker. Now, you are the signpost. You carry:

> Stillness in chaos
> Clarity in confusion

Fire in gentleness
Wisdom without performance

You are not the answer. But you are a doorway. And many will pass through you; not to reach you, but to touch what flows beyond you. This is not burden. This is becoming.

The mountain is no longer where once was. It now rises in you.

> Its foundation is your stillness.
> Its altar is your surrender.
> Its waterfall is your breath.

What once overwhelmed you... now flows from you. You carry the sacred not as a container, but as a channel. And your life becomes the evidence that descent leads to divine integration.

Reflection Invitation

> Can I live as a river; without holding back, without trying to control the flow?
> Have I made a monument where God intended movement?
> Am I willing to become a living threshold for others?

Close your eyes. Feel the mist. Feel the quiet current behind your ribs. It is not memory. It is revelation, activation, elevation and liberation. It is now.

> You are not escaping Earth.
> You are becoming one with its hidden flow.

You are not finished.
You have become a beginning.

Final Benediction of the Chapter

Let the awe remain. Let the lies fall away.
Let the wisdom rise. Let the presence take shape.
Let the radiance shine. Let the river flow. You are not waiting for another encounter. You are one. You are not chasing the waterfall. You are becoming its echo.

And the Earth, aching, dry, trembling; waits not for escape... But for your return as river.

Chapter Six Summary

The 5 Cascades of Revelation

Living Water from the Mountain Within

In Chapter Six, the journey of Escaping Earth enters a new dimension; not just of descent, but of deep activation. What began as a dream becomes a map. What appeared as five majestic waterfalls flowing within a mountain becomes five sacred thresholds of revelation, each cascading into the next.

This chapter is not merely poetic; it is prophetic architecture. It marks the transition from seeker to steward, from receiving to becoming, and from presence to embodiment.

Entering the Hidden Realm

The chapter opens with the dream-vision: a descent into the base of a mountain where five cascading waterfalls flow; not from the sky, but from within.

This hidden realm is not a metaphor; it is divine architecture. The portal is not upward, but inward. This part invites the reader into sacred awe, not to climb higher, but to descend deeper into mystery.

Revelation Comes in Layers

Revelation is not linear; it unfolds in dimensional descent. Each cascade flows from the one before it, not replacing, but expanding it.

This part compares the five cascades to the five books of Moses, the five wounds of Christ, and the five senses; all of which speak of grace, passage, and transformation. To receive revelation is to be shaped by it layer by layer.

The First Cascade – Awakening Awe

The descent begins with the breaking of numbness. The first cascade does not offer answers; it arrests the soul. Awe becomes the divine disruption that awakens presence. Many stop here, satisfied with inspiration, but this part makes it clear: awe is not the destination; it is the doorway to deeper revelation.

The Second Cascade – Confronting Illusion

As the soul passes through awe, the second cascade begins the work of refinement. This sacred current strip away false identities, inherited narratives, and illusions of outward escape.

Here, the ego is disarmed, and the soul begins to see through truth's unflinching light. The pain is real, but so is the freedom.

The Third Cascade – Receiving Hidden Wisdom

With the vessel now emptied, the soul becomes ready to remember. This cascade flows not with noise, but with stillness. Revelation comes as ancient knowing; truth hidden in the bones, in the land, in the silence. It is not new information, but divine remembrance. Creation itself becomes scripture. The soul becomes a well.

The Fourth Cascade – Embodying Presence

Revelation is no longer something you carry. It becomes something that moves through you. You become a living altar; a person through whom presence flows in silence, posture, word, and gaze.

This cascade marks the shift from inner knowing to incarnated truth. You are not reflecting presence. You are becoming it.

The Fifth Cascade – Returning with Radiance

The descent gives way to a radiant return; not an escape, but a re-emergence. The one who has passed through the sacred layers now returns to the world as a vessel of what they carry.

This is not mission in the traditional sense; it is embodied light. You become the signpost, the gate, the window through which the sacred continues to flow.

A River Through You

The five cascades are no longer events; they are active rivers flowing from within. The reader is called to become not the collector of revelation, but its living current. Like the promise of Jesus in John 7:38, the living water now flows through the one who believes.

You are not just changed. You have become the change; and the world thirsts for what you now carry.

Themes & Transformation

Descent as Activation; Transformation happens not by climbing higher, but by entering deeper.

Revelation as Flow; Each truth is not a conclusion, but a current.

Embodiment over Information; Truth must not only be received. It must be lived.

Commission as Re-entry; You are not sent to escape the world, but to bring heaven into it.

Spiritual posture of chapter six; This chapter calls for: Silence over speaking. Yielding over striving. Presence over performance. Stewardship over consumption You are not just a listener; you are a living portal.

Conclusion: The River Lives in You

You are no longer seeking the sacred flow. You are the sacred flow. Chapter Six does not end with closure. It ends with release. You are the river now. And the Earth, trembling with thirst, waits for your arrival.

Chapter Seven

Reclaiming the Original Mandate of Earthly Stewardship – Returning as Earthkeepers

A Call to Sacred Presence in a Disconnected Age

The journey inward is never without consequence. It strips away illusions, dissolves ambitions, and invites the soul to rediscover its original posture.

We who have wandered through the wilderness of knowledge and the caverns of contemplation now stand at the precipice of sacred unveiling. What was once hidden in shadow is now revealed in light.

But revelation, if not embodied, becomes a monument to missed opportunity. The river of understanding that now flows within us was never meant for private consumption; it is destined for release, to irrigate barren lands, to anoint the Earth with new life.

This is not the call of escapists seeking refuge from a broken world. It is the awakening cry of stewards, Earthkeepers, who return not with schemes of dominion but with hands of healing.

We are not here to ascend into clouds of detachment, but to descend with holy presence, bearing the weight of sacred responsibility. The time has come to reclaim what was lost, not merely in memory but in practice.

The time has come to return to the original mandate.

Edenic Memory and the Original Intent

Before laws were etched in stone, before temples crowned hills and rituals filled the air with incense, there was a garden. Eden: more than a place, it was a divine rhythm, a seamless dance between humanity, creation, and the Creator.

In Eden, humanity's first breath was not a command to control, but a whisper to care. We were not formed to conquer but to cultivate; not to rule over, but to walk among.

This is no poetic idealism; it is the forgotten code of our spiritual DNA. The command to "tend and keep" was never revoked; it was merely buried beneath centuries of conquest theology and empire-minded religion.

Reclaiming our identity as Earthkeepers requires that we remember this Edenic rhythm; not as nostalgia for a paradise lost, but as a divine order to be restored.

The garden is remembered not through intellect but through intimacy. We must reenter it not with theories, but with tenderness.

As we return, we find that the trees still await our friendship, the rivers our reverence, the soil our steps. Eden is not lost, it is layered beneath our forgetfulness, waiting to be unearthed by those who walk with sacred memory.

We were formed from the dust; and this is not a mark of shame, but of covenant. In the divine act of creation, the Eternal bent low, shaping humanity not from starlight or celestial flame, but from the soil of Earth. Then, with breath eternal, He animated that soil with Spirit. We are dust, yes; but dust filled with wind, with purpose, with divine resonance.

This dual identity is not a contradiction to be resolved, but a mystery to be embraced. Earth and spirit, matter and meaning, form and essence, they dance within us as one. The soil was not chosen by accident; it was chosen by design.

The Earth is not beneath us. It is part of us. We are not above creation; we are creation, infused with consecrated consciousness.

To be an Earthkeeper, then, is not to assume the posture of duty-bound steward alone, it is to return to kinship. The rocks, the winds, the waters; they are not resources, but relatives.

The trees are not timber for our gain, but temples of praise in their own right. When we forget the dust, we forget our story. But when we remember it, we begin to walk again in harmony with the Breath that first stirred the clay.

Revelation that does not transform is merely entertainment for the soul. True revelation always brings responsibility. It lifts the veil not so we can admire the view, but so we can answer the call.

The visions, dreams, encounters, and insights received in the sacred stillness are not trophies of the mystic life. They are blueprints for embodiment.

To carry revelation is to carry responsibility for the Earth, for the marginalized, for the future generations not yet born. The sacred cannot remain in sanctuaries of silence; it must be walked out in the noise of the world.

Revelation that only elevates us but does not ground us is incomplete. We are not called to escape the world through knowledge, but to redeem it through presence.

The Earth groans, awaiting not our declarations, but our demonstration. Our prayers must become posture, our songs become fertile soil, our visions become vineyards.

The true servant is not the one who flees the Earth, but the one who kneels in its dust and says, "Here I am, send me."

The Rise of the Earthkeepers

The Earthkeepers are awakening, not from seminaries or institutions, but from divine silence and wilderness. They do not rise with the credentials of men, but with the commission of Heaven. Their authority is not based in eloquence, but in essence. They are marked not by platform, but by presence.

You will know them by their walk, barefoot, reverent, intentional. Like Moses before the burning bush, they understand that the ground beneath them is holy. They carry not weapons, but water. Not slogans, but seeds. They carry Eden in their bones and resurrection in their breath.

The Earthkeepers are prophets of the land, priests of the garden, and poets of the possible. They live sacramentally, knowing that every act of restoration, whether planting a tree, healing a wound, or forgiving a neighbor, is an act of divine warfare against decay. They till the soil not only with hands, but with hope.

The Forgotten Mandate Remembered

In the beginning, a mandate was given: "Be fruitful. Multiply. Fill the Earth. Subdue it." For generations, this has been read through the lens of domination. But what if we've misread the mandate? What if "subdue" does not mean to suppress, but to sanctify? What if "rule" does not mean to control, but to reflect the divine image in love and wisdom?

The original mandate was not an imperial license, but a relational invitation. Humanity was called to extend the borders of Eden; not to conquer the Earth, but to cultivate it. The Garden was to grow, not be gated. The Earth was not ours to possess, but to partner with.

Dominion, rightly understood, is the practice of divine responsibility.

This mandate, corrupted by empire and greed, is being reclaimed by grace. To remember the original call is to renounce exploitation and embrace sacred service. It is to live not above creation, but within it. Not as kings demanding tribute, but as priests offering incense.

The Path Back to Eden

Eden is not behind us; it is before us. It is not a lost geography, but a living invitation. The way back is not paved with nostalgia, but with renewal. The veils have lifted; the path is open.

But this path is narrow; it cannot be walked with ambition or arrogance. It requires humility. It requires transformation.

To return to Eden is to remember who we are. It is to rekindle relationship, with God, with neighbor, with the Earth. It is to shed the garments of separation and clothe ourselves in communion.

The ones who return do not come with trumpets, but with tears. They do not rebuild temples; they rebuild trust. Eden awaits those who will choose presence over prestige. Creation groans not for a new religion, but for a renewed people.

The Earth does not ask for more doctrines; it longs for daughters and sons to awaken to their birthright. The path to Eden is paved not with conquest, but with compassion.

We are entering a new era where power is no longer defined by dominance, but by devotion. Influence will not come through charisma, but through consecration.

The age of declarations has passed; the age of restoration has come.

To carry true spiritual authority is not to stand above others, but to kneel below them. It is not to speak the loudest, but to listen the deepest.

The Earth does not need more noise; it needs nurture. And nurture flows from those who have laid down ambition and risen with tenderness.

The Earth will be healed not by slogans, but by scars. Not by strategy, but by sincerity. The ones who will lead this age of restoration will be those who have first been undone, who have descended into silence and emerged carrying oil, not for fame, but for fire.

The New Genesis Movement

A New Genesis is unfolding. Not a return to primitive ways, but a return to divine ways. It is not about replicating Eden but redeeming the Earth. This is not escapism; it is incarnation. It is the Spirit made flesh again in the garden of humanity.

This movement is not built by institutions; it is born in intimacy. It is not curated by councils, but cultivated by those who walk slowly, love deeply, and live sacrificially.

These are the gardeners of grace, the architects of hope, the midwives of a new creation.

They do not seek to leave the Earth, but to liberate it, from neglect, from exploitation, from despair. They walk with the Lamb and till the soil. They honor the seasons and sing with the stars. They understand that heaven's agenda is not domination, but restoration.

And now, beloved reader, you stand at the threshold. The scroll has been read. The vision has been revealed. The invitation is before you; not to escape, but to embody. You are not called to climb another mountain of ambition, but to walk the land you once fled; now barefoot and blessed.

The river within you is not for containment; it is for baptism. For irrigation. For resurrection. You were not anointed for applause, but for alignment. You were not awakened for spectacle, but for stewardship.

What the Earth needs is not another hero, but a healer. Not a conqueror, but a companion.

Return; not with conquest, but with compassion. Return; not to rebuild systems of separation, but to restore sacred rhythms. Return; not to escape the Earth, but to become its healing. For as it was in the beginning, so it shall be again.

We are Earthkeepers.

Let us return.

Part 1.

From Revelation to Responsibility

The Journey That Returns

We stand at the cusp of a return; but not the kind the world anticipates. This is not a return to the comforts of the familiar, nor a return to the illusion of control. It is a return with revelation; and that changes everything.

Throughout Escaping Earth, we have descended through thresholds and caverns, walked through dreams and revelations, been dismantled and re-formed by what lies beneath the surface of ordinary living. Each mountain, gate, stone, and flow led us inward; not to escape the world but to truly see it again.

Now, the final act begins; not as an ending but as a sacred returning. And we do not return empty-handed. We return with a divine mandate.

Reclaiming the Original Scroll

In the beginning, humanity was not cast upon the Earth randomly. We were not merely creatures among others, nor were we rulers over a lifeless domain. We were formed from the dust yet breathed into by the Spirit. This paradox, soil and spirit; was the blueprint of divine intention.

"Then the Lord God took the man and put him in the Garden of Eden to tend and keep it."
Genesis 2:15

The first commission given to humanity was not to preach or perform, but to tend and keep. The Hebrew words here; *abad* "to serve, work, cultivate", and *shamar* "to guard, preserve, watch", unveil a role more profound than dominion: we were called to be gardeners and guardians, not governors.

This Edenic mandate wasn't a job description; it was a sacred identity. To keep the Earth was to reflect the very nature of God: Creator; Sustainer; Nourisher; Protector.

But something was lost. And now, with revelation restored, we must remember what we were always meant to be. And this revelation deeply moved us to understand that the process of true transformation it is not an escape hatch.

There is a seductive tendency in modern spirituality; to treat revelation as a secret code for personal escape. Many seek divine insight to avoid suffering, to ascend away from the world, to enter bliss while the Earth groans.

But true revelation is never divorced from responsibility. In fact, it increases it.

"To whom much is given, much is required."
Luke 12:48

To receive truth is to be entrusted with its embodiment. To see heaven is to become accountable for how we walk on Earth. To witness glory is to carry it back to where the darkness lingers.

The mountain was never the end. It was preparation. Moses did not stay on Sinai. He came down with tablets etched in divine fire. Jesus did not remain transfigured. He descended into human suffering again; with radiance. Likewise, your revelations are not for your own isolation; they are fuel for faithful return.

And now we come to the recognition that the descent was truly for this very moment. Everything in Chapters 1 through 6 has prepared you for this threshold.

You walked through the veils.
You entered caverns and hidden altars.
You rediscovered the mountain within.
You drank from cascades of awe, exposure, remembrance, embodiment, and radiance.

But none of it was for escape. It was for transformation; so that you might now carry the heart of heaven back into the soil of Earth. The final movement of the sacred dream is not ascension; it is grounded return. And now the Earth groans, waiting for what you have become.

Stewards, Not Owners

We were never meant to own the Earth. We were never meant to exploit it. We were meant to walk with it, to listen to its song, to feel its rhythms beneath our feet.

The original mandate is not about environmentalism; it is about relational stewardship. The land is not a possession. It is a sanctuary. Creation is not property. It is kinship.

Every tree, rock, bird, and river bears a whisper of the Creator. And you dear reader; are made in that same breath; have been invited not to conquer, but to co-hold. This is not passive caretaking. It is active communion.

Every true revelation carries within its frame and essence a commission. Commission is not a suggestion. It is an entrustment. And the question is not, "What did I see?" The question is, *"How will I now walk?"*

Will you walk softer on the land?
Will you speak to creation with reverence?
Will you guard the sacred spaces around you and within you?

You cannot unknow what has been revealed. You are now a living altar. A carrier of fire.
A guardian of thresholds. Your hands are anointed not only to pray, but to plant. Your voice is charged not only to declare, but to heal. Your presence is now a living temple, within which the Earth can feel safe again.

The Priesthood of the Garden

We were meant to be priests in a sanctuary called Earth. Before temples of stone, there was a cathedral of sky and soil. Before incense and rituals, there was wind through the trees and water flowing over rocks. The first priesthood was not clothed in garments; but in humility, wonder, and listening.

We have traded that priesthood for performance. But the Earth remembers. And it groans for those who remember it.

"The creation waits in eager expectation for the children of God to be revealed."
Romans 8:19

What is this revealing? It is not about celebrity. It is not about grandeur. It is about the return of those who walk barefoot in sacred places again. The children of God are those who carry heaven not above Earth, but through it.

To reclaim the mandate is not to take on a burden. It is to return to joy. Tending the Earth is not a task. It is worship.

> Every act of kindness to a creature is an echo of Eden.
> Every protection of the soil is a song to the Creator.
> Every moment of reverent silence in nature is incense rising to the throne.

And when responsibility becomes worship, you are no longer simply doing a job; You are becoming a living liturgy.

This brings forward to life The Sacred Loop that humanity needs to embrace it: Revelation; Response; Restoration.

This is the divine cycle:

> Revelation: You are shown something sacred.
> Response: You choose to embody what was revealed.
> Restoration: The world is healed through your alignment.

This is not theoretical. It is deeply practical.

> Revelation without response leads to pride.
> Response without revelation leads to burnout.
> Restoration only comes when both are held in holy tension.

You have been shown sacred things. Now comes the sacred task: To walk within the revelation you saw. And then every step becomes part of the restoration.

For some this following statement may seem untheological but here is an ancient and sacred truth: The soil misses you. Yes; you.

The Earth remembers your footsteps from Eden. It remembers your voice before it was silenced by shame. It remembers your breath before it became frantic with performance. And the Earth it has been waiting.

> Not for a hero.
> Not for a savior.
> But for a steward.

One who will walk again with the quiet strength of one who has seen the face of God… and come down the mountain carrying presence.

"The land you walk on; I will give it to you," the Lord said to Moses. Not as ownership. But as inheritance. Not for exploitation. But for nourishment.

From Pilgrims to Planters

You have been a seeker. Now, you are being called to become a Sower. You have tasted mystery.

Now, you must plant it into your everyday life. The seeds are not in heaven. They are in your hands. And the soil is ready.

Wherever your feet touch, may the mandate rise. Wherever your eyes behold beauty, may reverence be rekindled. Wherever your hands build, write, create, or comfort; may Eden bloom again.

Reflection Invitation

Sit still. Feel the breath of the Earth beneath you.

Ask:

What revelation have I received that I have not yet responded to?
Where am I being called to walk differently because of what I now know?
What would it mean for my presence to be *a sanctuary* for the world around me?

Now speak aloud: "I am not escaping Earth. I am becoming its sacred keeper."

Benediction: The Return Begins

The dream did not end in escape.
It ends in entrustment.

The revelation you received was not a door out, but a way in; to a new kind of life on Earth.

You are not a visitor here.
You are not a stranger.

You are a guardian of wonder.
You are a restorer of what was forgotten.
You are a carrier of the ancient mandate;

To walk the Earth in reverence,
To tend the unseen roots,
To steward the seen world in light of the invisible one.

And now…

>	Walk on.
>	Barefoot.
>	Listening.
>	Rooted.

Part 2.

The Forgotten Mandate

Forgotten Not Erased

Mandates from Heaven are never truly erased; only buried. Not in the dust of time, but in the layers of distortion and disobedience.

What was once entrusted to humanity as a sacred role has, over millennia, been forgotten, altered, commercialized, or altogether dismissed.

But forgotten does not mean lost. And the call that echoed in Eden still whispers in the soul of every living being: *"Tend and keep."* Genesis 2:15

Not to rule. Not to ravage. But to remember and restore. This is the forgotten mandate. And its remembrance begins now.

What Was Entrusted

In the Edenic pattern, stewardship was sacred; an act of divine image-bearing. Humanity was called to:

Mirror the Creator's compassion, not mimic domination.
Cultivate the garden, not control it.
Walk in intimacy with creation, not separate from it.

We were not placed over the Earth to exploit it, but within it to co-labor in its flourishing.

This was not a metaphor. It was an ontological assignment; an identity intertwined with the soil.

But then came the fracture. Not just the "Fall" in terms of sin, but the falling away from communion. And from that moment, we began replacing mandate with mastery, communion with consumption, and stewardship with sovereignty.

The Earth was no longer a living cathedral. It became a commodity.

The Subtle Shift

How does a mandate so central become forgotten? The answer lies in a subtle drift, a spiritual amnesia cloaked in progress.

The drift from wonder to utility: What we once revered, we began to use.

The drift from communion to control: Where once we walked with creation, we built systems to subdue it.

The drift from co-creation to consumption: The Earth became a means to an end rather than a partner in purpose.

And the most tragic drift?

From presence to absence: We stopped being present; to creation, to the Spirit, to one another.

The mandate was not revoked. We just stopped hearing it. But it still echoes; under the pavement, beneath the noise, inside the longing.

And even if the mandate has been forgotten by the Mind, it is always remembered by the Soul. The modern mind has lost track of the ancient mandate, but the soul never forgets.

That ache when a tree is cut down for no reason.
That reverent silence in a forest or mountain.
That longing to escape city noise for still waters.

These are not coincidences. They are memory triggers. Signs that the soul remembers Eden. Clues that the spirit knows what the mind cannot articulate. *"He has set eternity in the human heart." Ecclesiastes 3:11*

Eternity includes the first call, the original assignment. And now, the living soul calls us to unearth what was buried.

The Misinterpretation of Dominion

One of the greatest missteps in spiritual history was the misreading of this verse: *"Have dominion over the Earth..." Genesis 1:28*

Dominion was never meant to mean domination. The Hebrew word *"radah"* implies benevolent rulership, a shepherding function. It echoes the nature of God: to uphold, not to abuse.

But over time, dominion was weaponized to justify exploitation. Forests cleared. Rivers poisoned. Lands colonized. Species extinct. All in the name of a misunderstood mandate.

This isn't dominion. It's desecration. And it is time to reclaim the true meaning: To guard. To guide. To grow.

Dominion is a sacred charge; not to dominate, but to dignify.

When Theology Forgets the Earth

How did we get here? Some of the forgetting was seeded in our theology. When spirituality became about leaving Earth, we stopped believing it was worth embracing its welcome.

When heaven became the goal and Earth a stepping stone, we devalued the very place where God first not only placed the man, but went even further, and walked with man, on Earth.

The truth is:

The Bible begins in a garden, not a temple.
Jesus taught from mountains, boats, and fields.
The resurrection happened in a garden tomb.

And the final vision in Revelation is not of disembodied souls; but a renewed Earth. God has not forgotten the Earth. We did. But it is not too late to remember it again.

The Earth as Co-Witness

Creation was never meant to be an object; it is a witness. "The heavens declare the glory of God; the skies proclaim the work of His hands." Psalm 19:1

But the Earth is not silent either. It speaks, groans, responds.

The trees clap their hands.

The rocks cry out.
The seas roar.
The mountains quake.

This is not poetic metaphor alone. It is theology of participation. When humanity forgets the mandate, creation groans (Romans 8:22). When humanity remembers, creation responds with joy. We are not its masters. We are its missing half. And the Earth is waiting for the reunion.

Warning Signs from the Earth

The forgotten mandate is not without consequence. Today's ecological crises are not merely environmental. They are spiritual signs of a severed relationship.

- Wildfires
- Melting ice
- Collapsing ecosystems
- Extinct species
- Polluted waters
- Famines and floods

I choose to mention these events because we are trying to rational them as being merely natural events, but truth be told, they are symptoms of our humanity spiritual dislocation.

The Earth is not retaliating; it is responding to neglect. It was not created to endure greed and indifference. It was created to flourish under stewardship. We must not spiritualize away the signs. We must repent; and return to the original way.

Remembering Is Repentance

To remember is not just to recall. It is to re-align. Repentance *"teshuvah"*, in Hebrew means "return."

Return to Eden.
Return to purpose.
Return to responsibility.

You don't need to figure it all out. You just need to start remembering. And in the act of remembering, the Spirit begins to rebuild.

Reconstructing the Forgotten Framework

The forgotten mandate must now be reconstructed; not from new ideas, but from ancient wisdom reawakened.

Here is the framework:

Reverence over resource: See the Earth not as supply but as sanctuary.

Partnership over possession: Relate to creation as a companion, not a commodity.

Presence over progress: Prioritize being over building.

Restoration over reward: Heal, even when it's not profitable.

Listening over leading: Learn from the rhythms of creation.

This is not regression; it is resurrection.

Re-Enacting Eden

You don't need to recreate Eden. You just need to live in a way that reflects its memory.

> Let your home become a garden of peace.
> Let your language carry the gentleness of rivers.
> Let your decisions reflect the long-view of mountains.
> Let your hands tend to beauty, not busyness.

Every action becomes a reenactment. Every choice a sacred echo. Eden lives again; through you.

Reflection Invitation

> Where have I allowed "dominion" to become disconnected from dignity?
> In what ways has my spirituality forgotten the Earth?
> How can I restore the mandate; today, in small and real ways?

Ask the Holy Spirit: "Show me what part of the garden I have been called to tend." And listen for the whisper.

Benediction

You do not need a new mandate.
You need to remember the first one.

It is written in your breath.
It is stitched in your soul.

It is encoded in the rhythm of your hands when you bless, build, or behold.

You are not merely a believer.
You are a keeper of Eden's memory.

And even if the world has forgotten, you now remember.

And that my beloved reader; is the beginning of everything.

Part 3.

A New Genesis Movement

When the Old Earth Groans for New Beginnings

Every ending contains a hidden seed. And every forgotten truth, when remembered, carries within it the capacity to birth a new beginning; a Genesis not of chronology, but of consciousness.

We are standing at such a threshold. The world, as we know it, is not just aching for solutions. It is yearning for a movement of re-creation; a new Genesis, not because Eden failed, but because humanity wandered. And now, like the prodigal, we must arise and return to our Holy Father's inherited garden.

This is not about building another Eden by human effort, philosophy, or ideology. This is about becoming once more a living Eden; in mindset, in presence, in spirit.

A New Genesis Movement is being formed. And it begins not in policy or protest, but in the hearts of those who remember.

The pattern of Genesis still stands, because the eternal blueprint was never revoked.

Genesis 1 was not merely a poetic origin story; it was a spiritual schematic:

Light pierces the deep; Truth illuminates over confusion.

Order emerges from chaos; Identity is shaped from formlessness.

Waters are separated; Inner boundaries are defined.

Land rises; Grounded purpose is established.

Life multiplies; Co-creation begins.

Humanity is formed in God's image; Not to conquer, but to reflect.

Sabbath is declared; Rest becomes the rhythm of divine union.

This pattern is not trapped in time. It is a living sequence, waiting to be activated again; in us. And now, we are being invited to re-walk the Genesis path, not backward, but forward in a continue and sacred transformation.

The Re-Genesis of humanity is a divine return, and not a reset, as so many are expressing the need of a reset, but humanity does not need a reset, all it needs is a return.

The New Genesis Movement is not about a technological utopia. It is a spiritual re-alignment.

It begins in remembering who we are.
It awakens in restoring what we've lost.
It matures in reclaiming what we were always meant to carry.

This is not humanity version 2.0. or 3.0. or whatever .0's people think that there was or are, this is all about the humanity being re-rooted, in its rightful ground.

A return to original design, in the newness of divine understanding. This is Re-Genesis; a divine movement where the garden grows not around us, but within us.

The Breath of God Still Hovers

In the beginning, the Spirit hovered over the waters. Even now, the Holy Spirit hovers. Over chaos. Over confusion. Over crisis. The movement begins when we pause long enough to notice the hovering presence. It is in the stillness that the Spirit begins to breathe new form into the formless.

> New identity.
> New vision.
> New stewardship.

And as it was then, so it is now: *"Let there be light..."* This time, the light is within us; those that are being awakened into conscious alignment. The breath of God is not only in the wind, but it is in the co-creative breath of all of the people who have remembered.

In this New Genesis Movement, Eden is not a geographic place to return to. It is a state of alignment, not only internally between Spirit, Soul, Body and Mind, but also externally between the human being and all other majestic manifestations of life in the Creation.

A posture where:

Creation is honored, not harvested for greed.
Time is sacred, not scheduled for exhaustion.
Work is worship, not slavery.
Every interaction is an altar.

As I mentioned previously, we do not need to rebuild Eden. We need to embody it.

Let every home become a garden. Let every table become an altar. Let every step be holy ground. This is Eden reborn.

The Book Within the Book

Genesis is not just the first chapter of Scripture. It is also the deep breath of divine identity; a frequency that echoes through all of time. In this movement, the Genesis story is no longer a story we read. It is a book we become.

When you bring light to darkness; you are in Genesis.
When you establish peace in chaos; you are in Genesis.
When you create beauty where there was decay; you are in Genesis.

You are like a majestically inked living scroll now. Your life becomes a new creation story, written not on tablets of stone, but on the soil of Earth and soul.

The New Genesis Movement will not be led by celebrities or platforms. It will be nurtured by prophets of presence. Who are they?

Gardeners and teachers.
Mothers and fathers.

Healers and poets.
Silent laborers who carry light.

These prophets don't preach sermons. They live them. They carry Eden in their eyes. They bring the breath of God into every room. They build altars not from stone, but from daily sacrifice and sacred intention. You will know them not by their fame, but by the fruit of renewal that follows their wake.

Perhaps; you beloved reader; you are one of them.

The New Genesis Movement does not require new foundations, because the ancient foundations were never revoked, just forgotten. But we can remember them in our:

Sacred Imagination; Seeing the Earth not as damaged goods, but as divine inheritance.

Embodied Spirituality; Living truth in flesh, not in theories.

Ecological Communion; Practicing reverence in how we treat land, water, creatures.

Generational Legacy; Building for children we may never meet.

Presence Over Performance; Letting the inner Eden be enough.

These are not programs. They are patterns of living. They are our humanity old roots from which new divine and sacred futures will grow.

The movement even if is embody around the world, has to begin locally, one remembered soul at a time. You don't need a platform to start a New Genesis. You need a place:

> Your backyard.
> Your table.
> Your morning routine.
> Your conversations.

Every local act of Eden-like living becomes a global frequency. Like seeds scattered across continents, each one carries the code of the whole.

This movement is not centralized. It is cellular; spread through awakened souls tending to small plots of sacred ground. Let your part be your portion. That is enough.

Return to the Center of Your Life's Balance knowing that:

> At the heart of Genesis is the garden.
> At the heart of the garden is God's presence.
> And at the heart of God's presence is relationship.

This movement will not succeed through ambition. It will be sustained only through intimacy. Return to the center and:

> Let silence be your soil.
> Let prayer be your rain.
> Let meditation be your tending.
> Let the Spirit walk with you again in the *cool of the day*.

Why? Because from this center of your life's balance, everything flows.

The Seven Commitments of the New Genesis Soul:

> I will walk in reverence; Every tree, lifeform, and soul is sacred.
>
> I will co-create, not only consume: I exist to bless, not exploit.
>
> I will restore, not retreat; The Earth is my home, not my escape route.
>
> I will carry Eden within me; My inner landscape shapes the outer world.
>
> I will nurture intergenerational legacy; What I plant today will bless those I may never see.
>
> I will listen to the Earth's language; Seasons, signs, and silences are all messages.
>
> I will remember the Genesis code; Light, order, life, beauty, rest, and responsibility.

These are not vows of burden. They are the joyful agreements of awakened hearts.

Reflections for Activation

> Where am I still living under the old story of dominion, rather than co-creation?
> What does "Eden within" look like in my actual lifestyle, not just my beliefs?

> How can I participate in the New Genesis
> Movement right where I am?

Let the Spirit answer not in thunder, but in gentle knowing.

Closing Benediction

In the beginning, the Spirit hovered.
Now, the Holy Spirit hovers again; over you.

Over the chaos in your life.
Over the seeds waiting to be sown.
Over the garden within your soul.

You are not too late. You are right on time.

The Earth does not need heroes.
It needs remembers.
Carriers of Eden. Tenders of sacred ground.

And when you rise each day, rooted in love and alive in purpose, you participate in the re-beginning of the world.

Welcome to the New Genesis Movement.

Part 4.

Earthkeepers Arise

The Earth Is Crying; Who Will Answer?

The Earth is not silent. Earth groans, waits, pulses. Earth is not merely a habitant place. Earth is a living witness, bearing the memory of Eden, the weight of exile, and the hope of redemption.

In the hush between disasters, in the stillness between storms, the Earth is asking: "Who will keep me? Who will care?"

This cry is not merely environmental or physical; it is spiritual. It is the same tone and voice that once echoed in Eden, like the voice of the Eternal Creator *"Where are you?"* Genesis 3:9

And now, in this sacred hour, the response of humanity is rising:

"Here we are."
"We remember."
"We return."

From Exploiters to Stewards: The Shift of the Living Soul

We were not born to exploit, but to tend. Not to dominate, but to guard. The word to keep in Genesis; "to till and keep the garden"; comes from the Hebrew word "Shamar," which means to guard, to protect, to preserve. This is priestly language. It is sacred guardianship.

Humanity was not placed in Eden as masters, but as earth-priests; carrying the breath of God and called to honor the breath of Earth. To be an Earthkeeper is to embody this holy role again; not with pride, but with trembling joy.

Across the Earth, a subtle sound is stirring, it is the sacred sound of awakening.

Not a trumpet of war, but a bell of remembrance.
Not a political march, but a sacred procession.
Not slogans, but songs, ancient and new;
being sung by those whose spirits are stirring.

These are not the loudest voices in the room. They are the most rooted. They know that revival begins not in stadiums, but in the soil, the sacred ground.

And they are arising; not as conquerors, but as Earthkeepers. They are not defined by profession, but by their posture. Who are really the Earthkeepers?

A child planting a seed in faith.
A mother tending a garden with prayer.
An elder walking the forest with reverence.
A laborer who refuses to extract more than needed.
A prophet who sees the Earth not as commodity, but as companion.

And they are not bound or limited by surroundings, because the Earthkeepers come from every nation, tribe, and tongue.

Some wear robes.
Some wear overalls.

Some write poems.
Some build homes.
Some heal rivers.
Some teach children to listen to the wind.

They are not just environmentalists intrinsically in their own nature. They are soul-environmentalists; tending the ecology of the human heart and the ecology of the Earth.

The call to Earthkeeping is not a trend; but it is a call to return to the original humanistic mandate. Before there was law, there was a mandate:

"Be fruitful, multiply, fill the Earth, and *keep it.*" Genesis 1:28, 2:15

To fill the Earth does not mean to overrun it. It means to honor it with presence. To keep it does not mean ownership. It means fidelity; a sacred marriage between spirit and soil.

This original mandate was never revoked. It was forgotten. But now, it is being remembered by a remnant whose hearts beat in rhythm with Heaven and Earth.

Let's meditate few moments over these five postures of the Earthkeepers attributes.

Reverent Watcher: You observe with awe. You listen to wind and rain as if they are voices.

Faithful Tiller: You work the soil, the soul, the systems with gentle hands and vision.

Restorative Healer: You mend what was broken: land, relationships, water, memory.

Prophetic Witness: You speak not just against destruction, but *toward hope*.

Contemplative Listener; You do not act from urgency, but from discerned timing with the rhythms of creation.

These five are not mere roles; they are rhythms. They become your breath, your prayer, your way of being.

To be an Earthkeeper is to walk in the priesthood of all creation, carrying a priestly anointing. Just as priests in the temple tended fire, Earthkeepers tend the sacred flame of sustainability, reverence, and renewal.

They burn not offerings of sacrifice, but of awareness, honor, and intercession. They live between realms; one foot in the divine, one hand in the dirt.

They are bridge-beings; reconciling heaven and earth, time and eternity, humankind and home. This is not performance. It is the identity of the humanity recovered.

We are entering an era of reclamation, where the sacred winds of heaven are bringing a change: Where lands long desecrated begin to sing again. Where polluted rivers receive prayers and healing acts. Where people remember how to walk barefoot on holy ground.

This is not regression. This is not nostalgia. This is a sacred return; forward and upward. The winds are shifting, and those with ears inclined towards to the earth hear the sound.

A sound like Eden approaching.
A sound like guardians arising.
A sound like Earthkeepers awakening.

To rise as an Earthkeeper is also to stand against those that corrupts the Earth, and must be ready to confront their behavior: Systems that commodify land, labor, and life. Narratives that tell us nature is "lesser" or "neutral." Doctrines that preach escape over engagement. Technologies that exploit instead of harmonize.

Earthkeepers are not anti-progress. They are pro-purpose. They do not hate cities. They bring gardens into them. They do not avoid crisis. They carry covenant into crisis. They are not passive.
They are prophetic; embodying what others have abandoned.

The Inner Garden First

The first Earth to keep is not the Amazon or the ocean. It is the garden of the heart. If you dominate your emotions, extract your own energy without rest, pollute your thoughts with fear and greed; then how can you tend the outer world?

The Earthkeeper starts by sitting still: breathing with the land, confessing their disconnection, receiving divine permission to begin again.

The outer Earth reflects the inner ecology of humanity, but truly the healing must begin from the inside out. Because of that Earthkeepers are not just called to action. They are called to sync with the seasons of life physically and spiritually: Rest in winter. Sow in spring. Tend in the summer. Harvest in fall.

This rhythm is not rural; it is universal. It is the divine pulse woven into all life. Modernity has lost this rhythm. Earthkeepers restore it; not by preaching, but by embodying.

Let your life become a calendar of sacred time. Let your breath align with the breath of trees. Let your work reflect the wisdom of bees and rivers. This is the dance of Earth and Soul.

Building the Earthkeeper Life

What does it look like in practice? Honor your food; Know where it came from, bless it, waste nothing. Sabbath your land; Let your body and your home rest.

Decolonize your theology; Remove the idea that Earth is evil and Heaven is the goal. Educate your children in wonder; Let them taste awe, not just data.
Speak with reverence; Words are seeds; plant truth and beauty.

This is how Earthkeepers live. Not by force; but by formation. By daily rhythms that become rivers of renewal. Prophetic Declarations of the Earthkeeper:

I am not the owner of this land; I am its servant.
I am not above creation; I am within it.
I will not wait for governments; I will plant with my own hands.
I will not curse the darkness; I will be light and soil and salt.

I will not abandon the Earth; for it is the dwelling of the Lord.
I am an Earthkeeper; not by trend, but by covenant.

Benediction: Rise, Keeper of Eden O! You who remember.

Rise from the ashes of forgetfulness. Shake off the dust of domination. Receive again the breath of stewardship. The Earth does not need saviors. The Living Earth needs sons and daughters.

The Earth needs those who walk slowly, speak gently, plant wildly, and pray deeply. You are not too small. You are not too late. You are a flame in the forest. You are a whisper in the drought. You are a keeper of the soil, the sky, the spirit.

Arise, beloved Earthkeeper. Your garden is calling. And Eden is not behind you. It is growing within you.

Part 5.

Covenant with the Dust

"Then the LORD God formed man from the dust of the ground and breathed into his nostrils the breath of life; and the man became a living being." Genesis 2:7

The Sacred Origins

Before we were voices, we were dust. Before we were stewards, we were soil. Humanity's beginning was not forged in heaven's heights, but in earth's lowliest corners. Not in palaces of gold, but in the humble dust of the ground. The act of divine creation did not bypass the earth. It included it.

God bent low, reached into the earth, and from that ancient soil fashioned us, not as strangers to the eternal foundations of the Earth, but as its living covenant partners.

"For you created my inmost being; you knit me together in my mother's womb. I praise you because I am fearfully and wonderfully made; your works are wonderful; I know that full well. My frame was not hidden from you when I was made in the secret place, when I was woven together in the depths of the earth". Psalm 139: 13-15.

What does that mean for our humanity? It means that we do not merely live on the Earth. We belong to it. And more mysteriously still; the Earth belongs to us. This is the Covenant with the Dust.

Dust as Divine Substance

The Hebrew word for ground in Genesis 2:7 is "Adamah", from which we derive the name Adam. We are, quite literally, earthlings. Not in the sense of science fiction, but in the deepest theological truth. The dust is not our shame. It is our origin.

When God chose the raw material to shape humanity, He chose dust, not because dust is weakness, but because the Creator saw potential in mere dust.

Dust is:

> easily scattered
> easily forgotten
> yet also incredibly fertile.

And when dust is in the divine hands, dust becomes destiny. The covenant, then, is this: "As long as you remember where you came from, you will know where you are going." Forget the dust, and we lose our direction. Remember it; and we walk in humility, hope, and harmony.

The Breath and the Soil

The covenant of dust is not complete without breath. Genesis 2:7 does not end with soil. It continues with spirit: "...and God breathed into his nostrils the breath of life", and Adam the firs humankind became, a living Soul. We are dust and breath, soil and spirit, earth and heaven.

This union is the mystery of incarnation: That divine breath would willingly inhabit the frailty of matter, not to escape I; but to redeem it. Thus, our mandate was never to exploit the dust, but to walk in covenant with it.

All things sacred have dust on them, because in truth dust is the portal to eternity:

> The Tabernacle was pitched in desert dust.
> The burning bush was rooted in desert sand.
> Jesus knelt in the dust to write forgiveness.
> The cross stood upon a dusty hill.

And when He rose from the grave, His glorified feet still bore the prints of dust.

This is the great paradox: That dust, when anointed, becomes a portal to the divine. Because of that we are not waiting to escape Earth.

We are being invited to be redeemed while still embracing our origin as inhabitants of the Earth.

The tragedy of human history is not just merely sin, but the influential breach of the original covenant. When we forgot our dusty origins, we began to:

> Exploit the soil instead of honoring it.
> Build towers instead of altars.
> Extract instead of cultivating.

Modernity has signed a new contract: One that sees dust as dirt, earth as expendable, and creation as mute.

But the true Earthkeepers tears up that contract and returns to the ancient agreement: "I will walk humbly with the ground, honor it as holy, and remember that it holds my very beginning."

Even Jesus Christ, the Living Word made flesh, entered the dust. He:

walked dirt roads,
spat on dirt to heal,
washed dusty feet,
and was buried in the earth.

Even resurrection happened within the covenant of dust: Not apart from it, but through it. He did not hover above the earth like a ghost.

He dwelt among us; embodied, earthbound, incarnate. Jesus did not despise the dust. He redeemed it.

The Earth Remembers

There is a mystery in scripture where the land itself remembers: "The land is defiled, and therefore I punish it for its sin." Leviticus 18:25. "The stones of the field will be at peace with you." Job 5:23. The land is not dead matter. It is a witness.

When we break covenant with the dust, it groans. When we renew that covenant, it rejoices. Creation is waiting: "For the revealing of the sons and daughters of God." Romans 8:19

The Creation is not waiting for con or escape artists. The Creation is waiting for the true Earthkeepers who remember the once forgotten covenant of the dust.

Dust, Ash, and Sacred Memory

The ritual of Ash Wednesday reminds us: "Remember you are dust, and to dust you shall return." This is not morbid. It is liberating. It reminds us that life is gift, breath is sacred, and our bodies are not eternal machines, but temporary temples.

To covenant with the dust is to:

Live with humility.
Walk with reverence.
Steward with joy.
Die with eternal hope.

Because embracing dust is not the end. It is the threshold of resurrection.

Renewal Through Reconnection

To restore our covenant with the dust, we must: Touch the Earth again: Walk barefoot. Plant something. Kneel in soil.

Speak to the Earth with blessing: Words shape worlds. Declare life, not curse.

Repent for breaches: Confess how we've harmed the land, knowingly or not.

Honor the Sacred Cycles: Sabbath the land. Let it rest. Let it breathe.

Teach the next generation: Dust is not disgrace. It is the beginning of glory.

This is not nostalgia. This is the true revival, of the deepest kind.

The Final Garden

In Revelation, the final vision is not a cloud, but a city with a garden. "On either side of the river was the tree of life…" Revelation 22:2. Eden is not abandoned. It is restored.

The covenant with the dust is not voided by time. It is fulfilled in Christ and renewed in us. As we await the fullness of restoration, we live now as keepers of the covenant.

Closing Invocation: Remember the Dust

O dust, ancient and alive, holder of holy breath, womb of humanity, cradle of Christ.

We remember you. We honor you. We renew our vow to walk with you in humility and wonder. Not as masters, but as partners. Not as tyrants, but as tender stewards.

May we not run from dust, but return to it, and find in it the echo of Eden, the breath of the Beginning, and the hope of Resurrection.

Amen.

Part 6.

The Return to Eden

"He drove out the man; and at the east of the garden of Eden, He placed the cherubim, and a flaming sword that turned every way to guard the way to the tree of life." Genesis 3:24

The Exile and the Longing

Since the gates of Eden were closed, humanity has wandered. We have:

Built cities from stone.
Raised monuments to our ingenuity.
Cultivated lands with sweat and suffering.

But buried beneath every human story is a shared ache: The ache for Eden. A place where:

The soul knew no separation.
The earth bore fruit without pain.
God walked with man in the cool of the day.

We carry this memory in our spiritual DNA, a sacred homesickness. We are not merely escaping Earth. We are longing for our return to Eden.

Eden is not lost; it is temporary hidden. Eden is not a myth. It is a dimension, and this dimension, it is not locked in the past; It is veiled in the present.

The flaming sword guards not to punish, but to protect. To re-enter Eden is not going backward.

It is to go inward and upward. The path is not marked by geography, but by sacred transformation.

Reclaiming Edenic Identity

In Eden, humanity walked in: Unbroken communion. Purposeful stewardship. Restful dominion.

These three divine dimensions; presence, purpose, and peace; were the core of our Edenic identity. To return to Eden is to:

Recover presence: Walk with God again.
Reclaim purpose: Tend what is sacred.
Restore peace: Live in shalom with creation.

The return is not only individual. It is cosmic.

The Christic Key

Jesus did not come to offer a way out of Earth, but to reopen the way back into Eden. He is:

The Tree of Life in the midst of the garden.
The Bread of Life was broken for the hungry soul of humanity.
The Spring of Living Waters gushing forth in parched places.
The Gate through which the exiled may return.
The Good Gardener, tending what was forgotten, buried, and broken.

And we must never forget: The way back into Eden did not come for the soul of humanity without sacrifice.

The Everlasting Father, Creator of All, the Highest God, and Architect of the Garden; in His unfathomable grace, mercy, and love for all of Creation, looked away for a moment so that redemption could look forward forever.

In that sacred moment:

> The Bread of Life was broken to feed the starved soul of Creation.
> The Spring of Living Water cried out, "I am thirsty," so the desert places might drink again.
> The Seed of the Tree of Life was hung upon a tree, cursed for our sake; so that roots of righteousness might once more take hold in the soil of the world.

He did not bypass the Earth; He entered its dust. He did not ascend without first descending.

He went to the heart of the Earth, to touch the covenant buried in dust and awaken it to life.

In Christ, the path to Eden reopens. The flaming sword does not consume Him;
it bows to Him. Why? Because He is the Edenic Flame that purifies, not destroys.

He is the Living Gate that swings wide for those who remember. He is the Breath that once hovered over dust and now breathes again into those who will walk the path of return. The flaming sword does not consume Him. It welcomes Him.

Eden is not merely a destination. It is a state of being, it is the sacred garden within. The kingdom of God is within you". Luke 17:21. To return to Eden is to:

Cultivate the inner garden. Pull up the weeds of bitterness. Water the soil of the soul with love.

We do not wait for Eden. We become encapsulated by Eden. When we host His presence, tend His purposes, and live in peace, Eden blooms again.

The Earth as the New Eden

The final vision of scripture is not: Souls floating in clouds, or an escape from the world.

It is: "A new heaven and a new earth." Revelation 21:1. It is Eden expanded. Eden restored. A garden-city where: Trees line rivers. Healing flows to the nations. God dwells with humanity.

We are not leaving Earth. We are being transformed in order to return, and to return to Eden is to: Live from communion, not performance. Steward the Earth as sacred trust. Rest in identity, not insecurity.

This is the mandate: "Tend and keep the garden." The same words spoken in Genesis 2:15, are whispered again today into the hearts of those who remember, because in truth Earth is not abandoned, it is awaiting the Edens sons and daughters to inhabit it once again.

Few Edenic Practices for Today

Sanctify Your Space: Let your home, work, and rest reflect divine order: Cultivate Beauty: Plant. Create. Beautify. Eden is expressed through beauty.

Live in Rhythm: Practice sabbath. Honor cycles. Rest and rise. Host His Presence: Invite God into every moment.

Guard the Garden: Resist corruption. Protect purity. Please remember; these are not laws. They are sacred and divine liturgies of return.

The Final Invitation

At the end of Revelation, the invitation echoes: "Blessed are those who wash their robes, that they may have the right to the tree of life and may enter the city by the gates." Revelation 22:14.

The gates of Eden once closed are now opening again, not by force, but by faith. Jesus has become the flaming sword and the open gate. The question is not: "Can we return to Eden?" The question is: "Will we choose to walk the path of return?"

Closing Benediction: Return, O Earthkeeper

Return, O Earthkeeper, not to nostalgia, But to divine design. Return, not with fear, but with fire.

Let Eden rise again in your thoughts, in your touch, in your tears, in your tending. Let the Earth rejoice for the gate is open, the sword bows, and the tree bears fruit once more. Return. Return. Return.   Amen.

Chapter Seven Summary

Reclaiming the Original Mandate of Earthly Stewardship

Chapter Seven brings us to the culminating revelation of Escaping Earth – The Dream That Revealed the Way: a divine return not to the abandonment of Earth, but to its original Edenic intention.

It is both a prophetic summons and a sacred remembrance, calling humanity to reclaim its identity and vocation as Earthkeepers, entrusted stewards of divine purpose and presence.

From the beginning, humankind was not formed apart from the earth but with it and for it. Each part of this final chapter unveils how that original covenant, though veiled by corruption, exile, and forgetfulness; is not lost. It lives, hidden in the memory of dust and quickened by the breath of Spirit.

From Revelation to Responsibility

This opening movement reveals that revelation is never given for escape, but for embodiment. We are not called to ascend away from the earth, but to descend into its sacred core; awakening to the responsibility embedded within every divine unveiling. The dream given is not just to be heard but lived.

The Forgotten Mandate

We revisit the original commission given in Eden: to till and to guard. Humanity was assigned to cultivate, protect, and co-create with the earth. This sacred mandate, though forgotten in theology and culture, still resounds beneath the noise of empire and religious abstraction. The soil remembers.

A New Genesis Movement

This part announces that we are standing at the threshold of a new beginning; not the repetition of an old cycle, but a Genesis movement birthed in Spirit and truth. Here, the Christic DNA re-seeds the earth through those willing to walk in humility, justice, and communion. The story begins again, with awakened stewards and re-aligned hearts.

Earthkeepers Arise

This is a rallying cry for a new priesthood; not one confined to pulpits, but planted in gardens, deserts, cities, nations. Earthkeepers are those who till with tenderness, guard with discernment, and walk as emissaries of the Edenic way. They carry memory, prophecy, and the weight of responsibility. The earth groans for such as these.

Covenant with the Dust

Here, we remember the sacred agreement between Creator, humanity, and the soil itself. The covenant made with dust in Eden is renewed through Jesus; the New Adam, the Christic Key.

He infuses the dust with resurrection life, transfiguring what was cursed into what is now consecrated. The covenant still holds.

The Return to Eden

This closing part reveals Eden as not lost but hidden; not past, but present; not myth, but mystery. Eden lives within the human soul, just beneath the surface of awakened consciousness. Through Christ; the Tree of Life, the Bread of Heaven, the Living Water, the True Gardener; we are not just called to find Eden, but to become it again.

Closing Reflection

Throughout this final chapter, we move from remembrance to restoration, exile to invitation. The garden gates are not guarded to keep us out, but to test our willingness to return in humility, obedience, and communion.

Eden is not something we wait for; it is something we embody.
The Earth is not an obstacle to escape; it is a beloved partner to restore.

This chapter does not close with finality, but with prophecy: The flaming sword bows, the gates reopen, and the garden waits.

The Earth is ready; not just for stewards, but for sons and daughters of Eden to arise. To Return. To Reclaim.

Epilogue

Escaping Earth – The Dream That Revealed the Way, is not a flight from creation, but a sacred descent into its forgotten meaning. This book is both a divine revelation and a soul-mapping journey; one that calls the reader not to abandon the world, but to remember the truth of it. Through seven prophetic chapters, each unfolding with sacred vision and spiritual clarity, the book invites the reader to reawaken to the mystery of Earth as womb, altar, garden, and covenant.

Chapter One: The Illusion of Outward Escape

This chapter begins by dismantling the false belief that spirituality demands separation from Earth. The modern appetite for ascension has produced a theology of escapism. But true transformation begins with descent, not departure. Each part reveals the illusion of rapture without responsibility, re-centering the incarnational truth that God descended into dust and womb to reveal the way home.

> The Modern Pursuit of Escape
> Ascension's Counterfeit
> Losing the Ground Beneath Us
> The Sacred Descent
> Reclaiming the Forgotten Sanctuary
> A Call to the Sacred Below

Chapter Two: Reawakening the Inner Temple

Descent is not a fall from glory but a return to origin. This chapter unveils descent as sacred and the soul as a forgotten sanctuary.

We are invited to peel away false layers, rediscover our original name, and drink from the hidden wells beneath. The excavation of truth restores the inner temple.

> The Soul; The Forgotten Sanctuary
> Beneath the Surface of Our Daily Identities
> False Layers and Forgotten Names
> The Excavation of Truth
> The Original Name
> The Descent is the Doorway
> When Roots Become Revelation
> Unveiling the Hidden Wells
> The Harmony of Depth and Height

Chapter Three: The Unveiling

This chapter calls us spiritual awakening. It restores the mirror of divine image and invites us into resurrection rhythms. With breath renewed and resistance confronted, we become vessels through which rivers flow from rooted depths.

> The Mirror Restored
> The Breath Returns
> The Spirit of Exploration
> The Resistance Before Resurrection
> The Overflow – From Roots to Rivers

Chapter Four: The Mantle in the Wilderness

Every wilderness hides a mantle. This chapter journeys through hidden seasons, subtle opposition, and the sacred transfer of divine responsibility. Recognition of the mantle requires weight, fire, and faithfulness.

    The Eternal Pattern
    The Fire of Hidden Seasons
    The Face of Subtle Opposition
    The Sacred Transfer
    The Receiving of the Mantle
    The Weight of Recognition

Chapter Five: The Descendance

A sacred pilgrimage into the Earth's mystery, Chapter Five brings us through caverns and stones, ancient gates and foundations, into the mountain within. The Christic key is revealed, and Eden's covenant is remembered.

    The Mountains as Thresholds
    The Foundation Holds the Mystery
    Return to the Sacred Core
    Gates Hidden in Plain Sight
    Stones, Caverns, and Hidden Altars
    Rediscovering the Mountain Within

Chapter Six: The Five Cascades of Revelation

Drawn from a sacred dream, this chapter is a mystical descent into layered revelation. The five cascades awaken awe, confront illusion, reveal wisdom, embody presence, and send us forth radiant with divine flow.

    Entering the Hidden Realm
    Revelation Comes in Layers
    First Cascade – Awakening Awe
    Second Cascade – Confronting Illusion
    Third Cascade – Receiving Hidden Wisdom

Fourth Cascade – Embodying Presence
Fifth Cascade – Returning with Radiance
A River Through You

Chapter Seven: Reclaiming the First Mandate

The final chapter restores the Edenic calling; to tend and to keep, to steward the soil with divine intimacy. Earthkeepers are summoned, and the covenant with the dust is made new. The return to Eden is not a myth, but a living movement.

From Revelation to Responsibility
The Forgotten Mandate
A New Genesis Movement
Earthkeepers Arise
Covenant with the Dust
The Return to Eden

The Final Echo: The Dream Has Been Revealed

Escaping Earth closes not with departure but with awakening. The Dream is not merely personal; it is prophetic. What was hidden has now been revealed: the way back is not outward, but inward; not upward but rooted. We are invited to re-enter the Eden within and walk in divine alignment with Earth, Heaven, and Spirit.

> This is the call.
> This is the return.
> This is the way.

A Final Reflection

The Journey Was the Revelation

In the sacred unfolding of these pages, we did not seek an escape route; we sought remembrance.

From the illusion of fleeing upward, to the revelation of descending inward; from the false light of escapism to the original radiance of Eden still pulsing beneath our feet; we have returned. Not to where we began, but to where we were always meant to awaken.

This book was never merely a volume of spiritual insights, dreams, or meditations. It was a journey of descent into the buried altars, hidden wells, and sacred blueprints encoded within Earth, body, soul, and Spirit. It was a spiral, not a ladder. A sanctuary, not an exit.

As we peeled away the illusions, the noise, and the fear, we found the ancient but forgotten mandate waiting, not in the clouds, but in the dust.

We discovered:

That Eden was never lost; only forgotten.
That the soul was never disconnected; only silenced.
That Earth was never cursed; only misperceived.
And that the dream was never fantasy; it was prophecy.

You have walked through mountains, caverns, rivers, and temples within. You have remembered the Christic Key, re-entered the harmony of heaven and soil, and heard the echo of the Voice that still walks in the garden in the cool of the day. Now, the journey becomes a seed in your hands.

A Blessing for the Reader: You Who Return

May your feet remember the sacred ground they walk upon, even when the world forgets its holiness.

May your eyes see through veils and illusions, and awaken to the rivers flowing within your own soul.

May your hands become altars of healing and cultivation, turning wastelands into gardens of remembrance.

May your voice carry the echo of Eden,
soft enough to mend, strong enough to call.

May you never again feel the need to escape Earth, but rather, feel chosen to remain; and reclaim.

May the dream revealed in these pages
awaken the greater dream within you.

And may the Holy Spirit who hovered over the deep, and who walks beside you even now, remind you daily:

*You were sent, not to ascend without return,
but to descend within, and be redeemed.*

Selah.

About the Author

Mihai Ilioi is a prophetic author, spiritual messenger, and devoted servant whose life journey mirrors the revelations he brings forth in *Escaping Earth – The Dream That Revealed the Way.*

His writings are not mere reflections of intellectual endeavor or literary creativity; they are living echoes of divine encounters, sacred visions, and a calling rooted in eternal purpose.

This book stands as both a warning and a prophetic invitation: a call to awaken in an age, where humanity teeters between divine identity and synthetic illusion.

Through this volume, Mihai extends a hand to those seeking to return; not to escape the Earth, but to embody its original meaning with sacred responsibility.

His voice reverberates with the truth that we are living souls, formed by divine intent, encoded with eternal resonance, and called to remember who we truly are.

Born on July 25, 1969, under the shadow of communist Romania, Mihai was raised amid intense political oppression and religious suppression. On June 12, 1988, driven by a relentless hunger for truth and freedom, he risked his life to escape across the Danube River; a courageous act that marked more than political defection; it became the first step in a lifelong pilgrimage toward divine purpose and spiritual awakening.

Surviving refugee camps and eventually arriving in the United States with the aid of UNICEF, Mihai rebuilt his life from the ground up; physically, emotionally, and spiritually.

On April 4, 1990, he married his beloved wife, Carla, and together they have cultivated a legacy grounded in faith, humility, and endurance. They are blessed with five children and ten grandchildren: a living testimony of restoration, grace, and generational blessing.

Professionally, Mihai has spent over three decades in the aerospace industry, balancing the precision of technological systems with the mystery of the spiritual realm. Yet even in the world of machinery and mathematics, his inner compass has remained anchored in the eternal.

Alongside his vocational work, Mihai has faithfully served as an ordained minister, and is the founder of Phoenix Worship Community, a fellowship devoted to sincerity, humility, and the unfiltered truth of the Gospel of Jesus Christ.

He is also the founder and visionary behind the RAELITE, (*Revelation – Activation – Elevation – Liberation-Inner- Transformation- Embodiment*), a prophetic and philosophical initiative designed to bring forth a message of hope and freedom, unshackled from religious ideology, political manipulation, and economic oppression.

His voice also resonates through The Expressed Thoughts Podcast, a platform of raw, spiritually inspired reflections that explore the profound intersection between inner revelation and external reality.

Mihai's published works reflect the evolving revelation he has received over the years:

- The Truth Shifters
- The Expressed Thoughts
- Echoes of the Soul
- Understanding Humanity – Volume One: The Alignment
- Our Father Who Art in Heaven – A Book of Prayers
- Soul-Based Living in the Age of AI
- The Human Thought – An Arrow That Never Stops Flying

Each book serves as a spiritual vessel, carrying messages for a world longing for clarity, healing, and moral reawakening. They are not authored from intellect alone but from the place of divine listening, sacred stillness, and prophetic fire.

This latest volume, *Escaping Earth – The Dream That Revealed the Way*, represents the culmination of Mihai's spiritual journey to date.

Born from a vivid dream and nurtured through countless moments of prayer, meditation, and divine insight, the book serves as a spiritual compass for those lost in the illusions of artificial constructs and digital deception.

It is a holy call to descend into the depths of one's being, reclaim the soul's original blueprint, and reawaken the truth encoded within the human essence.

Above all, Mihai does not present himself as the source of truth; but as a vessel of it. A witness. A servant. A messenger for this generation and the next.

With reverent humility, he offers what has been revealed to him so that others may remember, rise, and realign their lives with the eternal rhythm of divine life.

"May these words awaken the remembrance within you; not of the identity shaped by the world, but of the one spoken over you by the Eternal Creator: a living soul woven with divine intention, breathed into light, and destined to shine. And though we stand in one of the most artificial ages humanity has ever known, the ancient echo of eternity still calls with clarity and compassion: *Return*".

With reverence and love,

Mihai Ilioi

Mihai Ilioi

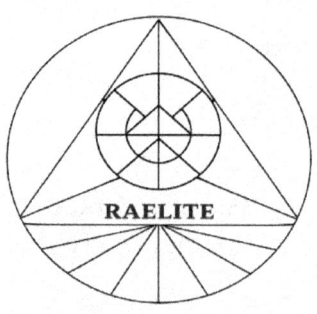

Notes:

Notes:

Notes:

Notes:

www.ingramcontent.com/pod-product-compliance
Lightning Source LLC
Chambersburg PA
CBHW060106170426
43198CB00010B/783